Law School

Law School

Getting In, Getting Out, Getting On

Michael Ariens
Professor of Law
St. Mary's University School of Law

Carolina Academic Press
Durham, North Carolina

Library of Congress Cataloging-in-Publication Data

Ariens, Michael S.
  Law school : getting in, getting out, getting on / Michael S. Ariens.
     p. cm.
  ISBN 978-1-59460-443-0 (alk. paper)
  1. Law schools--United States. 2. Law students--United States. 3. Law--
Study and teaching--United States. I. Title.

  KF283.A75 2010
  340.071'173--dc22

                        2010022590

CAROLINA ACADEMIC PRESS
700 Kent Street
Durham, North Carolina 27701
Telephone (919) 489-7486
Fax (919) 493-5668
www.cap-press.com

Printed in the United States of America
2019 printing

For Stephanie, Caitlin and John

Contents

Part II · Getting Out

Part III · Getting On

Introduction

This book takes you from the decision to take the LSAT (Law School Admission Test) through law school, the bar exam and getting the most out of your first job. It is a User's Guide to the law school experience, and so is divided into three sections: 1) Getting In to law school; 2) Getting Out of law school; and 3) Getting On with your life in the practice of law or in other work.

As of 2009, the American Bar Association (ABA) has approved 199 law schools offering a first degree in law, ordinarily called the juris doctor (J.D.). A few additional law schools will likely receive ABA approval in the next several years. Including part-time students, enrollment of first year law students in 2008–09 exceeded 49,000 persons at ABA-approved law schools. A person who obtains a J.D. from an ABA-approved law school is eligible to take the bar examination in any state. In all but a few states (California is the most notable exception to this rule), no person is eligible to take the bar examination without obtaining a J.D. from an ABA-approved law school. Nearly 100 law schools also offer advanced degrees in law, which are not required to practice law, but which may be helpful in obtaining expertise in specialized areas of law. The most popular advanced law degree is the LL.M. (Master of Laws) degree, which a full-time student can usually complete in one academic year. As already noted, most persons who take an advanced degree in law will specialize in an area of law (for example, tax law), although some students obtain an LL.M. in order to enter law teaching. A few law schools offer the equivalent of a Ph.D. in law, usually listed as an S.J.D., a degree rarely taken by American lawyers.

The business of educating lawyers is a big business. The average (and median) tuition at private ABA-approved law schools in 2008 is approximately $34,000 per year, with tuition increases likely to rise at least 3–5% annually. At state-supported law schools, the average yearly tuition is just under $17,000 for state residents and over $28,000 for nonresidents. Total annual revenue received by law schools exceeds $3 billion. Law schools awarded nearly $800 million in internal grants and scholarships in 2008, and external grants were also available to some students. This aid amount was more than double the value of grants and scholarships awarded in 2001–2002, as law schools both recognized the impact of the growing cost of legal education on students and as they competed more fiercely for the most desirable students. Even so, the average debt of law school graduates continues to rise. In 2007–2008, students at state-supported law schools borrowed an average of over $59,000, and students attending private law schools borrowed an average of over $91,000.

The most recent report of the Bureau of Labor Statistics (BLS) states that $110,590 is the median (that is, half made more and half made less) wage for all *employed* practicing lawyers as of mid-2008. The Great Recession of 2008, which began to affect the legal profession after this BLS report was issued, has likely led to a reduction in the median wage of lawyers. Even before the Great Recession, the BLS reported widely varying wage ranges for lawyers. The wages of lawyers ranged from $54,460 for the lowest 10% to $163,320 for lawyers in the 75th percentile in wages. Lawyers earn vastly different incomes depending on the lawyer's type of practice, experience and ability, and interests. One additional reason to look somewhat skeptically at the data reported by the BLS is that it does not include income for sole practitioners, a group that makes up roughly one-third of the legal profession.

Competition in the practice of law has intensified greatly in the last thirty years, requiring lawyers to spend much more time and effort marketing their skills and expertise to those in need of legal services than in previous eras. Thus, even though the future demand for lawyers will probably expand at a rate consonant with economic growth, you are forewarned that financial success is not guaranteed to all or even most lawyers.

If you have given any thought to law school, you have undoubtedly looked at the *U.S. News & World Report's Annual Guide to Law Schools*. The *Annual Guide* offers a ranking of ABA-approved law schools, numerically listing the top 100 law schools and dividing all law schools into four tiers. A number of commentators have noted both the manipulability of the methodology used by *U.S. News* and the lack of any substantial movement in the rankings over time, particularly in the first tier, both of which limit the value of the *Annual Guide*. The deans of many law schools have over the past decade jointly signed several letters rejecting the methodology used in the *Annual Guide* to rank law schools, and the annually produced *ABA/LSAC Official Guide to ABA-Approved Law Schools* argues against rankings. Because many prospective law school applicants pay attention to the *Annual Guide*, a number of law schools covertly (and a few overtly) try to take advantage of the methodology to improve their rankings in the *Annual Guide*. The *Annual Guide* is a tremendous revenue generator for *U.S. News*, and it is not likely to disappear any time soon. As I will discuss more fully in Chapter 3, for most prospective law students, the *Annual Guide* is irrelevant. Whether you should attend law school at Boston University (tied for 22nd), the College of William and Mary (tied for 28th), the University of Alabama (tied for 38th), or Southern Methodist University (tied for 48th) in the 2010 edition of the *Annual Guide* (which means that *U.S. News* has concluded that each of the above-named law schools is in the first tier of law schools), depends much more on financial, familial and geographic considerations than on some perceived competitive advantage found in one school rather than another. All of the schools listed above are strong schools offering a very good legal education. Each may have some comparative advantage over the others, but attempting to compare the strengths of Boston University with those of the University of Alabama will more likely result in confusion than enlightenment. A person who decides to attend the American University (tied for 48th), located in Washington, D.C., with the intention of moving to San Francisco (where the University of California Hastings College of the Law, tied for 42nd, is located) to find work, or attends the College of William and Mary in Williamsburg, Virginia in order to practice law in Dallas (where Southern Methodist University is located) should reconsider his or her decision. That is because legal employment remains, for all but those who graduate in the top 5% of all law schools or who graduate from a relatively few national law schools, a largely local and regional phenomenon. The *Annual Guide* is helpful to those considering law school not because it tells you how to compare the University of Iowa (26th) with Southern Methodist University, but because it simply confirms what you will find on any number of internet-based sites: what are consensually agreed as the top fourteen or so law schools. (For example, the very flawed website "The Best 100 Law Schools in the United States-Based on Qualitative, Rather Than Quantitative, Criteria," found at http://lawschool100.com and the much more trenchant (though still imperfect) site created by University of Chicago Law School Prof. Brian Leiter, *Law School Rankings*, found at http://www.leiterrankings.com, both offer very similar rankings of the top schools.) Even within the top fourteen law schools, the "national" value of the law school varies tremendously. A huge gulf still exists in the minds of many employers between Harvard Law School, which has a brand value recognized throughout the United States, and say, the Cornell University brand in the Southeast or the Duke University brand in the far West. Whether one in fact receives a better education at Harvard than Cornell or Duke (or many other law schools) is highly doubtful. And whether the graduates of Harvard will make better lawyers than graduates of Cornell or Duke is also highly doubtful. Because many schools can offer an excellent legal education and open doors to varied kinds of legal practice in a particular state or city, and because the costs of attending different law schools may vary widely, a law school applicant should think long and hard about what law school to attend.

One source of information prospective law school applicants may peruse for comparative purposes is the aforementioned *ABA/LSAC Official Guide to ABA-Approved Law Schools*. The *Official Guide* is a joint publication of the ABA and the Law School Admission Council (LSAC), a non-profit organization that owns the LSAT. The *Official Guide* publishes a profile for each ABA-approved law school. That profile begins with a two page presentation, in graphic form, of officially reported data on application deadlines and fees, admissions (number of applicants, admits, enrollees, and GPA and LSAT data for the 75th and 25th percentile of enrollees), enrollment (and attrition) figures, course offerings, tuition (including amounts for grants and scholarships) and living costs, faculty and library information, bar passage rates, and employment figures. The numbers for each school are presented in the same way, allowing a prospective applicant readily to compare different schools. Those two pages are followed by two pages consisting of a narrative written by the law school emphasizing its strengths, from its faculty/student ratio to its special programs to its location. Because the graduate of any ABA-approved law school can take the bar exam in any state, and the graduates of law schools not approved by the ABA can take the bar in just a few states, no law school will voluntarily cede its ABA approved status. Because ABA-approved law schools are required annually to give the ABA accurate data as a condition of continued ABA approval, the data found in graphic form in the *Official Guide* are less amenable to manipulation or obfuscation than the data voluntarily given by law schools to *U.S. News* for its *Annual Guide*.

One problem with the *Official Guide* is the difficulty a prospective law student will have in understanding the data in context. For example, the information regarding "Employment" offers the reader something of a breakdown of where graduates work nine months after graduation. Of those whose employment is known, the chart will state how many (and what percent) are working in law firms, in government, in business and industry, in public interest jobs, as judicial clerks and in academia. What the chart does not explain is the type of law firm graduates are working in. Are graduates largely employed in large law firms (colloquially called "BigLaw"), medium sized firms or small firms? Are the graduates self-employed as sole practitioners? Are the graduates employed by government working as municipal lawyers, assistant district attorneys, for state administrative agencies, working for the federal government in the Department of Justice or as an Assistant United States Attorney for the Southern District of New York? What kind of business and industry jobs are graduates engaged in? Are they law jobs in the business setting (known as corporate counsel positions), or jobs for which law is a helpful but not necessary condition of employment, such as labor or contract negotiators?

A similar problem arises in attempting to understanding the chart describing the curriculum of the law school. The *Official Guide* offers some numbers concerning the size of first year and upper level classes, but any explanation of the extent to which the school offers a coherent curriculum is lacking. And though the *Official Guide* notes the number of student slots for clinical courses, information about what the student does in any particular clinic may or may not be adequately explained in the two-page narrative written by representatives of the law school.

The *Official Guide* is a good place to start once you decide to attend law school. It is available in all law school libraries and in the undergraduate libraries of many universities, and can be viewed online at http://officialguide.lsac.org/. I encourage you to take a look at the *Official Guide* when making initial decisions about which law schools you might apply to. However, law schools vary considerably in their emphases, and to understand more completely whether a law school is right for you, you must go to the school's website and learn more about what the school offers both academically and professionally. Even better, if you have the opportunity, visit the school, attend a class, and see if it fits your educational needs.

This book will look at both the available data on the legal profession and go beyond those data to assist you in choosing the right school, in succeeding while in law school, and in obtaining your law license and thinking about your first job.

Part I

———

Getting In

Chapter 1

Thinking about Law School

Why law school?

Money?

Stories abounded in the first decade of the twenty-first century of the high salaries and bonuses paid first year associates by the largest American law firms. The peak came in Fall 2008, when those lawyers were paid an initial salary of $160,000 plus the opportunity to earn year-end bonuses based on the firm's profitability. Revenue at large law firms is ordinarily generated through billing the time of their partners, associates and paralegals. (Some large law firms are beginning to look to other revenue approaches, such as billing based on the result achieved, or on a flat-fee basis, a process accelerated by the Great Recession of 2008.) This is known as hourly billing (often done in six minute or fifteen minute segments). Under the traditional rule of thumb that an associate should be paid about one-third of the expected revenue generated by that associate, those highly-compensated first year associates would be expected to bring the firm a minimum of $480,000 in annual revenue. If the associate billed 2,000 hours in a year, which is an average of 40 hours a week for 50 weeks of the year, all of which was collected, the client would have to be billed $240 an hour for that associate's time (2,000 hours × $240 per hour). Firms rarely collect all the time billed by new associates, and a billing rate of $240 for a brand-new lawyer, while a possible hourly rate for new associates in some locations, is a ridiculously high billing rate for a lawyer with no experience. Consequently, those associates either billed substantially more than 2,000 hours annually or contributed a smaller profit than traditionally assumed. Both possibilities were realized. Associates at large law firms regularly billed well in excess of 2,000 hours. (Those billable hours should not be confused with the number of hours worked, for an associate will always work substantially more hours than can be billed, or that associate is padding his or her hours, a violation of professional ethics rules.) Even so, first year associates brought modest profits to the firm.

The Great Recession of 2008 spurred large corporate clients to scrutinize more closely their legal bills. Large law firms saw profits drop, and several counts claimed over 5,000 lawyers were laid off by the 250 largest American law firms. Many rising 3L law students who worked as law clerks in Summer 2008 and who accepted permanent offers from large law firms in early fall were later told the firm was retracting its offer, or the firm was delaying the starting employment date of those new associates for six months or a year. Large law firms were tight-lipped about 2009 starting salaries. Starting salaries for those associates joining large law firms in fall 2010 will range from about $100,000–$130,000. Starting salaries at medium-sized and small law firms will be lower than starting BigLaw salaries.

Beginning salaries for law graduates vary widely across the country. They differ based on type of job one takes (government or private practice), type of private law practice (criminal defense or corporate transactions), type of law firm (BigLaw or small (2–10 person) firm) and for other reasons. The most comprehensive work on new lawyer salaries by *NALP: The Association for Legal Career Professionals* (formerly the *National Association of Law Placement*) indicates a "bimodal" distribution for new lawyers. One "peak" is at $35,000–$40,000; the other is between $135,000–$140,000. This latter peak will fall in subsequent NALP surveys. A new lawyer working as an assistant district attorney or in a small law firm will earn substantially less than a fellow graduate working in a large law firm. The expected work load and experience gained will also differ markedly.

For many considering law school, money remains an important reason for spending three years in graduate professional education. As already noted, some will be handsomely paid upon graduation. But if money is your sole or dominant reason for applying to law school, you are cautioned that the practice of law is at best an indirect springboard to wealth. If you join a BigLaw firm (generally speaking, a firm with 100 or more lawyers) you will earn a healthy income, but at most such law firms you will also work nearly every day for nearly all of the day. In order to maintain (and to enhance) partnership profits, a large law firm must remain pyramidal in shape, that is, wide at the bottom (where the associates reside) and narrow at the top (where the equity partners reside). The owners of large law firms want more associates than partners (owners), so that those associates jointly can contribute profits in addition to the profits created by the partners themselves. The employment of more associates than partners allows the firm to leverage its profits. The desire to enhance profits makes it impossible for a large law firm to promote all or even most of its associates to partner, and the substantial risk that the new associate will not be made a partner after working incessantly for ten or more years is one reason for the high salary paid new associates in large law firms.

If you choose to work at a large law firm, you may make partner. However, you should recognize your chances of becoming a part-owner of the firm are modest, even if your work is uniformly excellent, for making partner is not just about excellent legal work but also about your ability to foster client development and retention. Further, many large law firms have created two levels of partner, an "income" or nonequity partner and a "participating" or equity partner. If you are made an "income" partner, you will receive a salary and bonus much as you do as an associate. A smaller minority will reach the level of "participating" partner, one who has a stake in the firm (since most law firms are now incorporated and not true partnerships, the use of the traditional term "partner" is actually a misnomer, for even these "partners" can be fired at most firms). Even participating partners can be ousted from their firms, and the ethos of many large law firms is "eat what you kill," which makes it crucial that you develop both excellent legal skills and a list of valued and valuable clients. This is discussed in greater detail in Chapter 8. The length of time to become a partner in a large law firm varies, but that time has lengthened in the past decade, and you should expect to spend at least a decade as an associate before becoming a partner in a large law firm.

At small and medium sized law firms your starting pay will usually be significantly lower than at a large law firm. You have to look carefully at the particular firm, but you may have more opportunities to develop advanced legal skills and a client roster at a mid-sized firm than at a large law firm, for mid-sized firms are usually less pyramidal in shape and often have a shorter partner track than is true in BigLaw. The variety of such firms makes it impossible to generalize, making it important that you consider thoroughly the particular firm when you receive an offer of employment or an offer to work as a summer associate.

One benefit of a job with the government includes more regular hours than in private practice. Lawyers in government practice can work many late nights and weekends, but ordinarily a lawyer in government practice sacrifices pay for more personal time. A second benefit is that government lawyers do not bill their time. Additionally, government lawyers (and small firm practitioners) may exercise greater autonomy in the manner in which they perform the work they are assigned. For those who wish to try cases, working as an assistant district attorney may get you to court more quickly and more often than if you work in large firm private practice. Government work is also conducive to those interested in how public policies are formed, for even relatively new lawyers may have a greater ability to influence (even if modestly) public policy.

Finding a Career?

Law can be a fulfilling career. You can help people protect themselves against an indifferent or hostile government, or aid the government against actions undertaken by powerful people. You can improve the society in which we live, making it both more economically effective and efficient and more just. In a society in which laws and regulations are numerous and often intrusive, lawyers assist individuals and entities who find themselves enmeshed, fairly or not, in legal entanglements. The many strands of law in our society give lawyers the opportunity to play a variety of different and important roles. The pervasiveness of law in our democratic society also means that lawyers wield a great deal of power, power that can be used for good or ill. A lawyer's expert knowledge of the legal system gives the lawyer the power not only to aid one's clients, but to harm others through legal but ethically dubious means. Lawyers can use the legal system to delay legal claims and use the law as a weapon rather than as a shield. Although some law work is a zero-sum game (for example, some civil trials), much legal work adds social value, and many lawyers are involved in work that serves both their client and the broader public. Even work that apparently serves only the interests of the lawyer's client usually benefits society.

For those graduates whose employment status is known, about 90% are employed nine months after graduation. Approximately 75% of those employed work in positions requiring one to be a member of the bar, and a little more than half of those employed are employed by private law firms. Of those employed by private law firms, roughly three out of eight (about one-fifth of all employed law school graduates) will join a law firm of a significant size. This percentage will shrink as a result of the Great Recession, which has forced large law firms to re-think their economic model. A majority of those entering private practice will join smaller law firms or enter the private practice of law as sole practitioners. Overall, about three-quarters of the lawyers who practice law work in private law firms, and a majority of lawyers in private law firms work in small firms, either as sole practitioners or in firms of ten or fewer lawyers.

Law can be a stressful profession, and the incidence of substance abuse within the legal profession is substantially higher than in the general public. Lawyers also suffer from depression and other illnesses in greater numbers than the public as a whole, and the demands of work can adversely affect one's physical health ("no time to exercise, I've got work to do") and one's intimate and family relations. Fortunately, the varieties of law practice provide a host of opportunities for a lawyer to find work that suits both his or her personal needs and professional desires, if the lawyer is willing to consider alternatives to some types of law practice.

Service?

A traditional reason to consider the practice of law is that lawyers can do well by doing good, serving the needs of others while earning a good living. Complaints about lawyers in the popular culture (going all the way back to Shakespeare's "The first thing we do, let's kill all the lawyers") are common. Further, bad news often drives out good news, and bad news about lawyers engaged in unethical or illegal behavior is reported much more often than news about the good things lawyers accomplish. All aspiring lawyers may be slightly comforted by the fact that public complaints about lawyers, including ever-present lawyer jokes, have existed since the legal profession has existed. In some respects lawyers deserve some of the attacks made upon their exercise of power. Most Americans, however, agree with the belief that the American desire for continued democratic (rather than autocratic) governance does not lead one to think it would be a good idea to rid our society of lawyers.

The traditional reason to become a lawyer in order to serve the legal needs of others remains a sound reason to spend the time and effort it takes to complete law school. You will likely not become wealthy if you enter the legal profession to serve others. You can, however, earn a good living in the service of others, and you may find that a life dedicated to serving those with pressing legal needs is one that is fulfilling even when not enriching. This duty-infused reason to practice law becomes even more compelling given the vast amount of legal services left unserved by the legal profession. Many middle class Americans believe they earn too little to afford private lawyers, and earn too much to qualify for legal services aid. Many who are poor are in great need of legal assistance that non-profit legal services organizations will not or can not take on. The United States is a nation replete with laws, and lawyers perform a signature role in ensuring that these laws do not generate harm to the people the laws are intended to protect. More lawyers are needed to serve those considerable unmet needs.

Prestige?

Another reason to attend law school is the prestige attached to becoming a lawyer. Even with a million or so licensed lawyers in the United States, the legal profession remains a prestigious occupation. Some persons attend law school not to practice law but for the title of attorney-at-law. This prestige factor may seem counterintuitive, given the abysmal status in which the public appears to hold lawyers. Despite the disdain held by some for lawyers, the general public knows that lawyers in general are both powerful (thus, the lawyer jokes) and smart (thus the abysmal ranking of the legal profession, which is based in part on the fact that some lawyers serve unpopular clients and causes and use their intelligence in behalf of those "undeserving" clients).

Prestige may be related to security, and security may reflect the fact that obtaining a license to practice law is difficult. Only those persons who have met stringent educational requirements and who have passed the bar exam are admitted to the profession, a process that excludes the vast majority of the public. A licensed lawyer has a relatively limited monopoly to act on behalf of others in preparing pleadings or appearing before a judge in litigation and to give advice and provide services requiring the use of legal skill or knowledge. The security of this limited "monopoly," however, is ephemeral. Lawyers are subject to competition from non-lawyers, from outsourcing, and from do-it-yourself software, as well as from fellow lawyers. A lawyer will succeed in the practice of law only upon developing a set of skills that make clients desire and value the work of that lawyer. Professional development continues throughout a lawyer's career, for most lawyers do not remain with the same firm or government office from cradle to grave, and movement requires lawyers to gain particular skills that enhance their prospects of practicing law successfully. Thus, while a prestigious profession, law is not a profession in which your income will always be secure and steady. For the foreseeable future, the practice of law will continue to be a profitable but competitive business.

Intellectual Curiosity?

The study of law presents the opportunity to ponder the nature of law, including the idea of the "rule of law," the nature of human beings, the structure of government, the idea of rights (natural, positive and constitutional) and a host of intellectual puzzles. Law is a practical intellectual discipline, for the exercise of legal power has actual consequences for those affected by its exercise. Legal education has traditionally focused on doctrine (What is consideration in a contract? What state of mind is necessary for this act to be first-degree murder?) rather than on either theory (Why is the legal system structured this way?) or practice (How does someone do this in a courtroom or in transactional practice?). That emphasis on doctrine has changed dramatically over the past two decades, and you will find that the study of law encompasses theory and practice as well as doctrine, providing a student with a host of varied opportunities to learn widely and deeply in law school.

For many law school graduates, law school is an experience one uses before entering another career, from investment banking to teaching cultural anthropology. While law school may sate one's intellectual curiosity, much of the learning in law school is prosaic, indeed dull. Unless you are independently wealthy, you should not enter law school just for the sake of satisfying your intellectual curiosity. If, however, your intellectual curiosity is joined by another reason to attend law school, you may find it an enriching and valuable experience.

No Idea What Else to Do?

Going to law school does not postpone the "what do I want to do with my life?" decision. Going to law school is itself a decision to do something with your life. You are deciding that you want to spend three additional years in professional school training for a profession for which you may have neither the interest nor aptitude. For some the decision to attend law school for a lack of better options will be serendipitous. The excitement of learning about law and the use of those analytical and writing skills honed in college may make law school the perfect choice. For most who attend law school to avoid deciding what to do, the time lost, the increased debt and the banality of some of the work of lawyers makes this the worst of all possible decisions. Unless you are free from financial worry and you would otherwise decide to waste three years of your life doing nothing, do not attend law school because you don't know what else to do. From the books *One L* to *Brush with the Law*, you can find stories about persons deciding to attend law school not because they hope to practice law, or to use their legal education to work in fields in which legal knowledge may be helpful, but in order to put off making a decision about a career. It is likely that such a student will find law school too alienating, unsatisfying, and unedifying to take this risk. And spending thousands of dollars, even if it is someone else's money, in order to live through an unhappy experience is a recipe for disaster, particularly if those thousands of dollars are not a gift but have to be paid back.

Some or All of the Above

Most persons who decide to attend law school do so based on some combination of the reasons given above. Law can be fulfilling and secure and enriching and intellectually challenging and stimulating and prestigious and a stepping-stone to other types of work. It will not always be all of those things and it may at times be none of those things. Law can be both demanding and unrewarding. As noted earlier, lawyers suffer from stress and substance abuse in numbers substantially greater than the general public. Simply becoming a lawyer exacts a significant cost in terms of time and money. If, however, you find that some of the reasons listed above speak to your interest in becoming a lawyer, you can find great satisfaction in entering the profession of law.

Law in America

The United States has been called, in the title of one book, "a nation under lawyers." Law permeates our society. From ERISA (pension) planning to mediation to international energy law to domestic relations (family) law, the work of lawyers courses through American society. The variety of law jobs is rivaled only by the importance of these tasks. Creative (and ordinary) legal work makes possible business ventures that will allow the economy to grow, gives individuals a voice to challenge the power of the government, and aids the government in expanding both the liberty and security of those within its borders. A nation that is devoted to a government that obeys the rule of law, not the whim or caprice of a government official, is one in which those who can understand, facilitate, analyze and interpret laws will possess a substantial influence. In a diverse, pluralistic society, lawyers provide many of the bonds that link Americans together in fashioning a civil society. The importance of law in American society gives law school graduates many options besides practicing law. Non-practicing lawyers use their knowledge to work for non-profit corporations, in business as managers and entrepreneurs, in finance and real estate, in government in non-law specific jobs, in academia (in law schools and in other university departments), and in various media.

It is never too early nor too late to think about law school. Over 15% of all applicants to law schools in recent years have been over 30 years old. Law schools enroll thousands of students who have worked for several years before deciding on attending law school, and one's age is not a handicap for law applicants. Instead, experience in the work force ordinarily benefits the chances of admission of otherwise qualified applicants.

However, neither law school nor the practice of law is for everyone. The efforts by faculty to inculcate analogical reasoning, to facilitate the ability to argue "both sides of a case," to separate the "artificial reason of the law" from one's emotional reaction to the events that led to the case may frustrate, tempt and annoy many law students, particularly first-year law students (1Ls). Dozens of law review articles and books have discussed and criticized the manner in which legal education may contribute to the tearing away of the ideals of students, and turn them into cynical relativists. Although this critique of law schools is overbroad, and may indeed simply be wrong, law school can have a substantial impact on a student's reasoning and emotional intelligence, and that impact is not always favorable.

Chapter 2

Getting Admitted to Law School

You've decided to apply to law school. How do you maximize your chances of getting into law school, and, more importantly, to the law school that best fits you? The information in this chapter applies to most law schools, but a few will explicitly embrace other criteria for admission to law school. Because some law schools may make their admissions decisions in a slightly different fashion than is discussed below, look closely at the admissions parameters publicly noted by the particular law schools to which you intend to apply. Go to the school's website, look at its narrative statement found in the ABA/LSAC *Official Guide* and take a visit to the school to learn about its approach to admissions and to learn about its program of legal education.

Between 2004 and 2008, the number of law school applicants declined from 95,774 to 80,213. The number of law school applicants will rise between 2010 and 2015 for several reasons. One, law school applications tend to rise or fall based on the number of Americans in their early 20s. The number of Americans between the ages of 22 and 25 will reach an all-time high during the next several years. Two, law school applications increase during difficult economic times. The impact of the Great Recession will likely also lead to an increase in the number of law school applicants during the next several years.

Current law school applicants apply to more law schools on average than applicants from a decade ago. The mean (average) number of applications per applicant was 6.5 in 2008, generating over 500,000 law school applications. Based on current enrollment figures one seat is available for every 1.6 applicants. That ratio that may rise slightly over the next several years, but is unlikely to change markedly. In general, this market slightly favors law schools, although it does so less than is commonly believed. A number of well-qualified admitted applicants choose to forego law school, and some applicants will not have the LSAT scores to compete effectively for admission to law school. More importantly, the recent increase in the number of applications per applicant requires law schools to admit more applicants, because good applicants are likely to have more choices among law schools. The result is that most law schools have a yield (that is, the number of admitted applicants who enroll divided by the total number of admitted applicants) of less than 50% (Yale and Harvard Law Schools are two exceptions, as is Southern University Law School). A law school with the excellent yield rate of 50% will still admit two applicants for every one it expects to enroll in the law school. Many highly regarded law schools will have a yield of less than 25%, so do not confuse a lesser yield with a judgment about the quality of the educational opportunity available to you. For example, in recent years Boston University School of Law has reported a yield of 17.5%. Georgetown University Law Center reported a yield of 23%. Both are excellent law schools. Because the market slightly favors law schools, not applicants, you must consider carefully which law schools you should apply to, and how many to apply to. Thinking about what law school is a "safety" school, what is a "reach," and at what law school your scores will be within the ordinary range of the applicant pool is a necessary step in deciding how to channel one's decisions about law school applications.

The two most important numbers in gaining admission to law school are your LSAT score (which ranges from 120–180) and your undergraduate grade point average (UGPA). You may be a smart, ethical and mature student, but if you have poor LSAT and UGPA numbers, you are unlikely to be admitted to law school. The better those numbers, the more options you will have. Because the types of undergraduate colleges and universities and kinds of undergraduate majors differ wildly among law school applicants, and because LSAT scores can be compared across all applicants, law schools place more stress on an applicant's LSAT score than on the applicant's UGPA. (LSAT scores are also an important component of the rankings of law schools in the *Annual Guide* published by *U.S. News*, so law schools pay close attention to the overall LSAT numbers of enrolled students to maintain or enhance their ranking in the *Annual Guide*.)

Obviously, law schools prefer consonant scores, that is, a good UGPA combined with a good LSAT score. ABA-approved law schools are required to report annually to the ABA the 75th percentile (meaning 25% of all enrolled students were at this or a higher number), the median (half of enrolled students were at or above this number and half were at or below this number) and 25th percentile (25% were at or below this number) for both UGPA and LSAT. As a result, all law schools are conscious of making these numbers look as favorable as possible. Unfortunately for law schools, an insufficient number of applicants come with a 3.95 UGPA and a 175 LSAT. Some applicants will have a 3.95 UGPA and a 149 LSAT. Others will have a 175 LSAT and a 2.10 UGPA. How a law school admissions committee or an Assistant Dean of Admissions will look upon these high/low applicants is idiosyncratic, but some decisions about what are called high/low applicants will be made based on how such an applicant might affect the reportable UGPA and LSAT numbers. If the low score is UGPA and the high score is LSAT, many admissions committees and admissions deans look very skeptically on that applicant if the applicant has recently completed college. This is because such an application record suggests a smart and lazy student. You do not have to be a genius to practice law; you cannot, however, practice law well if you are lazy. Of course, some schools are willing to take a chance on such an applicant, particularly if that LSAT score is at the top of its LSAT range, for LSAT score correlates higher with first year law school grades than does UGPA, and another high LSAT score may slightly boost the school's 75th percentile LSAT. Further, the greater the length of time between college and law school, the more likely an admissions committee will downplay an applicant's low UGPA and look at the accomplishments of the applicant since graduating that justify a heavier emphasis on the lopsided LSAT score.

If the applicant has a high UGPA and a low LSAT score, the question for the admissions committee is whether the apparent fact that the applicant is a hard worker is sufficient to overcome the caution of a low LSAT score. In this case, the applicant's chances of admission depend in part on how the school needs to portray its 25th/75th percentile UGPA and LSAT numbers. That is, the applicant may be in the 80th percentile in grades and in the 20th percentile in LSAT. Such an applicant might slightly boost the publicly reported UGPA number and will likely not affect the reported LSAT. If the applicant's undergraduate work indicates excellent grades in a strong major or at a strong university, that will bode well for the applicant in the admission process. If the applicant possesses other positive indicators, including work experience, ethnic diversity and strongly favorable academic letters of recommendation, the applicant's chances of admission increase substantially. In general, the chances of admission for a high/low applicant will be aided by work experience, excellent graduate work (given the understanding that graduate school grades are usually higher than undergraduate grades), effusive letters of recommendation and a strong personal statement.

Undergraduate Grades

If you are reading this having completed two or more years of college, there is little to say about undergraduate grades. Law schools always prefer applicants with good grades, and the more competitive the law school, the higher the grade point average expected of admitted applicants. For example, the

UGPA at the 25th percentile (again, 75% of enrolled students have a higher UGPA) of students at Harvard Law School is 3.75. Yale is even higher, with a 3.77 UGPA for the 25th percentile of enrolled students. It is impossible to graduate with a 3.75 cumulative UGPA if you have a 3.0 after your sophomore year. However, do not view these 25%/75% numbers as absolutes for at least two reasons. First, what Harvard is telling applicants is that 25% of its enrolled students have a UGPA of 3.75 or less. Because of Harvard's national reputation, Harvard has no difficulty in filling its classes with very bright students. But it and other national law schools can also take chances on some students who did poorly at the beginning of their undergraduate work but who performed well late in college and who offer other reasons for admission, such as graduate degrees, some unusual experiences that makes the applicant "interesting" (Harvard annually publishes in its law magazine profiles of a handful of new students, all of whom have "interesting" backgrounds, whether personal or professional) or diverse (which can mean either diversity on the basis of race or ethnicity or diversity in terms of background, geography and experience). And if Harvard can take a (modest) chance on such applicants, so too can other law schools. For example, a law school reporting a 25th percentile UGPA of 3.33 could consist of a class that includes 24% of its first-year (1L) student body with a UGPA of 2.50 or below. That is because the official reporting data are not averaged or averages, but percentile numbers. Applicants with high/low numbers can be often admitted without any adverse impact on the public reporting made by those schools and with some modest positive impact. Second, for those interested only in admission to an elite law school, another reason not to be deflated by the 25% UGPA number at Yale or Harvard is that this number falls quickly at other top ten law schools. For example, a recent 25% UGPA at Columbia University School of Law is 3.56. It was 3.49 at the University of Michigan Law School. Both are top ten law schools.

UGPA is used as one of the two most important factors in law school admissions because a number of studies have found a positive correlation between UGPA and first year law school grades. However, this correlation is relatively modest. This is due in part to the wide variety of undergraduate institutions from which law school applicants graduates. It is also due in part to the fact that law schools do not limit applications to those who focus in undergraduates studies on a "pre-law" curriculum. While courses in logic, philosophy, history and political science may benefit the entering law student, law schools embrace applicants from a vast number of undergraduate majors, making cross-comparisons of applicants difficult if not impossible. How you learn and how you are graded in law school differ greatly from undergraduate grading, and grade inflation that exists at one university or at one school or department within a university may provide a misleading assessment of the applicant. Some applicants may have a lower UGPA than others because they took more difficult courses or graduated in a field in which lower grades were the norm. To focus solely or predominantly on undergraduate grades would create a distorted incentive, telling law school applicants to find the easiest courses in undergraduate studies rather than the courses that may best prepare them for the rigors of law school. Law schools prefer students who challenged themselves as undergraduates, even if that means the applicant occasionally received a poor grade.

The combination of UGPA and LSAT provides the strongest correlation with 1L grades. Other research has found that first-year law school grades correlate with final law GPA and final LGPA correlates somewhat with bar exam success. However, the vast number of American undergraduate institutions (and universities elsewhere in the world) makes it extremely difficult to craft an "equalized" comparison of grades. For some admissions officers, an applicant's UGPA is less important than the "signal" sent by the applicant's major or the selectivity of the institution from which the applicant graduated. In other words, two applicants with a 3.50 UGPA from different universities or from different programs of study within a university will often be viewed very differently.

The lesson on UGPA is, do as well as you can as an undergraduate. Once that opportunity is gone, regrets about one's undergraduate grades are useless. You can overcome poor grades as an undergraduate with time and a record of accomplishments between college and law school. The most important factor will be demonstrating through one's work, volunteer and graduate record that you are now mature and ready to take on the obligations of law school. And, of course, a good LSAT score will go a long way.

LSAT

The LSAT is the single most important factor in determining whether you will be admitted to law school and to which law schools you will likely be admitted. DO NOT TAKE THE LSAT WITHOUT SOME STUDY PLAN THAT INCLUDES TAKING SAMPLE TESTS. This is because, unlike the use by undergraduate admissions officers of the SAT and ACT, law schools do not simply use the highest LSAT score in making admissions decisions. Unless you cancel your score (an event that will be sent to law admissions officers), all of your LSAT scores less than five years old will be reported to the schools to which you are applying. LSAT scores usually increase by 2–3 points on the second attempt, so law schools usually average the first and second LSAT scores in fitting that applicant into its applicant pool. A large jump on the second LSAT score will be viewed suspiciously, a possibility if you were unprepared when you took your first LSAT. Even if the consequence is a delay in applying to law school, do not take the LSAT unless you are well prepared. Law schools are not required to send the average of an enrolled applicant's LSAT scores when they report to the ABA. They can report the student's highest LSAT score only. However, in the admissions process itself, the vast majority of schools will average the applicant's LSAT scores in determining whether to admit the applicant.

It would be more egalitarian if LSAT prep courses did not work. For some they do, because doing well on the LSAT is not based just on "native" or "gathered" (obtained in one's formal education) intelligence, but also on understanding what types of multiple-choice questions are asked and how they are asked, and in learning exam-taking skills that will improve your chances of answering correctly those questions. Because LSAT prep courses cost a significant amount of money, some would-be lawyers may not be able to afford such a course, and they may not score as well as would be the case had the person taken the prep course. And law schools do not know who has taken an LSAT prep course. These courses do not work for everyone, however, and courses at different locations may vary widely in quality. If you cannot afford to take an LSAT prep course (the various providers can all be found on the Internet) or have heard the local program has received middling reviews from friends and acquaintances, you must become familiar with the LSAT through one of the many books that teach one how to improve one's performance on the LSAT. The LSAT is owned by the Law School Admission Council (LSAC), a non-profit organization. Go to its website, www.lsac.org, and read thoroughly the instructions about the LSAT. The LSAC has also published several books consisting of actual LSAT exams. If you cannot afford to buy one of these books, go to a university library, which will likely have available one or all of these books. You must, in some fashion, practice taking several LSAT-prep examinations before taking the actual examination.

The LSAT is given four times a year, in February, June, October and December. Law schools vary widely in setting application deadlines. Some use an April 1 deadline, or admit students in Fall, Spring or Summer. Others will require a completed application as early as the November preceding the beginning of classes in August. Most application deadlines are some time in late winter (January 15 to March 1). The usual deadline makes taking the February exam your least likely option for most applicants. Most applicants will take the exam either in June (during summer break from school) or in October (in time for all deadlines for admission the following year). If you are in undergraduate or graduate school, the December examination may conflict with final examinations, so consider carefully which exam you plan to take.

The LSAT takes about three and one-half hours, and consists of six section comprising five parts, each of which is 35 minutes in length:

- logical reasoning (two sections);
- analytical reasoning;
- reading comprehension;
- an experimental section; and
- an unscored writing sample.

The exam is divided into two halves, with a 10–15 minute break after the first three sections. That means that you will sit for 105 minutes, an hour and 45 minutes, get a 10–15 minute break, and then sit for another 105 minutes. All of the sections other than the writing section are multiple-choice questions with five answers given for each question. The LSAT asks an average of 25 questions in each of the five multiple choice sections, so you have approximately 84 seconds (1.4 minutes) to answer each question. The experimental multiple-choice section is just that. It is not scored, but is used to test new questions and to assess the current pool of test takers compared with previous examinees. It will be another logical reasoning, analytical reasoning or reading comprehension section. Unfortunately, you will not know which section is the experimental section and which is the scored section when you are taking the exam, so you must exert the same effort on each multiple-choice section. DO NOT GUESS WHICH SECTION IS THE EXPERIMENTAL SECTION.

Like the experimental section, the writing sample is unscored. How law schools use the writing sample varies not only by school, but often by the particular member of the admissions committee reading the application. The writing sample offers a limited time example of how an applicant organized and communicated his or her thoughts on the topic. In an attenuated sense this provides some insight into how an applicant may respond to a law school essay question, but its value is quite limited. If the writing sample is used in the admissions process at all, it will ordinarily be used as a very limited tie-breaker among a similarly situated pool of applicants, only some of whom will be admitted from this pool. Because schools vary greatly in the manner in which they use the writing sample, it may be useful to contact the Deans of Admissions at the law schools to which you plan to apply and ask them how the writing sample is used, if at all.

Your LSAT score is thus based on two sections on logical reasoning, a section on analytical reasoning, and a reading comprehension section. The LSAT score ranges from a low of 120 to a high of 180. It works as a bell curve, with about 2% of examinees scoring in the 120s, and 1% in the 170s, with a median of 151. About 70% of all test takers score between 141–160. A score of 161 or better will be in the top 15% of all test takers. The number of graded LSAT questions is ordinarily 101 (including the experimental section, somewhere between 120 and 130 questions are asked), and your score is based on the number of correct answers. DO NOT LEAVE ANY ANSWER BLANK, FOR YOU ARE NOT PENALIZED FOR A WRONG ANSWER! The LSAC takes the number of correct answers and uses a process called scaling to give you your final score. Scaling accounts for the relative difficulty of the examination, and equalizes the scores of test takers across different examinations, allowing a law school to conclude that a 155 score in October means the same thing as a 155 scored in June or December.

With five answers per question, you should get 20% correct simply by guessing. So, answering 20% of the questions correctly is not an accomplishment, and your score will be in the low 120s (if not 120 itself) if that is all you get correct. To receive the average score of 151, you need to answer correctly about 56 of the 101 scored questions. That means that the difference between an LSAT score of 151 and one of 180 (30 points inclusive) is based on the difference in correct answers on the other 45 questions. Because the LSAT is scaled as a bell curve, a difference of one in the number of questions answered correctly may add something close to one additional point to your scaled LSAT score, especially as you move toward the high end of the LSAT band. Further, the "perfect" score of 180 does not require perfection on the LSAT itself. An examinee may get a couple of questions wrong and still receive a scaled score of 180. The bell curve model, joined by the possibility of transcription error (you correctly believed the right answer was "B" but somehow you penciled in the "C" circle, or, even worse, you circled in "B" for question 18 when you meant to circle in "B" for question 17) and the randomness of taking an exam on that particular day, made the LSAC leery that slight differences in LSAT scores would be misunderstood as demonstrating qualitative differences among applicants. Consequently, the LSAC "bands" your score when it is sent to a law school. All scores are banded, that is, grouped, with scores three points below and three points above your actual LSAT score. If your score is 160, it will be banded 157–163, on the view that all test takers with a 160 are comparable to those who received a score three points below (157) and three points above (163). The LSAC began banding scores about a decade ago because both exam takers and some admissions personnel believed a qualitative difference existed between a score of 157 and a score of 158. If the difference between such scores represented just one more correct answer, surely no one would argue that the two applicants were qualitatively different in terms of the LSAT. The LSAC wanted admissions personnel to understand more fully that no qualitative difference on the LSAT exists among applicants with slightly different scores.

The LSAT, like the SAT and ACT used for undergraduate admissions, is relied upon by law school admissions officers and committees because it is the only comparable score for all applicants. With some exceptions it is used more heavily than UGPA not only because it is the only test that all applicants have taken but also because an applicant's LSAT score correlates more with first-year academic success than does UGPA. THE LSAT IS NOT INTENDED TO PREDICT AND DOES NOT PREDICT YOUR SUCCESS AS A LAWYER. As you know, correlation ranges from -1.0 (which is perfect negative correlation) to 1.0 (which is perfect positive correlation). A correlation of 0.0 means no correlation. You also will remember that correlation does not mean causation. No matter how much you think so, your decision to wear your lucky college shirt when your alma mater is playing does not cause the team to win. It may be the case that every time you wear your lucky shirt your alma mater wins, but that's correlation, not causation. The correlation between LSAT score and 1L grades varies among law schools, but ranges roughly between .30–.40. The correlation between 1L grades and UGPA and LSAT combined is somewhere around .50, although that again differs by law school. The extent of LSAT correlation means that a majority of the reasons for a first-year law student's academic success is unknown. Many students do better (and worse) in the first year of law school than is predicted by the LSAT and by the LSAT and UGPA combined.

The most important point to take away from this is that your LSAT score is not destiny. Your success or failure in law school will be determined much more by your motivation and by efficient and effective use of study skills than by that aspect of your aptitude for legal study as determined by the LSAT. Students with very high LSAT scores have failed miserably in law school, and students with very modest LSAT scores perform very well in law school, and, more importantly, in the practice of law. Some students test better than they perform, while others perform much better than they test. Once you are in law school, no one cares what you scored on the LSAT. Professors, fellow students and possible employers are interested only in your performance in law school.

The following discusses generally what is tested on the LSAT and how it relates to your 1L courses.

Logical Reasoning

Logical reasoning will constitute half of your LSAT score, so you should spend half of your time on logical reasoning. Logical reasoning tests your ability to think critically about the passages which you've read. Can you determine the central point of the paragraph? Can you spot the implicit syllogism in the paragraph? Can you assess the strengths and weaknesses of an argument?

Several types of logical reasoning are tested:

Syllogisms and Deductive Reasoning

A syllogism consists of a major premise, a minor premise, and a conclusion that follows from the two premises. The major premise is a global statement, the minor premise is a particular statement, and the conclusion follows from those premises. A famous syllogism is:

Major Premise—All men are mortal;
Minor Premise—Socrates is a man;
Conclusion—Socrates is mortal.

The conclusion follows automatically from the syllogism. This is a type of deductive argument, where the reasoning goes from the general to the particular. In reviewing the syllogism above, you can see how the major premise is a very general statement, the minor premise is a more particular statement, and the conclusion follows without any additional reasoning. The conclusion of a syllogism can be challenged only if one of the premises is inaccurate or incomplete.

Example:

Major Premise—All UPS vans are brown;
Minor Premise—The van that struck the pedestrian was brown;
Conclusion—The van that struck the pedestrian was a UPS van.

This conclusion can be attacked because the premises are incomplete. Even if one can prove that all UPS vans are brown (or at least all the UPS vans in the area where the accident occurred are brown), not all brown vans are UPS vans. The global nature of the major premise is thus unproven. It may well be that the conclusion is correct, but this conclusion is just one of several possibilities. To fix this syllogism, you must amend the major premise: "All brown vans in the area where the accident occurred are UPS vans." The conclusion then follows. The attack on this major premise is one of a lack of empirical proof: is it true that *all* brown vans in that area are UPS vans? Much like the syllogism involving fingerprints (Major premise: Each person's fingerprints are unique, excepting identical siblings; Minor premise: The fingerprints at the scene of the crime match those of the defendant; Conclusion: The fingerprints can only be the defendant's), the issue is whether the person challenging the syllogism can find one exemplar disproving the major premise. (This syllogism can also be attacked through challenging the minor premise, for the claim of a "match" may be faulty as an empirical matter.)

A second example:

> Major Premise—The person who will become President of the United States is sworn into office every fourth year on January 20;
> Minor Premise—John was sworn into office on January 20;
> Conclusion—John was sworn into the office of President of the United States.

The major premise is true. The minor premise is not necessarily true, for John may have been sworn into some office other than the office of the President of the United States on January 20. If the minor premise is not necessarily true the conclusion may not be true. The key to understanding syllogisms is understanding the validity or incompleteness of the major and minor premises, and learning how to analyze critically the assertions made in the premises.

Inductive Reasoning

Lawyers in the common law system rely heavily on inductive reasoning, reasoning from the specific to the general. In traditional common law reasoning, the court has a dispute in the form of a case before it based on some set of facts. It decides the case as a matter of law after making a decision regarding the facts presented by the parties. A second, third and fourth case involving somewhat different facts are decided by courts. Some of those later cases may be decided differently than the first case. From the decisions in these particular cases a more general legal "rule" of the common law arose. For example, if you find something (say, a ring), do you get to keep it and own it as a type of "finder's keepers" rule? Courts began to craft a rule by looking at the facts surrounding the finding (in part, to ensure that the "finding" was not in fact a theft), including where it was found, under what circumstances it was found, and what item was found. The use of factual differences and similarities, as well as more general policies concerning how ownership is gained (or lost) led the court from particular decisions about lost property to a general rule about who was the owner of lost property when more than one person claimed ownership. Once a general rule is created, then the courts will use that general rule as the major premise in a syllogism when deciding any further lost property cases. Thus, after a general rule is created, the courts will use deductive reasoning to decide any subsequent cases.

Here is an example of how a person takes particular examples and generalizes from those examples. Particular example: All fingerprints tested so far differ from one another. Generalization: When the next set of fingerprints not tested so far are taken, those fingerprints will differ from all others tested so far. Note that this can also be used deductively, for one can use the general proposition, All fingerprints are different from one another, to reach the specific conclusion, This new set of fingerprints will differ from all others known.

If-Then Reasoning

If-then reasoning is another form of inductive reasoning. If event X happens, it will cause Y effect. "If it is sunny, Dave will ride his bicycle to work." Note that Dave apparently will ride to work even if it is cold, as long as it is sunny. The "if-then" statement limits the assumptions one has to make. You could infer that the "if" statement is incomplete, because even if it is sunny, if Dave lives in a place where the temperature may hover near zero, Dave will not ride his bicycle to work. But you are not to make inferences that are not suggested by the facts as presented. The basis for "if-then" reasoning is that if the condition ("it is sunny") is met, then something will happen ("Dave will ride his bicycle to work").

You cannot invert or switch the "if-then" statement and be sure it is true: "If Dave is riding his bicycle to work, it is sunny." Not necessarily, for Dave may ride his bike to work on some days other than sunny days (say, warm but cloudy days).

You also cannot take the negative of each parts of the if-then statement and be sure it is true: "If it is not sunny, Dave is not riding his bicycle to work." Again, not necessarily true, for the reason stated above (it is warm but cloudy).

However, if you invert the statement and make both parts negative, the statement will be true. That is, it will be a mirror image of the original statement: "If Dave is not riding his bicycle to work, it is not sunny." You inverted (or switched) both the "if" statement and the "then" statement, and you used the negative for each part of the statement.

Reasoning by Analogy

Reasoning by analogy is a third form of inductive reasoning, and a type of reasoning extraordinarily common in law. Reasoning by analogy is the attempt to group "like" things together, and to separate "unlike" things from like things. This is a type of categorization, which we use all the time in thinking about ideas and objects in our general life. An old Sesame Street skit and song captures the heart of this form of reasoning. A child is shown four things, and in the background a song begins. The child is to guess which "one of these things is not like the others, [which] one of these things just doesn't belong." The point was reinforced by another lyric that stated that "three of these things belong together, three of these things are kind of the same." This last language is the key to reasoning by analogy. The things (ideas, policies, facts) are "kind of the same." They are not identical, but you are expected to see the correct grouping. So, if we have an apple, orange, grapefruit and bicycle, you are supposed to group the first three items into the broader category of fruits, which excludes the bicycle. The difficulty with reasoning by analogy is when the grouping can be made in more than one way. For example, if you have a red delicious apple, an orange, a red tomato, and a beet, you have two possible groupings. The apple, orange and tomato are all fruits (a botanist sees a tomato is a fruit, even though it is used as a vegetable in most cooking), while the beet is a vegetable. You can also group the apple, tomato and the beet as red food products, with the orange as the "unlike" food due to its different color (if it's not a blood orange). Reasoning by analogy requires a clarity in understanding what "grouping" or categorization you are trying to create and how another might categorize differently.

Proof-Based Reasoning

Several related types of reasoning involve statements based on empirical claims, claims supported by some type of proof. One type is the "cause-and-effect" claim. This is similar to the "if-then" statement, but cause-and-effect claims find some support in empirical proof, while the if-then statement may be a hypothesis only. A cause-and-effect claim is one that asserts a result (an effect) is a consequence of a particular event (the cause): "Taking music lessons from a famed soprano gave Sophie the musical qualities that sparked her singing career." Sophie's singing career (effect) was a result of receiving music lessons from an expert singer (the cause). Cause and effect claims are based on rational reasoning claims. A claim that sticking a pin in a voodoo doll that represents your enemy Hal (cause) led Hal to fall ill (effect) will not be accepted because Western thought rejects claims based on voodoo (or astrology or magic). A cause-and-effect claim will usually require a chain of inferences, that is, a chain of specific assumptions. Surely Sophie's singing career was aided by causes in addition to the singing lessons she received. A talent in voice, initial lessons, financial support from her family, an unsuccessful audition that was also heard by a producer looking for a singer for another production, and other causes created the effect of a successful singing career for Sophie. The number and validity of those assumptions will increase or minimize the probability of the relationship between cause and effect, and you will be tested on your understanding of the reliability of those different assumptions. Please remember that cause-and-effect claims differ from correlation claims. Correlation does not mean causation.

A second type of proof-based reasoning is the empirical claim based on statistical models. Experts in legal cases usually limit claims of cause and effect to statistical relationships that have a high degree of statistical likelihood (often a 95% degree of confidence). Once you are in law school and then in the practice of law, you should become familiar with statistical tools, in part to examine the validity and reliability of the claims made by experts. For purposes of the LSAT, you simply need to understand broadly that, as stated by Mark Twain and others, "There are three kinds of lies: lies, damned lies, and statistics."

Logical Fallacies

One of the most common logical fallacies is the *post hoc, ergo propter hoc* fallacy. This Latin phrase meaning "after the fact, therefore because of the fact" is a common logical fallacy and can be tested on the LSAT. The *post hoc ergo propter hoc* fallacy is usually a mistaken or at least unproven claim of cause and effect. For example, if someone claimed that "after Social Security was created the number of persons over 65 doubled," one must prove that Social Security was the cause that led to the effect of the doubling of the number of persons 65 or older. We can also return to our example of sticking a pin in a voodoo doll that represents Hal. If Hal dies after his enemy sticks pins in the voodoo doll that represents him, that doesn't mean that the cause (sticking pins in the doll) led to the effect (Hal's death).

A second logical fallacy is *to err in making an analogy*. A false analogy exists when the comparison (this event is like this other event) is unsupported by the facts or when the categorization strains reason. For example: "The way to win a political election is to take the same approach as a team takes in winning the Super Bowl." Is the approach taken in winning a championship in professional football the same as in a political contest? Other than the fact that there is a winner and loser, and that the contest is usually between two parties (since we have a two-party political system), is there anything that allows a comparison of these two events? All sporting contests are games played according to certain rules of the game. They are not decided by which team's fans are more passionate in voting for a winner. A political contest is decided by voters, and the intensity of those voters may make the difference in the election in a way that is not as relevant in sports. This appears to be a false analogy.

A third logical fallacy (at least some of the time) is the *"slippery slope" or the "parade of horribles" claim*, which is an extension of the "cause-and-effect" form of reasoning. If event X happens, then Y will happen, then Z will happen, then all sorts of terrible things (thus, a "parade" of horrible events) will happen. How far one can trace the causes of certain effects is very uncertain in the real world, so be wary of this form of argument. You can think of this type of argument by remembering the nursery rhymes "The House That Jack Built" and "For Want of a Nail": "For want of a nail the shoe was lost. For want of a shoe the horse was lost. For want of a horse the rider was lost. For want of a rider the battle was lost. For want of a battle the kingdom was lost. And all for the want of a horseshoe nail." This is an old but recurrent argument, one attacked as long ago as 1800 in a letter written by Thomas Jefferson on April 30: "Congress are authorized to defend the nation. Ships are necessary for defence; copper is necessary for ships; mines, necessary for copper; a company necessary to work the mines; and who can doubt this reasoning who has ever played at 'This is the House that Jack Built.' Under such a process of filiation of necessities the sweeping clause makes clean work." Jefferson was referring to a proposed bill in Congress to create a copper mining company, which he believed was beyond Congress's constitutional authority. The slippery slope/parade of horribles argument is, however, used regularly in law, including constitutional law.

A fourth type of logical fallacy is *"begging the question."* When a person is "begging" the question, it means the person is smuggling into the question certain unproven facts, conclusions or beliefs. Those unproven facts are then used to support the questioner's conclusion. The classic (and sexist) question, "Have you stopped beating your wife?" assumes a fact or condition (assaulting one's spouse) that may not be true, and a person falsely accused of such an act cannot answer the question either yes or no, for the conclusion smuggled in the question makes either answer an affirmation of the conclusion. Assuming a conclusion without any proof may also be called *circular reasoning*.

Another logical fallacy is a *non sequitur*, a conclusion that does not follow the premises. Example: "The state allowed automobiles to turn right even though the stoplight was red if no oncoming traffic was present. Thomas then decided travel by rail was now safer than travel by airplane." How a change in the state's law allowing a right turn on a red light led Thomas to consider the relative merits of rail and air travel is a non sequitur.

Several other logical fallacies, which work in conjunction with other types of arguments that have not yet been discussed, are not central to the LSAT.

They do arise regularly in law school, however, and are discussed in Chapter 4.

Analytical Reasoning

The analytical reasoning section of the LSAT constitutes one quarter of your LSAT exam. The LSAC defines this section in the following way: "Analytical reasoning items are designed to measure your ability to understand a structure of relationships and to draw logical conclusions about the structure. You are tasked to make deductions from a set of statements, rules, or conditions that describe relationships among entities such as persons, places, things, or events."

If you are required to make "deductions," then you need to understand the general premises or "rules" of the argument to reach a particular conclusion. The idea is to determine whether you can use your organizing skills to "see" whether your "deductions" follow the limits of the question. In the analytical reasoning section, you are given a set of rules within the question. You must accept these rules. Based on the rules that you must accept, you are to reach the logical conclusion that follows from those rules.

The types of questions asked in this section include 1) grouping questions, that is, questions about what persons or things go with other persons or things (a type of reasoning by analogy), and 2) questions placing persons or things in a certain order, that is, taking a group of people or things and, based on the "rules" set forth in the game, deciding in which order (or at least in which partial order) the persons or things are in (which includes syllogistic and if-then reasoning). These analytical questions are a type of math ordering question framed in verbal language rather than in the symbolic language of mathematics.

Reading Comprehension

The section on reading comprehension will also constitute one quarter of your total LSAT score. It consists of four lengthy (each passage will consist of 600 or more words) written passages. The LSAC states the purpose of this section is to "assess your ability to read, with understanding and insight, passages comparable in terms of level of language and complexity to materials you are likely to have to deal with in the study of law." You will be asked to answer between five and eight questions based on each passage. As noted by the title, this section is designed to determine whether you can comprehend this written passage, including its central point, its implicit and explicit arguments supporting the central theme of the passage, and its organizational structure.

The key to reading comprehension is a pencil, for you need to read the passage and annotate, criticize and underline the points made in the passage. This is known as active reading, and will keep you focused, particularly because some of the passages may otherwise be boring, incomplete or confusing.

Because the reading comprehension section consists of multiple questions based on four passages, you have both the opportunity and problem of time management. If you can read quickly and actively (again, in a focused manner), you should have little difficulty completing this section, for you have just under nine minutes to complete each written passage. However, should you have to read the passage three or more times, you will likely find it difficult to complete the 25–28 questions in the 35 minutes you have to complete this section. Practicing the pace at which you need to proceed will enhance your chances of answering more questions correctly. You must familiarize yourself with actual reading comprehension passages.

One way to use your time efficiently is to begin by skimming several of the questions asked at the conclusion of the passage. Looking at the "call" (the point or goal) of some of the questions may give you a better sense of what to look for in the passage. If the passage is followed by eight questions, however, understanding the call of so many questions is too daunting. Divide your skimming by looking at the call of two or three questions at a time. This should allow you to read the passage more quickly or even to skim the passage for some of the answers. In addition, because each question is worth the same, make sure you get to each of the four passages so you are able to answer correctly some of the easier questions asked in each passage.

If you find yourself spending too much time on any given passage (or even any question, given your regular quota of 1.4 minutes per question), have a default answer available and then move on. Your default answer may be any letter; just choose one before you begin the exam. You use a default to ensure that you do not bubble in the line for question 14 when you meant to answer question 16. You also use a default because you may be running out of time. You might get lucky and answer correctly by guessing. Remember, you are not penalized for a wrong answer, so no answer should *ever* be left blank. On questions that you think you can answer if you have sufficient time after completing the section once, put an asterisk next to the question. On questions that you found difficult to answer, put a check mark next to these questions. If you have time, go back and answer those questions in order: first the questions with asterisks and second, the questions with check marks next to them.

Writing Section

As discussed above, the writing section is at most a tiebreaker used at the end of the admissions process. Law school admissions committee members will not use a poor writing sample to bar the admission of an applicant with a very good LSAT. Admissions committee members will also not use an excellent writing sample to admit an applicant if one's LSAT score is poor. But particularly when the law school uses an admissions committee consisting of faculty members, it is a terrible idea to assume that no one will look at your writing section. The faculty member will likely forgive errors in thinking, but egregious errors in grammar and syntax may serve as a red flag for some faculty. This can be the case because faculty at a number of schools are involved in deciding the "maybe" applicant pile. Some law schools divide their applicants pools into three categories: likely admit, likely exclude, and maybe. Sloppiness in a "maybe" applicant's writing sample can suggest a laziness or immaturity that cautions against admission. Carefulness in the writing sample allows the committee member to acknowledge that you have done what you were supposed to do. However, this carefulness in the writing sample will not ordinarily improve your application. In a strong sense, then, the writing section sample can hurt your chances of admission, but likely will not aid your chances of admission. Another use of the writing section is to assess non-American or non-native English speaking applicants. If an applicant went to a non-American university, universities that often have very different grading systems that are difficult to comprehend, the writing sample may be used to determine whether this applicant can write at a level necessary to perform well in law school.

The LSAT and Law School

The LSAT reflects some of the skills and abilities that first year law students are expected to learn. Most first year courses are taught through the "case method." For each class session you will be assigned to read several cases, cases that are published opinions of appellate courts. The opinions may be well written, but some are poorly written or poorly reasoned, providing the student with various examples of how appellate decisions are made and should be interpreted. These opinions from different state or federal courts may in fact reach opposite conclusions (or you may be required to read both a majority and dissenting opinion), forcing you to think why one decision or opinion is or appears better reasoned than another. Law is supposed to be based on reason, and thus logical reasoning is central to appellate opinions. As you read more and more cases, you will have to keep track of various legal rules and doctrines, and see how they fit or conflict in practice. You will also have to keep in mind the differences between legal principles, legal policies and legal doctrine, as well as factual differences among cases, all of which will bring to bear your ability to order, using analytical reasoning. Of course, because judges are human beings, court opinions may also be tinged to a greater or lesser degree by emotion. Though you will focus on honing your reasoning skills you should never forget the important role of human emotion in the law. Finally, your ability to read closely and carefully will be tested on your final examinations (often the only evaluation tool you will have the entire semester), so reading comprehension is also important in learning the study of law in the first year of law school.

The LSAT does not reflect a number of other skills or traits that make one a successful lawyer or a successful first year law student. The ability to listen well is a tremendous asset to possess as a lawyer, and is very useful as a first-year law student, especially the difficult task of listening closely to your classmates in class. Your ability to manage your time is also quite valuable, a value tested only very indirectly in the LSAT. Additionally, your ability to communicate with and understand the emotional positions of clients and fellow lawyers and to work well with others are crucial in succeeding in the practice of law. To re-iterate, your LSAT score is not your destiny. It may be that you are not admitted to the law school you most wanted to attend. However, your success as a lawyer will be determined by your work ethic and your motivation, not your LSAT score and not the name of your law school alma mater.

Other Criteria

Although the law school admissions process focuses heavily on the applicant's LSAT and UGPA, many schools use other criteria to fill a class, particularly among the group of candidates that are in the "maybe" pile of applicants. These criteria should not be ignored, for they can mean the difference between admission and rejection. What are those other criteria?

- Graduate Education
- Letters of Recommendation
- Personal Statement
- Work/Voluntary/Other Experience
- Diversity

A significant majority of law students are in their middle 20s. However, law schools look to enroll a class that is diverse in terms of age and experience and otherwise. A number of law schools find the fact that the applicant has taken graduate level courses or received a graduate degree a helpful sign that the applicant possesses the maturity to succeed in law school. It is not that graduate school and law school are similar in educational approach that makes graduate work a positive admissions indicator. The signal that is sent is that the applicant has shown the ability to set long-term goals (and thus the applicant is used to delayed gratification), and may have a better sense why he or she wants to attend law school than someone who is just completing an undergraduate degree.

Letters of recommendation are much like the writing sample on the LSAT. They ordinarily do not aid the applicant's chances of admission, but they can harm the applicant's chances of admission. On occasion they can make a positive difference. I have in some cases used letters of recommendation as a tipping point favoring admission of the candidate. Invariably this is the result of reading an effusive and cogent letter of recommendation from an undergraduate or graduate professor who taught and knows the applicant well. These are the hand-crafted letters of recommendation, not the *pro forma* letters that are often sent on behalf of the application for admission. Getting two such letters can clinch a decision on a candidate whose LSAT and UGPA scores place the applicant in the "maybe" pool of candidates.

More often than one might expect letters of recommendation impliedly suggest the paucity of academic achievement of the applicant. Too many applicants send in letters of recommendation from politicians or religious leaders, letters that ordinarily indicate little or nothing about the applicant's academic abilities. (Some applicants will have also have a graduate of the law school send a letter of recommendation, which is rarely helpful in determining the academic abilities of the applicant.) The applicant may be a nice person with excellent character traits. What the admissions committee wants is some sense that this applicant's LSAT/UGPA scores are an incomplete indicator of the applicant's academic abilities, and some belief that another academic believes this applicant can do the work expected of him or her in law school. When the applicant fails to include any academic letter of recommendation, that absence can sound the death knell on that candidate. Of course, if you are a number of years away from your undergraduate or graduate education, you may not have kept in touch with faculty who can write a letter of recommendation (although you might be surprised at what faculty members can remember about you with some slight prompting). In that case, obtaining letters of recommendation from your work supervisors or from someone who knows you well from volunteer activities will serve as an adequate substitute for academic letters of recommendation.

You should provide the law school at least two letters of recommendation. Four is too many. The letters of recommendation should be from undergraduate or graduate professors. If a letter of recommendation is from an undergraduate professor, it makes no difference whether that professor taught in the applicant's major area of study or taught the applicant an elective course. Further, if the professor knows well the applicant's academic abilities, it makes no difference whether the professor is a distinguished professor or an adjunct professor.

The personal statement is the opportunity for the applicant to reveal something about his or her interests, passions and goals. It should not be longer than one-and-a-half single-spaced printed pages, and preferably no longer than one page. The applicant should focus positively on the reasons for attending law school, but claims that the applicant only cares about serving others and not about earning a living as a lawyer generally appear insincere (such claims might be sincere, but usually don't appear so). If one has an idea what he or she wants to do in the practice of law, saying so is fine. However, most applicants do not have a clear sense of how they want to use their law degree, and saying you do in an unclear fashion is worse than saying nothing at all. Your personal statement can also reflect on some of the experiences that led you to apply to law school, and those experiences can be intensely personal. Of course, members of the admissions committee do not require your personal statement to take on the tone of a confession, and a personal statement that serves as a passionate cry of the heart can often backfire. The personal statement will be read as much for how it says it as for what it says. In other words, take the time to make sure your personal statement is well written. This is not like the writing sample on the LSAT. If your personal statement is poorly organized, is replete with grammatical and spelling errors, and lacks a theme, that will be counted against you in the admissions process.

Work experience, experience as a volunteer and other experiences (for example, having been a student-athlete or having engaged in important co-curricular activities as an undergraduate) are all valuable. Formal work experience, whether part-time or full-time, provides a signal of seriousness in intention and maturity. Consistent work as a volunteer may serve as a proxy for service, which law schools are interested in fostering (some require volunteer service as a condition of graduation). Other kinds of activities can be slightly helpful (doing well as an undergraduate while spending twenty hours per week as an athlete shows dedication and organizational skills), but service as an elected leader in a social (not service) fraternity or sorority will be viewed neutrally or

slightly negatively. Further, an applicant's declaration that his or her engage-
ment in other activities explains modest or poor grades will signal the applicant failed to arrange his or her priorities well as an undergraduate, a signal that
may portend difficulties for the applicant in law school and which cautions
against admission.

Diversity comes in a number of packages. Law schools, as indicated above,
prefer an enrolled class that consists of persons with diverse backgrounds.
Diversity in terms of work experience between college and law school will
assist some candidates. Further, law schools encourage applications from
"second career" applicants, which diversifies the student body in terms of
both age and experience. Law schools also look favorably at geographical diversity. If you can find a way to explain that your socio-economic status created some adversity in obtaining either a college or legal education (say,
explaining that you are a first-generation college graduate), that explanation
can modestly assist your chances of admission. The difficulty is doing so in
a way that provides some evidence of your claim other than your bare assertion. Most law schools (some state law schools are prohibited from doing so
as a matter of state constitutional law) engage in some affirmative action for
applicants on the basis of race and ethnicity. The extent to which any law
school's admissions committee engages in affirmative action is not quantifi-
able. The Supreme Court of the United States upheld the use of affirmative
action on the basis of race in the admission of law students in *Grutter v.
Bollinger* (2003), allowing race and ethnicity to be used as a "plus" factor in
determining who to admit to law school. Most law schools have adopted
Grutter implicitly or explicitly. Again, the extent to which each uses this "plus"
factor is unclear.

What Is the LSDAS?

The Credential Assembly Service (formerly the Law School Data Assembly
Service, but still known as the LSDAS) is owned by the LSAC, the owner of
the LSAT. The vast majority of ABA-approved law schools require you to register with LSDAS if you are applying to that school. LSDAS requires a fee for
its services. Your LSAT score(s), UGPA by academic semester and year, attached official transcripts for all academic work in college and graduate school,
your writing sample, and letters of recommendation written in behalf of your
application will be compiled by the LSDAS and sent to any school to which
you have applied. The LSDAS form will be used in conjunction with your
school-specific application to determine whether to admit you to law school.

The LSDAS form is identical for applicants, and allows admissions staff and faculty to assess applicants using the same set of materials.

According to the LSAC, "Your LSDAS period will extend for five years from your registration date. If you register for a Law School Admission Test (LSAT) at any time during your LSDAS period, the LSDAS period will be extended five years from your latest LSAT registration."

Chapter 3

Choosing Which Law School to Attend

The good news about choosing a law school is that every ABA-approved law school can offer you an excellent legal education. All teach students the skill of "thinking like a lawyer." All teach students large amounts of substantive law and legal policy, and all provide training in lawyering skills. All ABA-approved law schools offer a thorough educational program providing opportunities for students to learn about vastly different areas of law. All law schools offer resume-building and skills-enhancing co-curricular activities such as law journal, moot court/mock trial competitions and *pro bono publico* (for the benefit of the public) law-related volunteer opportunities. All law schools have a career development office (which is rarely a jobs bank), and most have some kind of mentoring program linking students with practicing lawyers. In terms of the courses you take, you will find that most of your teachers will have significant strengths in teaching (yes, some may not be entertaining, but you may be surprised at how much you learn from them). Some excellent teachers are found at every American law school, teachers whose passion and drive you will remember long after you've forgotten the substance of what was taught. You are also likely at any ABA-approved law school to run into some professors who are weak teachers, and into some whose pedagogical goals are unclear or undeclared. If your only decision is whether to attend the single ABA-approved law school located where you live (for example, if you cannot move for personal or professional reasons), you can take comfort in the fact that this local law school can provide you with an excellent legal education.

The bad news is that it is too easy to make a less than optimal choice about which law school to attend. This is largely because too many law school applicants spend too much time thinking about a law school's putative national reputation rather than the law school's actual regional reputation, and too little time thinking about how well a particular law school's strengths meet the applicant's particular educational needs. The national reputation of a law school may be very good, but its value to a person intending to practice law outside of the region in which that "national" law school is located may make the nationally recognized school the wrong choice for that applicant. A law school with a strong regional reputation, though less well-known nationally, may provide the applicant with a better legal education, more developed legal skills and more employment opportunities within the region than the nationally recognized school. More importantly, too few law school applicants consider whether the strengths of a particular law school fit their needs and goals. Just as a law school will focus on some areas or aspects of law and legal education, law school applicants have different needs in terms of educational focus. For example, a number of law schools have reduced the number of hours its faculty teaches so those faculty will have more time to spend on legal scholarship. Some law schools have made this decision because legal scholarship is occasionally used as a marker or proxy for the school's overall reputation. This reduction in the number of hours a faculty member spends teaching has several consequences: 1) it will substantially increase the cost of the law school, for you will need more full-time faculty to teach the same number of course hours; 2) it will increase the number of adjunct professors who will teach some basic and many advanced course offerings, and adjunct professors, most of whom are practicing lawyers, will range the gamut from the sublime to the ridiculous in teaching ability; 3) office hours for personal interaction with full-time and adjunct faculty may be lessened, for full-time faculty may spend more time outside of the office while engaged in legal scholarship and adjunct faculty are already making a sacrifice of their personal time simply by preparing for and teaching their class; and 4) this may lessen (it doesn't have to, but it might) the value accorded teaching by that law school.

Part of the reason for this disconnect in choosing the right law school is that the qualitative differences among law schools are much less pronounced than the *U.S. News Annual Guide* and other ranking publications claim. The *Annual Guide* claims to provide a listing of law schools from one through 100, with the remaining 100 or so law schools unranked. The reader of the *Annual Guide* may first take from this the view that she should attend any ranked law school rather than any unranked law school. Not only is this false, it can have a pernicious effect on the education received by the student. Your success in the practice of law depends on how well you learn, not where you learn it. The advantage of going to law school at Harvard or the University of Michigan is not that you will learn from better teachers or generally receive a better education there than at any unranked law school. You won't. Instead, the benefit of going to Harvard or Michigan rather than to an unranked law school is that you will have an increased chance of gaining employment as an associate with a large law firm, as a judicial clerk working for a federal judge or as a lawyer with a public interest law firm. What is significant about what nearly all interested observers (law faculty, large law firm lawyers, federal court judges) agree are the top 5% of law schools (even the second 5% is subject to significant disagreement) is that employers do not have to sort through the class in order to find new employees. The graduation of over 45,000 law students every year makes it important for large employers of new lawyers (mainly large law firms located in large metropolitan areas) to sort through who should be interviewed and, among those interviewed, who should be hired. A student who graduates from what most agree is one of the top ten or so law schools has been sorted by her admittance to that law school rather than sorted by her law school grades. Sorting students by their grades is the norm for at least 90% of all law schools. The sorting function as used for graduates of the top ten law schools does not mean that those graduates will become more successful lawyers than graduates from lower ranked or unranked law schools, either in terms of financial success or in terms of the reputation of that lawyer within the legal community in which the lawyer practices. The vagaries of admissions decisions, of how persons learn and how one gains the practical wisdom that is essential to successful lawyering ensure that no intelligent client will make a decision about which lawyer to hire based on the diploma that hangs on the lawyer's wall. What the *Annual Guide* mimics is an already existing informal ranking of schools with the broadest reputation nationally. The *Annual Guide* did not create this ranking of law schools, it just profitably exploited it.

Sorting by law school works as part of the employment process. It is a blunt rather than a refined process. Many employers also use the sorting function of grades to make hiring decisions, with relatively little thought given to the rank of the law school. For example, a major Los Angeles law firm may interview students at most of the top ten law schools in sorting out who to hire. It may also interview students at other law schools across the country, occasionally chosen in part because one or two partners in the firm graduated from that law school. The major Los Angeles firm will additionally interview at nearly all of the law schools located in the greater Los Angeles area, and decide who to interview at those schools based on the grades received by the student. Sorting by grades may differ based on the regional reputation of the law school (that is, depending on how the different schools are perceived in comparison with one another on a regional basis), but rarely will a law firm decide not to interview at a law school in the area. Hypothetically, a law firm may be interested in interviewing students in the top half of the class at UCLA and USC and those students in the top third of their class at Loyola (Los Angeles) Law School or Pepperdine University. It may limit its interviews of students at other law schools in the LA area to those in the top 10% of their class. This regionally-dominant method of hiring, even at large law firms, has been successful throughout the United States for over fifty years. One result of the recent Great Recession is that national recruiting of students (say, recruiting in Los Angeles if your firm is located in Chicago, or vice versa) is likely to decline, while regional recruiting is likely to increase Tightened recruiting budgets will make regional recruiting more important and appealing. The Great Recession will also lessen the hiring of summer law clerks for several years, but it may also increase the number of local students hired by law firms to work part-time during the academic year.

A second and related concern about using ranking systems to choose a law school is that the data used to rank schools are not transparent. For example, the 2009 *Annual Guide* declared as the thirtieth best law school a tie among Fordham University, University of Alabama, University of North Carolina at Chapel Hill, University of Washington and Washington and Lee University. These are schools located across the country. Can they really be tied? The forty-ninth ranked law school in 2009 is a tie between Southern Methodist University in Dallas and Yeshiva University Cardozo School of Law in New York City. Can any good reason be given why these two schools are ranked lower than any of the five schools ranked thirtieth? The 2010 edition listed six schools as tied as the 28th best law school. Only the University of North Carolina at Chapel Hill was in both groups. The remaining four from 2009 were either tied for 34th or 38th in the 2010 edition. What happened to the University of Alabama, which dropped from a tie for 30th to a tie for 38th? It seems highly unlikely that anything happened to lead to this shift. The numerical differences among these schools appears modest, indeed statistically insignificant. A glance at the entire list of law schools in the *Annual Guide* also indicates a significant number of "unranked" schools have a better reputation within legal education than many ranked law schools. Although *U.S. News* provides some explanation of its scoring system, several professors have reverse engineered the factors used by *U.S. News* to show the significant flaws in its scoring system. Professor Theodore Seto showed that the criteria used for one edition of the *Annual Guide* was such that if the lowest ranked law school had a one percent drop in its employment rate for graduates (which would mean a change in employment status for one student), and no other change took place at any other school, that small change in the graduate employment percentage of the lowest ranked school would dramatically alter the rankings of a number of ranked law schools. Some would rise in rank (one from 32nd to 27th) and others would fall in rank, some by four places. Professor Seto also demonstrated that if Yale's median LSAT score was the same as a fourth tier law school it would still rank first in the *Annual Guide*! How is this possible? How is it possible that an insignificant change at the lowest ranked school could affect the rank of other law schools when nothing changed at any of these other schools? How could it be that drastically changing Yale's median LSAT score would make no difference in its ranking?

More to the point, the *Annual Guide* fails to account for notions of regional reputation. Should a law school applicant equate the University of Washington (Seattle), Washington University (St. Louis) and Washington and Lee University (located in rural Virginia) if that applicant wants to practice law in Seattle? There may be law graduates of Washington University and Washington and Lee University successfully practicing in Seattle, but the number of such graduates pales in comparison with the number of successful law graduates of the University of Washington practicing there. This likely difference among the three schools does not make any a lesser law school than the others; it just means that desired practice location can and should affect one's decision about which law school to attend. If you wish to practice law in New York City with a large law firm, will you have a better chance of doing so if you attend the unranked New York Law School or the twenty-eighth ranked University of Georgia?

Making the right decision about law school will depend more on your answers to the questions listed below than on basing your decision on a rankings guide. You may be slightly harmed if you do not look at the *Annual Guide* to determine whether a law school has a national reputation, but you will be greatly harmed in using the *Annual Guide* without thinking clearly about your goals in law school and in the practice of law.

Choosing a law school should take time. It is an expensive proposition, both in terms of money and, more importantly, time. As you think about law school, you should narrow the list of law schools you would consider attending to about ten. Most students do their initial homework about law schools by looking at the law school's website and from word-of-mouth from family or friends. Once you have received your LSAT score, you will likely be able to eliminate several schools from your application pool. You should strongly consider applying to a few law schools that are a reach, a few that appear to be well within reach ("safety" schools), and several in which you have a good chance of gaining admission.

For readers considering applying for admission to the California bar: California allows the following persons to take the California bar exam: 1) graduates of ABA-approved law schools; 2) graduates of law schools approved by the Committee of Bar Examiners of the state of California; 3) those who have learned law through office study (study with a lawyer or judge) and met all requirements of such study, including passing the First Year Law Students' Examination, also known as the "baby bar"; and 4) graduates of law schools that do not meet the first two categories, including those graduating from unaccredited correspondence law schools, from distance learning law schools, and from California-based but unaccredited fixed facility law schools as long as those graduates have passed the First Year Law Students' Examination. The First Year Law Students' Examination consists of questions on the subjects of Contracts, Criminal Law, and Torts. The contract law question includes both the general law of contracts and Articles 1 and 2 of the Uniform Commercial Code. The baby bar is not based on the particularities of California law, but on generally applicable law. It is offered twice yearly, and is a one day examination. The morning session takes a maximum of four hours and consists of four essay questions. After a lunch break of one hour, the afternoon session takes a maximum of three hours, during which the exam taker must answer 100 multiple-choice questions. A student must score at least 560 points to pass the baby bar, which then allows the student to complete his or her legal studies, making the person eligible to take the California bar exam. Each of the two parts of the baby bar is worth a maximum of 400 points. The applicant receives one raw point for each correct multiple-choice answer, making 100 the maximum raw score. The raw score is converted to a 400 point scale. It is not simply multiplied by four, but is adjusted to account for the relative difficulty of the exam. Each essay question is scored from 40–100, meaning a maximum essay score is 400. The raw score is again adjusted (slightly in this case) to account for the relative difficulty of the essay exam. The adjusted scores from each part of the baby bar are added together. A student must take and pass the baby bar by the third administration of the exam (again, it is offered twice yearly) after becoming eligible to take the baby bar. If the examinee passes the baby bar, she "shall receive credit for all law study completed to the date of the administration of the examination passed." If an applicant fails to pass the baby bar within three administrations after first becoming eligible to take the examination, when she finally passes the baby bar she will receive credit only for the first year of her law study.

California annually publishes statistics on the success rate of bar exam takers from the law school in each of the categories above (as well as the passing rate of graduates of out of state ABA-approved law schools with ten or more exam takers). Overall, the passing rate among California-based ABA-approved schools is much higher (in July 2009, the passing rate was 79.3%) than it is for California-accredited (32.2% in July 2009) and California-unaccredited (26.5% in July 2009) law schools. More importantly, if the law school applicant may end up moving outside of California, choosing to attend a California-accredited law school rather than an ABA-approved law school may have other consequences. All states allow a graduate of an ABA-approved law school to take that state's bar exam. Relatively few states allow a graduate of a law school that is not approved by the ABA (such as a California-accredited law school) to take its bar exam. If you have few options (for example, if you live in a city with no law school and you cannot commute (or move) to a city with an ABA-approved law school) regarding law school, attending a California-accredited law school may be your best option (and this option allows you to avoid taking the First Year Law Students' Examination). If that is not possible, then your best option may be enrolling in a California-unaccredited law school. If you choose this last option, there are significant differences in learning law through correspondence, distance learning, and fixed facility ("bricks and mortar") law schools. You must know your strengths and weaknesses as a student to determine which of these three options is best suited to the manner in which you learn.

What Are the Most Important Reasons for Choosing a Law School?

You should choose a law school for some mix of the following three reasons:

1. Does This Law School Fit You?

This is the most difficult reason to evaluate, and the most important. All ABA-approved law schools must meet certain minimum criteria to retain ABA-approved status, which narrows differences among schools in the overall curriculum, in assessment (grading) of students and in the law school's available co-curricular and extra-curricular activities. In addition, nearly all law schools are modeled on the Harvard Law School program of legal education initiated in 1870 by Dean Christopher Columbus Langdell. The "socratic" method of teaching law, particularly in the first year of law school (discussed in more detail in Chapter 4) consolidated its hold on legal education by the early twentieth century. American legal education settled on a three year program almost a century ago, and student-edited law journals (which are used as a tool by law firms as demonstrating a student's talent for writing and analytical ability) have existed for over a century and are found at every law school. Further, the bar exam also constrains differences among law schools. The bar exam is required everywhere but in Wisconsin. Even in Wisconsin only the graduates of the state's two law schools are currently exempt from the bar exam. The existence of the bar exam requires, to a greater or lesser extent, law schools to offer courses on most if not all of the subjects tested on the bar exam in the state in which the law school is located. One result of the history of American legal education is that the required courses in the first year of law school remain quite similar among American law schools.

Despite their many similarities, law schools vary substantially in a number of important respects for the student, and those differences will emerge if you spend time assessing the strengths and weaknesses of the school. For example, if you have some thoughts about the work you may be interested in doing after law school (say, civil litigation or banking/corporate work), you will find a number of differences among law schools. Students pursuing a J.D. do not "major" in a particular area of law, and your license to practice law allows you to offer legal advice on any law of that state (and any federal law) as well as to represent any client in a court of that state in any matter (of course, you are subject to a charge of legal malpractice and professional discipline if you give incompetent legal advice or perform incompetently in court). Most lawyers, however, eventually limit their practice to a relatively narrow area of law (that is, they will focus on bankruptcy law, or, even more particularly, on consumer bankruptcy law) or on a type of practice (say, criminal defense practice, or particular fields within criminal defense, such as "white-collar" or DWI/DUI criminal defense).

One consequence of the increase in specialization in the practice of law is that a number of law schools now offer their students a chance to "concentrate" (and to receive a "certificate of concentration" along with a diploma at graduation) in a particular area. For example, the law school may offer a concentration in property law. In the final two years of law school the student may take courses in land use planning, environmental law, natural resources law (including water law and oil and gas law), real estate finance and similar courses. The capstone of the concentration is often a research paper or other project focused on some aspect of that area of law. A second consequence of legal specialization is that a number of law schools have opened "Institutes," "Centers" and "Programs" focused on a particular area of law. These Institutes are staffed by one or more faculty members and others who teach and write in the area, giving students the opportunity to take a number of different courses in the area. For example, several law schools have established a Health Law Institute, and the faculty associated with the Institute may offer courses in Bioethics, Mental Health Law, Medical Malpractice, Food and Drug Law and other courses. Institutes often collaborate with other departments with the University (or with other universities in the same city) to create a joint degree program between the law school and other graduate school, offering a student the opportunity to obtain both a J.D. and a master's degree. For example, a law school with a Health Law Institute may have a joint degree program with a medical school or School of Public Health offering the student a chance to receive a joint J.D.-M.D. or J.D.-M.P.H. (master's degree in public health). Further, Institutes sponsor conferences, lectures and other programs attended by practitioners in the field. An active and engaged director of an Institute can assist students in making contacts with practitioners, particularly alumni active in this area of practice, can give students some sense of the type of work expected of the lawyer practicing in this field, and can introduce those students to a lawyer who may serve as a mentor providing an understanding or context concerning this field of law. The Institute may also generate opportunities for graduates to enter the area of practice. A third consequence of specialization is the rise of LL.M. programs, advanced programs of study (usually completed in one year of full-time study) after receiving a J.D. Law schools with LL.M. programs allow students studying for a J.D. to take most or all of the LL.M. courses offered by the school, giving J.D. students a way to focus in an area of law even absent a formal concentration.

Given the number of areas of legal specialization, law schools are constrained to limit the number of programs offered for its students. The applicant who has given some thought to considering which career path to take should evaluate which of the law schools she is considering offers a concentration or an Institute in a desired area of study. Determining which law school offers the best program in that field may lead the applicant to assess general employment data for graduates, the reputations of Institute faculty (conduct an Internet search), and even calling well-known alumni who practice in the field (most law schools have printed materials that highlight noted alumni who practice law in the field in which the law school offers a concentration or Institute).

Most law school applicants do not know in what area they plan to practice law. How should you determine whether the law school will fit you when you are not sure what kind of law you want to practice or, in some cases, whether you want to practice law?

One consideration is geography. A counterintuitive approach may be to think about law schools after first deciding on where you want to live, at least where you would like to live for the next three years. Your decision about which law school to attend will narrow to those law schools in that location. So, if you have an affection for the Bay Area (San Francisco, Oakland and environs), either as a native or from afar, you may limit your decision to those law schools located in the greater metropolitan area. One consideration in focusing on a particular location is that the number of law schools which you might attend will quickly dwindle as the metropolitan population decreases. The Bay Area is the home to a large number of law schools that serve very different populations of students. This approach also works well for about seven other metropolitan areas (New York, Los Angeles, Chicago, Washington, D.C., Boston, Philadelphia and Miami) and moderately well in a few other metropolitan areas (Houston, Dallas, Seattle and San Diego). Although more than fifty ABA-approved law schools are located in these areas, this leaves a large number of law schools unaccounted for. If you are particularly interested in attending a state-supported law school, most are found in medium-sized metropolitan areas (Gainesville, Austin, Columbus, etc.). If you want to live outside of the top ten most populous metropolitan areas, your choice of law schools will be limited. Even a city like Phoenix is home for but two law schools. Outside of those listed cities, a slightly different way to use geography is to consider location in terms of state rather than metropolitan area.

Washington, D.C. is a special case. Six law schools are located in the District of Columbia. Another is in Arlington, Virginia, just across the Potomac River, and two law schools are in Baltimore, about an hour's drive from Washington. You may decide to attend law school in Washington because you've always wanted to practice some type of law prominent in the area (say, as a lawyer practicing before the Federal Communications Commission (FCC)), or because you just like the idea of learning law in a place where lawyers are prominent figures (and occasionally where its most prominent resident, the President, is a lawyer), where Congress makes law and where the Supreme Court and other important federal courts, including the United States Court of Appeals for the District of Columbia Circuit and the United States Court of Appeals for the Federal Circuit are located. Because Washington is a magnet for lawyers trained across the country, competition for jobs is fierce. Attending law school in Washington will allow you opportunities to find internships or part-time legal work during law school that may give you a better chance of finding work there upon graduation.

A second consideration is to look at the type of school you would like to attend. Although all law schools will teach the basic building blocks of the law in the same way, some will add components as a result of conscious choices regarding their institutional mission. In this measure, state-supported law schools are bound more tightly than private law schools. More than half of all ABA-approved law schools are private. More than thirty of those law schools are religiously-affiliated. Most of these are affiliated with Roman Catholic universities, but other schools are affiliated with the Church of Jesus Christ of Latter-day Saints, or are schools within Baptist and Methodist universities or are part of a Jewish university. Religiously-affiliated law schools vary widely in the extent to which they incorporate legal theories or ideas that may have some religious basis (for example, the extent to which natural law is discussed may range from never to often, and how religious faith informs the teaching and understanding of human rights thinking may be great or little).

Relatedly, some schools are well-known for their focus on particular social justice issues, including immigration and poverty law clinics, or for their integration of international law in the curriculum. A few have blended law and economics in their program of study, while others are known for their co-curricular advocacy programs, in which students learn about trying and appealing cases through mock trial and moot court competitions that often are national competitions in which dozens of law school teams will compete. Most law schools publish, in addition to their namesake law review, one or more law journals dedicated to specialized topics in law. These specialized law reviews, once known as "secondary" law journals, provide both a sense of an area of focus within the law school as well as an additional opportunity for law students to improve their writing and analytical skills.

Most law schools have little political tilt or cultural bias. However, some law schools may be dominated by some particular political views. Even if a law professor has pronounced political views, those views are rarely made part of the learning process. Enough stories exist about the politicization of undergraduate classes that law professors have largely (not completely) avoided injecting their political views into the learning mix. However, students may not be as shy as professors, and in some law schools students offering minority viewpoints have been hissed for their class comments. However, if a law school has a political bias it is ordinarily found not in the classroom but in extra-curricular organizations. If you have a strong interest in joining the school's ACLU chapter or Federalist Society, you should find out how that organization is viewed in the law school.

In terms of cultural bias, law schools differ quite a bit. The extent to which an LGBT student will find the law school a comfortable place will vary widely at different schools. Law schools will also offer very different experiences to evangelical students. As a formal matter, law schools are not interested in discriminating against students or appearing to discriminate against certain students. Informally the student may feel fellow students (and some administrators) are either quite welcoming or quite distant. Scouring the website and taking with current or former students will give you the best sense of how politics or culture may affect your law school experience.

Several law schools are part of historically black universities, and those law schools were initially created as a consequence of legalized segregation. These law schools are now the among the most diverse law schools in the United

States, with students of all racial and ethnic groups in attendance. Other law schools have strong Hispanic/Latino/a student populations, or significant Asian-American student bodies.

About a dozen law schools are not affiliated with a university. They are called "free-standing" law schools because they operate independently of any university. The Dean of the free-standing law school is also often its President, and ordinarily reports directly to the law school's governing body, the board of trustees. Four free-standing ABA-approved law schools are for-profit schools. Three of the four are owned by the same company. All law schools, whether non-profit or for-profit entities, work to achieve a surplus of revenues over expenses (if they didn't, they would eventually go bankrupt). Whether a for-profit law school has a greater interest in maximizing the extent of revenues over expenses than a non-profit law school is unclear, given the existence of for-profit law schools is a recent phenomenon. It was only in 1996, after the ABA entered into a consent decree with the United States Department of Justice regarding an antitrust claim made by the DOJ against the ABA that the ABA agreed to approve for-profit law schools if they met the ABA's other criteria for approval.

A third consideration concerning fit is the size of the law school. Law schools range in size from under 300 students (thus, fewer than 100 students per entering class) to over 1,500 students (thus, over 500 students per entering class). Very small law schools will not have the resources to provide a wide-ranging number of co-curricular and extra-curricular activities. They offer the advantage of closeness among classmates, who will often take the same course or set of courses (for example, the school may offer just one section of Evidence each year, instead of several sections taught by several faculty), and the small size of the class may present closer ties between current students and alumni, as well as with faculty. Large law schools will offer a much broader array of courses than a small school will, including a host of advanced courses on very specialized topics. Those schools will also provide an abundance of co-curricular and extra-curricular options, from legal and quasi-legal organizations of all types to a large number of law reviews to many other opportunities. Your familiarity with your classmates and faculty in a large law school may suffer in comparison with those who attend a small law school, and your sense of anonymity is likely to be greater at a large law school. Medium sized law schools can reflect either or both the best and worst of small and large law schools. What is the culture of competition or cooperation at the school? How do faculty interact with students outside of class? Is it easy or hard for students to find faculty mentors or alumni who will serve as mentors? What organizations might I join that are of interest to me? What organizations can I join that may be helpful to my future career? What co-curricular options do I have? Does the school have an Office of Academic Support if I am struggling with some of the material? What are my course options after completion of my first year of law school? What clinics exist, and will they provide me with the knowledge and skills I am likely to need in the practice of law? Will I be prepared to take and pass the bar exam? All these questions should be asked in light of the size of the law school.

2. Is the Opportunity Cost Best at This Law School?

Law school costs both time and money. Once you decide to attend law school, the time spent pursuing a law degree is largely static. A very few schools now offer a two-year degree track, which means twenty-four straight months of study. A larger number of law schools will permit a student to accelerate studies by one semester, allowing a student to take the February bar exam rather than the July bar exam. At most schools you will spend three years in law school, so the opportunity cost question is largely whether a significant difference in the monetary costs of two or more law schools should affect your decision. This is not to suggest that your decision should be determined solely or evenly predominantly based on which law school costs the least amount. Your calculation of costs is, however, a factor that must be weighed along with your answers to the first and last questions.

Law schools are expensive. As noted in the *Introduction*, the average (and median) tuition at private ABA-approved law schools in 2008 is approximately $34,000 per year, with tuition increases likely to rise at least 3–5% annually. At state-supported law schools, the average yearly tuition in 2008 was slightly under $17,000 for state residents and over $28,000 for nonresidents. Law schools awarded nearly $800 million in internal grants and scholarships in 2008, but students will likely find law school expensive.

The absolute expense of law school is an important factor in making your initial determination about whether to attend law school. Once you have decided to attend law school, you must look more closely at the comparative expenses of law schools. Began by comparing the cost of tuition less any scholarship awarded you. If your choices are located in different cities, what are the comparative costs of living in those cities? Many students will work part-time during the second and third years of law school (called "clerking" or serving as a "law clerk"), giving them some sustained work experience and generating some income to contribute to their living expenses. Are the law schools you are considering located in very differently sized metropolitan areas, making one better than the other in generating clerking opportunities? If you plan to enter relatively low-paying public interest work, does the law school have a loan for-giveness program or other benefit that would allow you to choose that kind of work without facing an overly burdensome loan repayment schedule?

3. *What Kinds of Opportunities Will Be Available to Me if I Attend This Law School?*

Even during law school you are building a career, not just preparing for a job. Evaluate the kinds of careers fashioned by successful graduates (most schools have some print or electronic publication spotlighting its graduates) of the schools. All ABA-approved law schools count many superb graduates, from those engaged in needed public-interest law to those who are handsomely re-warded for their work as private firm lawyers or in other businesses. Ask the admissions office whether, and if so how, the law school creates opportunities for its students to gain the kinds of contacts and enter into mentoring pro-grams that will facilitate success in the practice of law.

Most lawyers, whether in private practice or engaged in government work, perform work that is local or regional in nature rather than national. Most personal injury lawyers do not take cases outside of the state in which they practice. Assistant United States Attorneys almost always limit their work to that found within the federal district's geographic boundaries. Consequently, one component of your success in the private practice of law will be your abil-ity to integrate yourself into the appropriate community of lawyers, a com-munity based either on geography or on type of practice. If you have some idea of the state or locality in which you want to practice law, your opportu-nity quickly to enter that community of lawyers is likely to be greater if you at-tend law school in that state than if you attend law school elsewhere. Some lawyers from all law schools move about the country, and if you end up, for personal or professional reasons, moving away from the state in which you went to law school, you should expect to make a more concerted effort to enter into those professional communities. It is, however, easier to enter a commu-nity if you are familiar with that community.

The importance of considering the community of lawyers in which one may practice law is one reason why it may be better, both professionally and edu-cationally, to attend a law school that is either "lower" ranked or unranked by the *U.S. News Annual Guide* than most law schools listed in the first tier in the *Annual Guide*. Only a few law schools have a "brand" that is sufficiently rec-ognizable nationwide that makes geography unimportant to your decision. If you plan to work in South Carolina, deciding to attend New York University School of Law rather than the University of South Carolina School of Law is likely not the best choice to make. If you are considering practicing law in South Carolina, New York, or Washington, D.C., and you are thinking about both large firm private practice as well as government work, then the decision to attend NYU rather than South Carolina is likely (but not always) the correct decision.

The strongest reason to choose to attend a top ten law school is not because you will receive a better education there than another law school but because your employment possibilities will be more widespread geographically and in terms of practice. An excellent student at a regional law school will have a number of employment opportunities within the region, but fewer outside the region. A graduate of a national law school will have fewer employment options within the same region as the graduate of the regional law school, but more employment opportunities generally. But if you want to practice law in Jacksonville, Florida, your chances of finding work there are better having attended law school in the state than by graduating from the University of California, Berkeley School of Law (Boalt Hall). More pointedly, the advantage of graduating from top ten law school is not the first job you take, but the second job. Being a graduate of an elite law school confers an advantage in terms of "getting in the interview door," not because that graduate has demonstrated that he is a better lawyer than a comparably experienced graduate of a regional law school, but because legal recruiters and employers will recognize the name brand of the law school. This advantage quickly dissipates at the workplace (you will be judged based on your work product and, at some point, on your client-generating skills, not your diploma). Further, within five years or so of graduation, the name of the law school from which you graduated will be unimportant to future employers. The question clients and employers will ask is, Does this person perform excellent legal work? Private law firms will also ask, Does this person have the ambition and personality to bring in legal business to the firm?

Law School Location and the Bar Exam

Every year thousands of law graduates take the bar exam in a state other than the state in which their law school is located. Most will pass the bar on the first attempt. However, your chances of passing the bar in a state outside of the state in which you went to law school will likely be lower than an applicant who is taking the bar exam in the same state in which she graduated from law school. Of course, students who graduate at the top of their class are highly likely to pass the bar exam no matter which state's exam they take, and applicants who finish in the bottom quartile of their class are at some risk of failing the bar exam. Those who graduated in the third quartile of their class are at a slight risk of failing the bar exam. Despite the homogenization of the law tested on the bar exams of many states, specific state law is tested by every state but Missouri, and more exposure to that specific law is better than less exposure. Because matriculating students have no idea how well they will perform in law school, it is impossible to ask students to think about attending a different law school in light of the possibility that the student may need more exposure to state-specific law. The greater the likelihood that you will practice law in a particular state, the better off you are attending law school in that state. If you are unsure and you have been very successful in both undergraduate work and in your performance on the LSAT, the less important law school location becomes.

Some modest differences in the passing rate for graduates of in-state and out-of-state ABA-approved law schools exist in most states. For example, in the July 2009 Florida bar examination, 75.2% of first-time examinees who graduated from non-Florida based law schools passed. Those first-time examinees who graduated from a Florida-based law school passed at 82%. Similar data are found in the July 2009 bar exam results in Texas (84% to 89.4%), California (69.4% to 79.3% when evaluating solely those who graduated from an ABA-approved law school in California or elsewhere) and New York (84% to 88.1%).

Consequently, if you are sure you want to practice law in a particular state, you will slightly enhance your chances of passing the bar exam by attending law school in that state. Again, this in large part is because you are likely to be exposed to state-specific law at the law school located in that state. In addition, it is possible that routine may make it easier to pass the bar exam in the state where you attended law school. If you graduated from a New York law school, and decided to take the California bar, you will either take the bar prep course through distance learning while still in New York, and then travel to California to take the bar, or you will immediately move from New York to California after graduation, a stressful event that may adversely (even if slightly) affect your chances of passing the California bar exam.

How Many Law Schools Should I Apply To?

The number of applications per student has been rising for the past decade. The average applicant sends applications to six or seven law schools. Your decision about the number of applications should be based in part on the competition for law school seats. Competition for law school seats varies particularly on the location and general reputation of the school. Overall competition for seats varies based on both national economic concerns and trends in popular culture, including the popularity of lawyer shows on television. Most broadly, competition for law school seats depends on national demographic data, particularly the number of young adults. The baby boomlet of children born in the late 1980s through the mid-1990s will create a greater competition for law school seats from 2010 through 2015 or so. This national number, however, is likely to differ greatly among different regions in the country. The percentage increase in applications to law schools in New England may differ greatly from the increase in applications in the Southwest. During the admissions cycle (October through May) the LSAC regularly publishes data concerning the overall number of LSAT exam takers and provides initial numbers on applications nationally and by region of the country, data that can inform you of the extent of the competition in gaining admission.

You will have to pay an application fee to each law school to which you apply. Most schools allow poor applicants to request and obtain a fee waiver, but only if you fill out a fee-waiver request with the LSDAS. The application fee is usually between $50–$100 and is nonrefundable.

When Should I Hear from the Law School?

Unlike elite undergraduate admissions processes, most law schools do not wait until April 1 to notify applicants about their admission status. Three types of admissions processes are common. First, several schools have moved to a type of early admissions process. Like undergraduate early admissions programs, the applicant agrees, if admitted, to forego seeking admission at other law schools. Second, many schools have adopted a rolling admissions process, making admissions decisions on applicants shortly after the receipt of a completed application. A law school using a rolling admissions process may decide not to decide on some "borderline" applicants but wait until all applications are in before making a decision. Third, the school may adopt a staccato-type admissions process, with admissions decisions issued every two to three weeks, usually beginning in late winter. The website at most law schools will give you a sense the particular timing of admissions decisions of each.

When Do I Have to Decide?

LSDAS member law schools have agreed to a code of conduct regarding the time frame in which it makes admitted applications choose a law school. If an applicant is admitted through an early admission program, the member school is permitted to require the applicant, as a condition of admission, to send in a nonrefundable deposit and withdraw other law school applications. If an applicant is admitted through the ordinary admissions process, as is true in the vast majority of admissions decisions, LSDAS member schools will not require the admitted applicant to make a nonrefundable seat deposit before April 1. Thus, if an applicant is admitted on February 15, the letter of admission will almost certainly include a statement indicating that the applicant must reserve her seat by sending in a nonrefundable deposit by April 1. If the applicant is admitted on March 20, the letter of admission will ordinarily allow the admitted applicant about three weeks to decide whether to accept the offer by sending in a nonrefundable deposit, thus pushing the deadline for sending in the deposit from April 1 to mid-April.

The customary nonrefundable deposit is $350. An admitted applicant is free to send a nonrefundable deposit to more than one law school as long as he or she is willing to forfeit the deposits made to schools other than the one the applicant finally chooses. If you are unsure about which law school to attend, you may be able to defer your final decision to as late as mid-June. That is because many schools do not require admitted applicants to send a second, refundable deposit until June 1 or June 15. Although refundable, this second deposit is ordinarily a significant amount of money, which provides admitted applicants an economic incentive to make a final decision about that law school.

How Do I Pay for Law School?

You will be able to borrow money to pay for tuition, books and living expenses to attend any ABA-approved law school. You will need to fill out the FAFSA (Free Application for Federal Student Aid) application. Recent federal initiatives will alter the manner in which educational loans are requested and made, and may increase the amounts available to borrow. It is highly unlikely that any such changes will adversely affect the ability of law students to obtain loans that allow the student to pay tuition and books and provide a modest amount for living expenses.

Part II

Getting Out

Chapter 4

Getting Started in Law School: The First Year

In the 1971 novel *The Paper Chase*, written by Harvard Law School graduate John Jay Osborne, Jr., the frightening Professor Kingsfield tells his first year Contracts students, "You come in here with a skull full of mush, and you leave thinking like a lawyer." Kingsfield was enunciating a statement of purpose that remains at the core of legal education, particularly the first year of law school: Law school is designed to instill a type of thinking in its students, one that is sharp and nuanced, able to see the general (theories of law and legal policies) and the particular (what facts are relevant and which relevant facts are most important). When a student learns to "think like a lawyer," that student understands the relationship among legally important facts, legal rules (doctrine), and broader legal policies. Thinking like a lawyer also means knowing the limits (or weaknesses) of particular legal rules and policies, limits that may be exposed in the student's subsequent study of this doctrine. Thinking like a lawyer allows one to frame in legal terms the facts related to the lawyer by the client, and to consider possible solutions to the problem facing the client. Thinking like a lawyer gives one the ability to analyze problems quickly and thoroughly, and teaches one how to use a number of tools of rhetoric, the use of language and argument, in formulating arguments concerning legal issues.

The facility of lawyers in the use of language, together with the duty to advance the interests of their clients even at the possible expense of the public's interest, has made some skeptical of legal education. Criticism by insiders and outsiders of teaching students to think like a lawyer has become more prominent in the past several decades, for thinking like a lawyer does not teach students the skill to communicate effectively with clients, nor how to consider the moral implications of their actions as lawyers. Further, the ability to frame a client's problem in legal terms may constitute only a partial understanding of the client's broader needs. Finally, if not properly understood as a tool, instilling in students the ability to think like a lawyer can create lawyers who are nothing more than amoral legal technicians, bereft of any sense of how law actually affects people and of the practical wisdom that makes lawyers valuable problem solvers in American society. Despite these often valid criticisms, thinking like a lawyer remains the dominant purpose of legal education, for it has great value in the practice of law. Legal educators supplement such training by training students in other skills, including client communication, the foundations of law and the moral dilemmas that lawyers may face.

For better and worse, the Kingsfield-type (the outwardly autocratic, intimidating professor) is nearly extinct in the 21st century law school. His statement of intent, however, remains valuable. Many law students enter law school with the belief that the professors will teach students "the law," and after each course is completed, they will know "the law" on that subject. This idea is premised on the belief that students are passive learners whose "empty" brains are filled with a plethora of legal rules by the fount of legal knowledge, the professor. Although 1L students will learn and be expected to understand (even memorize) plenty of legal rules, such as the doctrine of consideration in Contracts and the doctrine of *respondeat superior* in Torts, first year law school classes are not designed with passive learning in mind. Law school courses generally, and first-year classes particularly, are designed to provide you with a framework about how lawyers and judges (who were trained as lawyers) think and argue. This framework is based on learning by reading and evaluating many different cases in which appellate judges disagree about the facts, the applicable legal doctrine and legal policy. A 1L student does not begin at the beginning. Law students learn *in media res*, a Latin term for "in the middle of the thing." If you are not confused when you first begin reading appellate cases, you are not trying hard enough. This active learning includes learning a set of tools about how to think about the law, and how law is both made and reshaped by repeated exposure to those various tools. Active learning requires that you engage in active thinking about the meaning of each of the particular cases you have been assigned to read and about the relation of those cases to one another. In addition, you are to glean from those assigned cases the often unspoken policies that led the court to reach its conclusion. The common law system in which law is made by judges in deciding cases has been joined by statutes adopted by legislatures and administrative regulations promulgated by the executive branch that affect this judge-made law. The result is that legal doctrine regularly changes. The amount of law on any subject is so great that "mastery" is unlikely to occur after a student takes a four or six credit hour class in a subject. After completing Contracts or Torts a student will understand how much more law exists than the professor was able to explore in class. The benefit of the active learning approach to law is that learning to think like a lawyer allows the student to consider how the law may change tomorrow.

Even "mastery" of current legal doctrine is good only for today. The analytical skills you develop in law school and hone in the practice of law will provide you with a complex mental network allowing you quickly to understand and account for doctrinal changes.

We will return to how you learn to think like a lawyer later in this chapter. For now, we will begin at the beginning of your law school experience.

About Your 1L Courses

Harvard Law School made a big splash in 2006 when it announced it was reorganizing its first year curriculum to include a required course in international law (chosen by the student from three options), a course in Legislation and Regulation, and a course in Problems and Theories, joining its first-year courses in Contracts, Torts, Property, Criminal Law and Civil Procedure. We will overlook the fact that it took Harvard 136 years to alter its first year curriculum and focus instead on what this change tells us about the first year of law school.

The modern law school began in 1870 with the appointment of Christopher Columbus Langdell as Dean of the Harvard Law School. Langdell is credited with creating both the "modern" first year curriculum and the "socratic" method of teaching law students. The first year curriculum was to consist of courses in private law (contracts, torts, and property, legal topics in which private individuals were involved as the parties to disputes). These private law courses focused on opinions written by common law judges (English and American) providing the result and the reason(s) for the result. These were appellate decisions, cases in which the losing party appealed a judgment adverse to them by challenging a ruling of law made by the trial court. This "law" decided by the trial court was common law, law ascertained by judges, not law based on statutes adopted by legislatures. Once a case reaches an appellate court, most of the debate over contested facts (who had the green light at the intersection?) is over. As a general matter, if the plaintiff and the defendant disagreed about who was properly in the intersection, the decision of the finder of fact (usually a jury but sometimes the trial judge if the parties do not request trial by jury) was final. The job of the appellate court was to determine whether the trial court erred in its legal decisions. Some of these decisions were about what evidence was admissible. In other cases, the question for the appellate court was whether a legal rule required the trial court to rule in favor of the defendant without any trial. In Langdell's day, these appellate cases reprinted in the newly created "casebooks" (also a Langdell invention) exemplified "certain principles and doctrines" of the law. The number of principles of law, in Langdell's view, were few in number, and the "vast majority [of cases] are useless, and worse than useless, for any purpose of systematic study." The purpose of this systematic study was to understand the "science" of law. The first year curriculum, then, was to 1) focus on private, common law subjects, 2) emphasize the study of principles and doctrines found in printed appellate cases, and 3) teach those principles and doctrines through the "socratic" method.

The late nineteenth century Harvard Law School method of teaching law faced a number of obstacles. First, most prospective lawyers obtained their legal training through apprenticeships with practicing lawyers, not in a law school. The advantage of spending 18 months (later increased to a recommended three years in 1876) in a law school instead of apprenticing oneself was then unclear. The later argument in favor of the Harvard method was that it was "systematic," giving the student a structured system of learning and training that differed from the hodgepodge of apprenticeship training wholly dependent on the lawyer's interest in the apprentice. Second, for those students in law schools, the lecture method, one in which the student simply recorded the commentary of the professor talking at the head of the classroom, remained popular through the early twentieth century. (Another method, the "textbook method," requiring students to memorize parts of assigned texts, withered by the late nineteenth century.) Eventually the socratic method, which appeared both scientific and cost-efficient (one professor could teach 150 students at a time using this method, making its cost relatively low), became the dominant approach to American legal education. The socratic method, as described below, focused on active learning, contrary to the passive learning found in the lecture method.

The 1L curriculum at nearly all American law schools remains heavily weighted in common law subjects. Contracts, Property and Torts are all common 1L courses, and remain primarily based on the judge-made system of the common law. Substantial changes in how law is made has increased the importance of understanding statutes (and how to interpret statutes), but this is a lesser source of the law of these subjects than judicially-created doctrines. Most law schools also require students to take a course in Civil Procedure during their first year of law school, a course about the process of how civil cases (including all contracts, property and tort cases) are begun, continued through trial and completed.

It is harder than one might expect to craft brief working definitions of your common law subjects. The following is a modest and incomplete effort. Contract law focuses on the study of the law of agreements between persons, agreements that create some kind of obligation in both parties. Contract law also studies the law applicable when one party to the agreement claims the other has violated ("breached") the agreement in some fashion or when one defends claiming no agreement exists. A tort is a civil wrong other than a breach of contract. This nicely divides "civil wrongs" into just two categories (contractual wrongs and tortious wrongs) and divides tort law from criminal law by defining tort law as a civil, not criminal, wrong (you will learn that some conduct can be both a civil and criminal wrong). This definition also fails to describe tort law. Tort law is generally about involuntary interactions between strangers, in which one claims the other committed a wrong that caused harm and that wrongdoer should compensate the injured person. In this tort law differs (again, generally but not always) from contract law, which is largely about voluntary interactions among persons. The study of Property law includes a study of the nature of what constitutes ownership of things or, more accurately, what rights persons may have in those things called personal and real property. Property law examines a person's (owner's) right to control, use or dispose of what is legally defined as property. Civil Procedure is the study of processes by which a complaint about a violation of substantive law (which includes contracts, property or tort law) is made, how that dispute is developed and clarified and how it is resolved. Criminal law is the study of the substantive law of crime, a public law course because it involves the state as one of the parties. (Criminal procedure is usually an upper level course on the processes by which persons are charged with and tried for a crime, the rights a person has in the investigation of a crime, and constitutional rights the accused has during and after trial.)

Private law continues to dominate the first year curriculum, with public law second and theories about law and legal decisionmaking a distant third. Public law subjects are those that concern the relationship of the individual and the state, and include the above-mentioned Criminal Law, Constitutional Law and Administrative Law. Most schools require students take Criminal Law in their first year of study, and though criminal law was a common law subject in England, it is now statutory law in nearly all American states and in the federal system. Courses that are primarily based on reading and interpreting statutes are known as "code" courses, and Criminal Law is a classic "code" course. Constitutional Law focuses on the how the Constitution of the United States creates the structure of government (including separation of powers among the three federal branches of government and federalism, the relationship between the federal and state governments) and how it protects individual rights against government interference, particularly Fourteenth Amendment due process and equal protection guarantees and First Amendment rights, including freedom of speech and free exercise of religion. The Constitution is not self-executing, and Constitutional Law largely focuses on how the Supreme Court has interpreted the provisions of the Constitution. About half of all law schools offer Constitutional Law in the first year of law school. A few law schools offer a 1L course in Administrative Law, the study of how government regulates aspects of the economy through agency regulation based on general statutes. It is a common and popular upper-level course.

Third, few law schools teach 1L students through lectures. Most will use a modified version of what is called the "socratic" method.

The "Socratic" Method

The socratic method of teaching is named after the type of questioning by the Greek philosopher Socrates. His success in gathering young Athenians to his philosophical investigations made him enemies in Athens, and after his conviction for corrupting the minds of the young he was ordered to kill himself by drinking hemlock, a poison. The socratic method of instruction as traditionally used by law professors requires the professor to act almost solely as an interlocutor, not as a fount of answers. The professor asks a student to engage in a colloquy with the professor, one in which the student attempts to answer increasingly difficult questions. Students are expected to thoroughly read and try to understand the assigned case(s) before class. During class students will learn whether their initial understanding is correct, and will learn more clearly what the impact of the decision means for this area of law and how the doctrine taken from that and related decisions will be applied in future cases, all through questions by the professor. It is rare today, but formerly one student was called on to answer questions during the entire class, after first being required to stand. A professor would (and today still often does) begin by asking the student to state the facts of the case. This statement of the facts means only those facts relevant to the legal issue discussed in the opinion. After coaxing out of the student the relevant facts, the professor might ask what result was reached by the appellate court. Then the professor might ask what legal policy justified the result. Now the fun (or excruciating) part began. The professor might ask the student to compare the result in the case the class was studying with another case decided by another court, a case that might have been studied earlier in the semester. Were the two cases compatible? If not, why not? The professor might change a few facts from the case under discussion (called a hypothetical) and ask whether the result would be different. If so, why? The professor might ask the student whether the stated justification for the rule declared in the case was an adequate justification, or whether the actual reason for the rule was absent from the court's opinion. The professor might then ask whether another policy, a policy that justified a result contrary to that reached by the appellate court, was actually a preferable policy? To many of these questions it did not matter what the student's answer was, for the goal was to test the reaches of the policy, and all legal policies have a limited reach. Often the colloquy between professor and student ended with the student and the class baffled, mired in apparent confusion or incomprehension.

This exchange between teacher and pupil had a purpose other than sowing confusion. When used by a skillful questioner, the class was led to considerations about the purpose and meaning of legal rules, not just memorization of the rules themselves. These purposive considerations gave students some answers about the content of legal rules; more importantly, these purposive considerations gave students an understanding of the reasons for the existence of that law. Understanding the reasons for the law were crucial because law is not static. Knowing the policies that justified a particular legal rule, or, just as importantly, knowing when policies might justify a change in a legal rule, are more important than memorizing a set of rules.

Today few professors use a traditional socratic method to teach 1L students. Many will use a "modified" socratic method. Most will not require the student stand and recite (though some still do), and most will call on numerous students (some will call only on volunteers but many will call randomly on 1L students) during a single class. The modified socratic method may include not only questions from the professor but an introduction to the material under study, one that provides a context for understanding the material. Some professors will use the introduction to explain to students how the "notes" in the casebook that follow most excerpted cases help frame one's understanding of the primary material, the excerpted case opinion. Others will provide a written summary of the day's material before or after class. What remains the same is a requirement that the student engage in close and active reading of the cases *before coming to class*, for the cases are just the tip of the legal policy iceberg. You must know how the policy justifying the decision in the case works, and understand the premises or bases of that policy because both are highly likely to be tested on the final examination and will be the focus of the class.

Casebooks

The cases you read in your 1L classes are compiled and edited by one or more law professors for use in a casebook. Because casebooks are sold nationally and because law school is designed to teach you the general doctrine of Contracts, Property and Torts in your 1L year, these casebooks do not focus on any particular state's Contracts or Torts law. Because *general doctrine* does not mean *universal doctrine* in American law, your professor may require you to read additional cases decided by the state appellate courts in the state in which you attend law school that exemplify differences between the law as stated in the casebook and your state's law. Thousands of published appellate cases discuss the doctrines you will learn in your first year. The authors of your casebook ordinarily attempt to find the most trenchant and memorable cases from those many cases. Your authors will ordinarily edit the cases to pare them down to the discussion about the meaning and interpretation of a particular doctrine. Consequently, you will rarely read an entire appellate opinion. If you do, you will realize quickly that an ordinary appellate opinion discusses more than one legal or factual issue, issues that are not immediately crucial to your education. An unedited opinion will also often include a substantial amount of procedural information, information usually excised from an edited version designed to demonstrate how a court interprets substantive law. This excerpted case in the casebook is known as a *primary* case, and your professor will usually assign two to four primary cases for each class session. Most of your class time will be spent on the primary cases. After each primary case the casebook will include a section titled *Notes* or *Notes and Questions*. This section may cite other cases decided contrary to the result in the primary case, may inform you that the primary case states the rule adopted by the majority of states, and likely will offer some statements about similar but slightly different cases. This last aspect of *Notes and Questions* is intended to get you to think contextually, about how the primary case may be applied or limited depending on whether some facts are different. You must read the primary case with the purpose of both understanding what it declares and how it relates to other cases which present some different facts.

Casebooks are usually required (many now have electronic versions in which all cited cases are hyperlinked; if so, spend relatively little time on the hyperlinked cases or you will find yourself lost in a maze of decisions). Law school publishers have flooded the legal education market with a number of outstanding books that serve as study aids to students in the study of their first year substantive courses. These books have slightly different goals: some offer a general overview of the material a student is likely to study, some provide detailed outlines of doctrine, and some are written to provide specific examples of concepts and ideas in common 1L subjects. You will find several examples of each of these supplementary materials for each first year class. Nearly all are available in your law school's library, and it is useful to check out several before deciding whether to purchase one. Nearly all are thoughtful, accessible and thorough, and you may decide to base your outline on the outline you find in one of these supplements. Your professors may favor some and dislike others, however, and you should speak with your professor about which sup-plemental book, if any, your professor recommends. Some professors will rec-ommend a supplement in the syllabus to the course.

Reading and Briefing a Case before Your First Day of Class

You will learn during orientation that some of your professors will post an as-signment for the first day of class. The old-fashioned way is to post assignments on a bulletin board organized by first year section, for 1L students are assigned to particular letter sections (for example, three 1L sections called, A, B and C). Some professors now post such assignments electronically. In either event, make sure you are aware of any such assignments given by your section's professors be-fore attending class on your first day as a law student. Relatedly, make sure you obtain and read (skim) the syllabus for each of your 1L classes. A few professors will wait until the first day of class to hand out a syllabus, but most make it avail-able ahead of time. The syllabus will give you information on the exam, mate-rial that will be focused on, class attendance rules, and requirements for recitation.

Your assignment for the first day of class will likely include some introductory material and possibly one or two appellate cases offered as exemplars of the sub-ject. Because legal education begins by having you read cases, and because those cases will use legal language that you are unlikely to be familiar with, you should purchase a legal dictionary (the most well known is *Black's Law Dictionary*) to as-sist you in understanding those terms of legal art. Below is a so-called "slip-and-fall" case you might read in your Torts class. After actively reading the case, consider creating a "brief" of the case. A "brief" is a summary of the essential aspects of the case which you can use to get ready for class, to use if called upon during class, and for use when creating an outline and studying for the final examination.

Jasko v. F. W. Woolworth Co.
494 P.2d 839 (Colo. 1972)

GROVES, Justice.

Petitioner Jasko (plaintiff) was injured when she slipped and fell in respondent's (defendant's) store. The plaintiff brought an action against the defendant to recover damages for her injuries. At the close of the plaintiff's case, the defendant's motion for a directed verdict and dismissal was granted. The dismissal was affirmed by the Col-orado Court of Appeals, 29 Colo.App. 338, 350 P.2d 810. We granted certiorari and now reverse.

We view the evidence in the light most favorable to plaintiff. Bailey v. King Soopers, 142 Colo. 338, 350 P.2d 810 (1960). She was leaving the defendant's Denver store by a main aisle after shopping there. As she walked past a pizza-hoagie counter, she slipped and fell heavily against an up-right counter injuring herself. She testified that she had slipped on a piece of pizza which was on the terrazzo floor.

An associate manager of the store testified that 500–1000 individuals per day purchased one or more slices of pizza at the pizza counter. There were no chairs or tables by the pizza counter. Many customers stood in the aisle and ate their pizza slices from the waxed paper sheets upon which they are served. When pizza was being consumed, according to this witness, porters 'constantly' swept up debris on the floor.

The trial court and the Court of Appeals followed the well-known rule of law that, before there can be liability for injuries resulting from a dangerous condition, it must be shown (1) that the defendant in control of the premises had actual knowledge of the condition and failed to correct it, or (2) that the defendant had constructive knowledge of the condition and failed to correct it (i.e., that the condition had existed for such a period of time that the defendant, in the exercise of due care, could have and should have known it). We address ourselves solely to the necessity of notice of the specific condition, which under the facts of this case is of first impression in this court.

In her attempt to meet the requirement of notice, plaintiff did not claim or show that the alleged pizza was placed or dropped on the floor directly by the defendant or its employees, or that defendant knew of its existence. Van Schaack v. Perkins, 129 Colo. 567, 272 P.2d 269 (1954). Rather, it was her contention that defendant's method of selling pizza was one which leads inescapably to such mishaps as her own, and that in such a situation conventional notice requirements need not be met. We agree.

The dangerous condition was created by the store's method of sale. The steps taken to constantly clean the floor show that the store owner recognized the danger.

The practice of extensive selling of slices of pizza on waxed paper to customers who consume it while standing creates the reasonable probability that food will drop to the floor. Food on a terrazzo floor will create a dangerous condition. In such a situation, notice to the proprietor of the specific item on the floor need not be shown.

The basic notice requirement springs from the thought that a dangerous condition, when it occurs, is somewhat out of the ordinary.

Such was the case under the facts of Woolworth v. Peet, 132 Colo. 11, 284 P.2d 659 (1955), and Denver Dry Goods v. Pender, 128 Colo. 281, 262 P.2d 257 (1953), which the defendant has urged upon us. In such a situation the storekeeper is allowed a reasonable time, under the circumstances, to discover and correct the condition, unless it is the direct result of his (or his employees') acts. However, when the operating methods of a proprietor are such that dangerous conditions are continuous or easily foreseeable, the logical basis for the notice requirement dissolves. Then, actual or constructive notice of the specific condition need not be proved. Bozza v. Vornado, 42 N.J. 355, 200 A.2d 777 (1964).

We approached recognition of this principle with a slightly different setting in Denver Dry Goods Company v. Gettman, 167 Colo. 539, 448 P.2d 954 (1969). There the plaintiff slipped on a wet stairway of defendant. We held there (albeit without an extended discussion) that defendant's knowledge that there was snow outside, that the stairway became slick when wet, and that snow customer's shoes would be deposited inside, was enough to allow the question of negligence to go to the jury.

In order to recover, the plaintiff must establish that the conduct of the defendant was negligent. This, of course, is a jury question.

'The mere presence of a slick or slippery spot on a floor does not in and of itself establish negligence, for this conditions may arise temporarily in any place of business. Kitts v. Shop Rite Foods, Inc., 64 N.M 24, 323 P.2d 282 (1958). Nor does proof of a slippery floor, without more, give rise to an inference that the proprietor had knowledge of the condition. Kitts v. Shop Rite Foods, Inc., supra. But we are not dealing with an isolated instance.

'Plaintiffs were not required to prove either a specific act of conduct or an obvious dangerous condition. Such proof was not required once there was proof of a continuing messy condition—a pattern of conduct. Shaver v. Ray Bell Oil Co., 74 N.M. 700, 397 P.2d 723 (1964); Lewis v. Barber's Super Markets, Inc., 72 N.M. 402, 384 P.2d 470 (1963).

'The proof of the pattern of conduct does not, of course, established the defendant's negligence. Williamson v. Piggly Wiggly Shop Rite Foods, Inc., 80 N.M. 591, 458 P.2d 843 (Ct. App. 1969). Taking the evidence in the light most favorable to plaintiffs, not only was there proof of the pattern of conduct, there was evidence or inference of defendant's knowl-

edge of a continuing hazard, that invitees might fail to protect themselves against that hazard and that defendant failed
to exercise reasonable care to protect them from that hazard.
Williamson v. Piggly Wiggly Shop Rite Foods, Inc., supra. In
the light of the evidence and inferences, it would have been
error for the trial court to have sustained defendant's claim of
'no negligence.' Factual issues on defendant's negligence had
been raised.' Garcia v. Barber's Super Markets, 81 N.M. 92,
463 P.2d 516 (1969).

For other cases in accord, see Thomason v. Great Atlantic and Pacific
Tea Company, 413 F.2d 51 (4th Cir. 1969), Rhodes v. El Rancho Mar-
kets, 4 Ariz. App. 183, 418 P.2d 613 (1966), Wollerman v. Grand
Union Stores, Inc., 47 N.J. 426, 221 A.2d 513 (1966), Mahoney v. J.
C. Penney, Co., 71 N.M. 244, 377 P.2d 663 (1963), and Forcier v.
Grand Union Stores, 128 Vt. 389, 264 A.2d 796 (1970).

The ruling of the Court of Appeals is reversed and the cause re-
manded to it for further remand to the trial court and new trial.

Let us start at the beginning and work our way through the case, then structure a brief of the case. First, the names of the parties are Jasko (the injured
person and plaintiff) and F. W. Woolworth Co. (the defendant, which claims
it is not legally responsible for the injuries suffered by Jasko). Immediately
below the title of the case is a notation, "494 P.2d 839 (Colo. 1972)." This is called
a case citation, and lawyers use a consistent type of case citation so they can
find the original printed version of this case if they need it. The citation begins
"494," which always means the volume number. Jasko is found in volume 494.
The next notation is "P.2d." "P" stands for Pacific Reporter. Beginning in the
1870s John B. West began to collect, bind and sell to lawyers the decisions of
every appellate court in each state in the United States. All states had some private entity publishing the appellate decisions of each state, but the timing of
such publications was often sporadic. Further, the compilers of state appellate
court decisions often provided little or no summary of the law stated in the
case, a summary some lawyers used in lieu of reading the entire case. The West
Publishing Company not only reprinted the decision, it eventually added some
material before the beginning of the opinion called "headnotes," brief summaries of the law as expressed in the opinion by West. These headnotes were
categorized within something called the West Key Number system. West published a decennial digest of summaries, so that once you found the right Key
Number, you could look in that digest to see if any other appellate court any-

where in the United States had written an opinion discussing the same point. West Publishing Company, which still exists as a division of the publishing giant Thomson Reuters and is likely the publisher of one or more of your 1L casebooks, provided lawyers with the opinions of state courts gathered by region of the county. For example, opinions printed in the Pacific Reporter are from the state appellate courts of Arizona, California, Colorado, Idaho, Kansas, Montana, Nevada, New Mexico, Oklahoma, Oregon, Utah and Washington, for when West started publishing state appellate cases the population of those western states was modest, which is why so many were gathered together. In addition to the Pacific Reporter, the West Publishing Company regional publishing system includes a North Eastern Reporter (N.E.), an Atlantic Reporter (A.), a South Eastern Reporter (S.E.), a Southern Reporter (So.), a North Western Reporter (N.W.) and a South Western Reporter (S.W.). West also publishes federal decisions, from decisions by the district or trial courts (Federal Supplement, abbreviated F.Supp.) to decisions of the circuit courts of appeals (Federal Reporter, abbreviated "F.") and decisions of the Supreme Court (S.Ct.). The notation "2d" after "P." means the opinion is found in volume 494 of the Second Series of the Pacific Reporter. ("P." standing alone would mean the case is found in the initial or first series, and "P.3d" stands for the Third Series of the Pacific Reporter.) The number "839" after P.2d is the page at which the *Jasko* case begins. If there was listed a second number after "839," so it looked like this "494 P.2d 839, 841 (Colo. 1972)," "841" would stand for the page location at which a specific statement of law referenced by the person making the citation. This is called a "pinpoint" citation. Finally, "(Colo. 1972)" means the case was decided by the Supreme Court of Colorado and the opinion was issued in 1972. If the end of the citation was "(Colo. App. 1999)" that would mean the case was decided by the Colorado Court of Appeals rather than the Colorado Supreme Court and publicly released in 1999. (An aside: In the state of New York the highest court is the "Court of Appeals," and the "Supreme Court" in New York is the trial court. Thus, a citation to a decision of the New York Court of Appeals would be "539 N.E.2d 570 (N.Y. 1989)".)

In the second paragraph of the opinion the *Jasko* court cites "Bailey v. King Soopers, 142 Colo. 338, 350 P.2d 810 (1960)." This is a complete citation, required by some state courts, complete in the sense that it cites the location of the case of *Bailey v. King Soopers* in both the Colorado Reports (142 Colo. 338), which publishes only decisions of Colorado appellate courts, and in the Pacific Reporter (350 P.2d 810). When a complete citation is given, you need only to state the year of decision (1960), not both the state and year of decision (Colo. 1960). West is a private company, and its reports of issued opinions are often not the official citation accepted by the courts. The official citation is usually the state-based citation (142 Colo. 338). In the days of print-only media, because it was difficult to obtain the official reporters of each of the states, many states allowed a lawyer to cite only the West Regional Reporter citation for any out of state case. Today, with the rise of electronic media, this has begun to change, for some state appellate courts now file all their opinions on the Internet, and several private companies now post appellate opinions online. The form of electronic citations differs from print citations because one no longer has pages in electronic format. Instead, the citation may begin with the year of decision, 2010, the name of the state, Wis. (Wisconsin), a number, say 29, standing for the chronological order in which opinions were released that year (the 29th opinion released in 2010), and then a specific citation to the paragraph number stating a proposition of law, for example, ¶ 13, making the complete electronic citation 2010 Wis. 29 ¶ 13.

Second, in all capital letters is "GROVES," followed by "Justice." In the American system of appellate opinion writing, the person who writes the opinion for a majority (or the entirety) of the court is generally named. The name of the judge writing the opinion for the court in most cases is unimportant. But some deceased state and federal judges (and a few living judges) are well-known within legal circles, even though they never served on the Supreme Court of the United States. The late Learned Hand, a federal district judge and later a circuit court of appeals judge, is one. Roger Traynor, late Chief Justice of the Supreme Court of California, was another. These judges are the exception, not the rule. In a few cases you will not see a judge's name but the words *per curiam*. *Per curiam* is Latin for "by the court," and means the opinion should be ascribed to the entire court. Ordinarily a *per curiam* opinion is used when the opinion is simply a disclosure of the result without any formal opinion of the reasons for that result or when the court is attempting to signal that the issue resolved by it was not one of great difficulty or controversy.

Third, the Supreme Court of Colorado begins its opinion as most appellate courts do, with a quick review of the way in which the case arrived at the Supreme Court. The court tells us what happened, or at least what the plaintiff says what happened (she was exiting the store when she slipped and fell on a slice of pizza). It notes the legal basis for the plaintiff's (usually abbreviated by law professors and students with the Greek letter Pi, π) lawsuit against the defendant (usually abbreviated with the Greek letter Delta, Δ), and the decision of the trial court to dismiss the case by granting "[a]t the close of the plaintiff's case, the defendant's motion for a directed verdict." That statement means that the trial court ended the case without giving it to the jury to decide. The trial began as most civil trials begin, with the plaintiff's case-in-chief. The plaintiff is the first party to offer evidence at the trial because the plaintiff has the burden of proof or burden of persuasion (you will learn later that the more accurate term is "risk of nonpersuasion," but lawyers will use burden of proof and burden of persuasion interchangeably). The plaintiff wants the jury to decide in her favor, and in order to have the judge give the case to the jury for a decision about disputed facts (*e.g.*, what was the cause of the plaintiff's fall?) the plaintiff must produce some evidence on each element of the law concerning its claim. If the plaintiff fails to offer some evidence on one element of the claim and then "rests" (that is, tells the court she has no more evidence to offer in her case-in-chief), the judge must dismiss the case and enter a judgment in favor of the defendant. In civil cases such as this (a negligence slip-and-fall or premises liability case), the burden of proof on the plaintiff is "a preponderance of the evidence," or "more likely than not." (In criminal cases you will learn that the burden is on the prosecution to show the defendant is guilty by evidence "beyond a reasonable doubt.") The trial court in *Jasko* held that the plaintiff failed to offer evidence on an element of the case (evidence that the defendant knew or should have known that the floor was slippery) and thus it had to dismiss the plaintiff's case and enter a judgment in favor of the defendant. That decision of the trial court was "affirmed" by the court of appeals, meaning its (when speaking of any court, even a one-person trial court, we use "it," not "his" or "her") decision was accepted as correct by the court of appeals. The final sentence of the first paragraph of the Supreme Court's opinion is, "We granted certiorari and now reverse." Reverse obviously means that the decision of the court of appeals (and implicitly the decision of the trial court because the court of appeals affirmed the decision of the trial court) was rejected by the Supreme Court of Colorado because the decision of the court of appeals was inaccurate in some way. To "grant certiorari" is to issue to the petitioner a type of "writ," a process of initiating a hearing that originated in the English common law. A "writ" was necessary to begin any legal case. A party that challenged its loss in the trial court asked a higher court to issue a particular writ, the writ of certiorari to the lower court. If the higher court granted the petition for a writ of certiorari, then the party that lost was able to gain a hearing explaining why it believed the lower court was incorrect in its ruling. When a higher court grants a petition for a writ of certiorari, it requires the lower court (the court of appeals) to send a certified record to the Supreme Court of Colorado to examine the record and decide if any problems exist in the decision(s) below. In general, a court that has the power to issue a writ of certiorari (the most famous court with this power is the Supreme Court of the United States) has the discretion to decide whether to issue the writ. That is, it is not required to hear the claim of the losing party, but may choose to do so. All states grant to parties in civil and criminal cases the ability to appeal as a matter of right (rather than discretion) to the first level of appeals courts (usually an intermediate court of appeals, as was true in the *Jasko* case). In the writ system, the person asking for the writ is the "petitioner," and the opposing party is the "respondent." The petitioner may be either the original plaintiff or defendant, and when the case is heard by an appellate court on a writ of certiorari, the petitioner's name is listed first, no matter how the case was styled in the trial court. Because Jasko is both the plaintiff and the petitioner, the style of the case, *Jasko v. F. W. Woolworth Co.*, remains the same. Had Woolworth lost and successfully petitioned the Colorado Supreme Court for a writ of certiorari, the name of the case would have been *F. W. Woolworth Co. v. Jasko*. When a case is taken to a higher court through an appeal, which is how most states currently allow a party that loses at the trial court to challenge that decision, the names of the parties remain as they were in the trial court. In a system of appeals, the party challenging the decision below is called the appellant and the party that won below is called the appellee.

Fourth, the second paragraph of the opinion begins with a statement of the *standard of review*, or standard of appellate review. In general, the trial court is the place where decisions about disputed facts are resolved. When an appellate court reviews a party's challenge to a factual decision made by the jury, it will defer greatly to the decision of the jury. The appellate court can declare in civil cases that the jury's decision about the facts was contrary to the great weight of the evidence and overturn the factual conclusion of the jury, but this power is rarely exercised. When a party challenges a decision that is called a mixed question of fact and law, that is, a question that requires the trial court to make some initial factual decision before making a legal decision (these are often found in evidentiary decisions made by trial courts; for example, was the person who made the out of court statement, called hearsay, under the stress of excitement when the person made the statement is a factual determination; if the answer to that question is "yes," should this hearsay statement be admissible as an exception to the hearsay rule, the answer to which is a legal conclusion), the appellate court will ordinarily reverse only if the trial court abused its discretion. The trial court has discretion (that is, judgment) to ascertain the facts necessary to decide the legal issue. Even if the appellate court disagrees with the legal conclusion reached by the trial court, it must uphold that decision unless the trial court abused its discretion, that is, failed wholly to account for some fact, or refused to exercise its judgment. The abuse of discretion standard is intended to make it difficult for the appellate court to overturn the mixed law-and-fact decisions of the trial court. That is in part because no trial is perfect, and if appellate courts are reversing decisions in the trial court because of imperfections, the justice system will grind to a halt. When the issue before the appellate court is solely an issue of law, the appellate court will analyze the legal issue *de novo*, Latin for "anew," for a trial court's decision on an issue of law is not subject to any deference by the appellate court. In *Jasko*, the issue about the proper standard of appellate review is what deference, if any, must the Colorado Supreme Court give to the trial court's decision to hold in favor of Woolworth and dismiss the case? The court notes, consonant with other courts, that it must review the "evidence in the light most favorable to plaintiff." That is because the common law system favors decisions by juries, and the court dismissed this case without any decision by the jury. As discussed above, in a case such as this, the plaintiff, the party who brought the lawsuit, has to prove by a preponderance of the evidence that the defendant negligently caused plaintiff harm (the four general elements in negligence law are 1) showing a defendant had a duty of care to the plaintiff, 2) proof that the defendant breached that duty of care, 3) the defendant's breach of the duty of care was a "proximate" cause of 4) the damages, or harm suffered by the plaintiff).

The court completes this paragraph and the following paragraph by noting what it believes are the relevant facts: the store served pizza on waxed paper during the day to many people, they ate the pizza while standing because no tables or chairs were made available to customers, and pizza debris was constantly being swept up off the terrazzo tile floor. Looking at the facts in "the light most favorable to the plaintiff," the court also accepts as a fact the plaintiff's claim that she slipped on a slice of pizza on the floor, injuring herself.

The court then notes the trial and appellate courts followed the "well known rule of law" concerning when a defendant is liable to a plaintiff in a slip-and-fall case: Did the defendant have actual or constructive knowledge of the dangerous condition and fail to correct it? This well known rule of law, the Supreme Court states, is a rule of notice. As the Colorado Supreme Court notes, even looking at the evidence in the light most favorable to the plaintiff, it is clear that the plaintiff offered no evidence that the defendant knew (actual knowledge) or should have known (constructive knowledge) of the "dangerous condition" of one or more pizza slices lying on the floor ready to be slipped on. And if the defendant Woolworth Company had neither actual or constructive knowledge of the dangerous condition, it did not owe the plaintiff any duty of care under this well known rule of law, a duty that is the first element of the plaintiff's claim.

The plaintiff's lawyer is well aware of this well known rule of law, and claims that it should not apply in these circumstances. Instead, plaintiff should be given the chance of obtaining a jury verdict even without showing the defendant possessed any actual or constructive knowledge of the dangerous condition of pizza slices falling to the ground. The Court notes that in two previous cases, one from 1955 (*Woolworth v. Peet*) and one from 1953 (*Denver Dry Goods v. Pender*), it (that is, the Colorado Supreme Court of that time) adopted the "well known rule." These precedential cases, Woolworth claims, should be followed by the Court to resolve *Jasko*. The Court notes that the rule of notice disappears if the method of sale makes dangerous conditions easily foreseeable, and cites a New Jersey case for support of that rule of law. Whether Colorado law dispenses with the element of notice (actual or constructive knowledge) in some premises liability cases is, the court states, a matter "of first impression in this court." A case of "first impression" means that the legal issue as framed by the court has not been adopted or rejected by the highest court in Colorado. The issue as stated by the court is: Does the defendant owe a duty of care to the plaintiff even though the defendant had no actual or constructive knowledge of the dangerous condition due to the manner ("method") in which it is selling pizza? The Colorado Supreme Court concludes that the plaintiff's evidence concerning the method of selling pizza showed defendant created a dangerous condition.

The Colorado Supreme Court thus concludes that the plaintiff did not have to prove that the defendant had notice of the dangerous condition in order to avoid a motion for a direct verdict and have the jury decide the case. This is a legal question, and no deference need be given the conclusions of the lower Colorado courts. The Supreme Court also notes that the court of appeals relied on the "well known rule of law" for its conclusion requiring plaintiff to prove defendant's actual or constructive knowledge. In general, "new" law, of which *Jasko* is an example, is the province of the highest appellate court of the state. A trial court has the duty to follow the law then in existence (in this case, the law that required plaintiff to present proof of the defendant's actual or constructive knowledge). An intermediate appellate court (a court of appeals) also has the duty of following the law that currently exists, though on occasion you may it making a new rule of law. One difference between the judicial systems of states and the federal judicial system is that you are likely to find a federal intermediate appellate court (the circuit court of appeals) more ready to make a new rule of law than a state intermediate appellate court.

In reaching its eventual conclusion that the method by which the defendant sold pizza created the possibility of liability for plaintiff's injuries even without proof of knowledge of the dangerous condition (pizza or other debris on the floor), the court offers several initial conclusions. One conclusion of the Colorado Supreme Court is that "extensive selling of slices of pizza on waxed paper to customers who consume it while standing creates the reasonable probability that food will drop to the floor." That conclusion leads to the next conclusion: "Food on a terrazzo floor will create a dangerous condition." The court's final conclusion is that "notice to the proprietor of the specific item on the floor need not be shown."

The court explains the policy for the notice rule (that a "dangerous condition" is "somewhat out of the ordinary") and why that policy does not apply in this situation. The court finds support for its conclusion by noting that it had recognized this "principle" (actually a policy) in a "slightly different setting in *Denver Dry Goods Company v. Gettman*, 167 Colo. 539, 448 P.2d 954 (1969)." The *Gettman* case involved the liability of the defendant-owner for injuries suffered by the plaintiff after he slipped and fell on the stairway of the defendant. The stairway was slippery because other persons tracked snow into the stairway. The court declared that the facts in *Gettman* were analogous to the decision of the court in *Jasko* because in neither case did the plaintiff have to prove the defendant had actual or constructive knowledge (notice) in order to have the jury decide whether the defendant was negligent. The court's reliance on *Gettman* as a prior decision supporting is conclusion in *Jasko* is, however, strained. The court implicitly acknowledges that its decision in *Gettman* may not actually be analogous to *Jasko* by noting its conclusion was "(albeit without an extended discussion)." This statement is also a concession that the opinion in *Gettman* did not thoroughly consider its implications.

The court then reiterates that the plaintiff retains the burden of proving the defendant's action constituted negligence, a question of fact for the jury. In other words, proof by the plaintiff of the defendant's method of selling pizza (no tables, waxed paper, terrazzo tile floor) means the defendant owed plaintiff *Jasko* a legal duty of care (our first element in negligence law). Clearly Jasko suffered injuries (damages, our fourth element in negligence cases). Whether Woolworth breach its duty of care (duty and breach constitute negligence) and whether that breach of duty caused Jasko's injuries are factual decisions for the jury. Proof of the dangerous method of sale is sufficient to have the jury decide the case. The jury is free to decide that the defendant Woolworth was negligent or that it was not negligent. That factual conclusion will not be subject to reversal by any appellate court. The Colorado Supreme Court then extensively quotes a 1969 decision of the New Mexico Supreme Court as additional support.

Finally, the court declares in "accord" five other cases, all of which were decided by courts other than the Colorado Supreme Court. "Accord" means that the other cases cited accept the same legal conclusion that was reached in Colorado (or to state this conversely, that Colorado agrees with the decisions of five other courts on whether the plaintiff must prove the defendant had notice when plaintiff claims the method of sale creates a dangerous condition). Four of those cases in "accord" are written by other state appellate courts; one, *Thomason*, is written by the United States Court of Appeals for the Fourth Circuit. That court decides appeals from federal district courts located in Maryland, North Carolina, South Carolina, Virginia and West Virginia, but not Colorado. Each of these decisions in "accord" are dated from 1963 to 1970, which suggests this rule that dispenses with the requirement that a plaintiff prove the defendant's actual or constructive knowledge of the dangerous condition is a relatively new legal rule when *Jasko* was decided. The court's citation of these cases in accord with its decision is offered to alleviate any concern on the part of lawyers (particularly lawyers who represent defendants in similar negligence cases) that the court is adopting a legal rule that no other court has followed.

The final sentence of the opinion tells the reader what will happen next. The decision of the Court of Appeals is reversed. Because the case is before the Supreme Court on a writ of certiorari, the Supreme Court remands (that is, returns) the case to the Court of Appeals, for that is the court to which the Supreme Court officially issued the writ of certiorari. But because the case was dismissed by the trial court before being given to the jury for its decision, the Supreme Court additionally instructs the Court of Appeals to remand the *Jasko* case to the trial court for a new trial.

This expansive assessment of the opinion suggests you can write more about the case than the court wrote in the opinion itself. That is due in part to learning terms of legal art (again, obtain a legal dictionary), but also because the decision must be understood both in terms of what it does, and how it relates to larger legal matters.

A brief is a structured outline or summary of a case, hence the term "brief." The brief is for your own personal use as you prepare for class, recite during class, write an outline and study for the final examination. The following items are typically contained in a brief, although you should choose the briefing style that best suits your approach to studying.

1. **Citation**
   - Name of Case.
   - Jurisdiction (federal or state)?
   - Court (if state, what level of appellate court; if federal, is it a district, circuit, or Supreme Court case?)
   - Year case decided.

2. **Facts**
   - Who are the parties (*e.g.*, plaintiff and defendant)?
   - What was the plaintiff seeking at trial?

- What is the factual basis of the plaintiff's claim? (It is helpful to associate a few key facts with the name of the case so you can quickly recall the case.)
- Include only the legally relevant facts.

3. Procedural History
- Who won at the trial level?
- Who won at the lower appellate level if case has already been appealed?
- Is there other important information about the procedural posture of the case?

4. Issue(s)
- What issue does the court address?
- How is the legal issue precisely stated in light of the relevant facts?

5. Holding
- What did the court decide?
- What is the holding and what is *dicta*? The holding is law; *dictum* (plural, *dicta*) is the court's conclusion about a matter not necessary for it to decide, but about which it offered an opinion. *Dicta* is not binding on any court in that jurisdiction in deciding any future case that requires resolution of the issue which was dictum. You will find distinguishing between the holding and *dicta* is often difficult.

6. Reasoning
- What legal justifications or arguments does the court offer?
- What policy grounds support the court's decision?

7. Procedural Result
- Did the court affirm (agree with) or reverse (disagree with) the lower court's decision?
- What happens next? (*e.g.*, plaintiff collects money, defendant goes to jail, new trial, *etc.*)

8. Other Opinions
- *Concurring Opinion*—Judge agrees with the result but writes to address another issue or to offer a different reason for the legal conclusion.
- *Dissenting Opinion*—Judge disagrees with the result.

A brief of *Jasko* (lawyers regularly refer to cases by one name, and use the name most likely to be distinctive or used less often—thus, Woolworth, a company named as a party in a number of cases, including appellate cases, would not be as distinctive for purposes of the shorthand signal that Jasko is) might look something like the following:

TITLE/CT./YR.: Jasko v. F. W. Woolworth, Colo. S.Ct. 1972

PROCEDURAL AND FACTUAL BACKGROUND: Petitioner-Plaintiff (π) Jasko allegedly slipped on a slice of pizza while leaving the defendant (Δ) Woolworth store, injuring herself. No tables were available to sit at while eating pizza. Testimony offered that porters were constantly sweeping up debris. At trial Jasko offered no evidence of defendant's actual or constructive knowledge of a "dangerous condition" and trial court granted motion for a directed verdict. Ct./App. aff'd ("The Colorado Court of Appeals affirmed." Using abbreviations will become commonplace.)

HOLDING: Colo. S/Ct. reverses, holding no need to prove actual/constructive knowledge when "method" of business creates "dangerous condition." "Well known rule of law" requiring notice eliminated in this type of case based on "reasonable probability" of creating dangerous condition by method of sale. "Method of business operation" rule competes with rule of notice, application of which rule depends on how broadly court interprets "method of business operation."

ADDITIONAL NOTES: S/Ct. cites five other cases reaching same result (trend?) dated from 1963–70.

If you are asked to recite on *Jasko*, you will be asked a series of questions. The questioning may begin with, "What are the facts in *Jasko v. Woolworth*?" You may then be asked what the "well known rule of law" was (no duty of care unless plaintiff shows defendant had actual or constructive knowledge of dangerous condition of premises), whether the court followed that well known rule of law (no), and if not, what rule of law did the court in *Jasko* accept or adopt (see holding above). But what your professor is really interested in is exploring the meaning of the *Jasko* for future similar cases.

The first difficulty you may find in *Jasko* is in stating, clearly and concisely, what the court meant by "method" of selling pizza. The court looked a several conditions of the sale of pizza: 1) no tables, so persons ate the pizza standing up; 2) pizza was served on waxed paper; and 3) the flooring adjacent to the counter where pizza was sold was terrazzo tile. What the court notes but does not focus on was the fact that the plaintiff was exiting the Woolworth store by a "main aisle." This must mean that the pizza-hoagie counter was located on or next to a main aisle. A main aisle is designed to channel more customer traffic than the other aisles in the store. The location of the pizza counter on a main aisle might have been further evidence that the method of selling itself created a dangerous condition. But the court does not use this fact in its determination. This is one of those stray facts that tends to bother law professors. Why does the Supreme Court of Colorado mention it if it is not important to the resolution of the case? It is possible that the location of the pizza counter was an important fact to other courts that looked at this issue. The court also mentions as a fact that, "When pizza was being consumed, according to this witness, porters 'constantly' swept up debris on the floor." That "witness" was the associate manager of the store. It appears that the court is implicitly using this testimony to demonstrate the weakness of the traditional notice rule. If porters were "constantly" sweeping up debris, then it is unlikely the defendant was aware of a dangerous condition and failed to do anything about that condition. And if the porters were constantly cleaning up debris and the plaintiff still slipped on a slice of pizza and was injured, then the notice rule may not be doing the job it was given: protecting innocent persons from dangerous conditions on premises. This testimony assists the Supreme Court in reaching its conclusion because it shows that pizza or some other debris was "constantly" found on the floor. An additional difficulty that may be lurking in the background (that is, never explicitly stated by the Supreme Court) is that the court is aware of the difficulty facing the plaintiff in finding evidence that the defendant possessed actual or constructive knowledge of the dangerous condition. As a corporation, Woolworth acts through its agents, its employees. Evidence that Woolworth was aware of the dangerous condition would ordinarily come from an employee of the defendant. In an unusual case you might obtain the following proof: The plaintiff slips. Before leaving the store, the plaintiff is approached by another customer. That customer gives the plaintiff her name and address and says, "Fifteen minutes before you slipped I told the manager that pizza slices were all over the floor and he told me not to worry about that. If you need me, I will be happy to testify for you if you sue Woolworth." The odds of coming across a disinterested witness with such strong evidence are slight. Ordinarily, proof of actual or constructive notice will have to come from an employee who admits learning of the dangerous condition and doing nothing about it, or who learned about the dangerous condition, informed a supervisor and again nothing was done. This difficulty in finding proof (evidence) requires the plaintiff's lawyer to engage in extensive pre-trial work (called "discovery") to learn whether any such employees exist. Discovery costs money, reducing the total amount recovered by the plaintiff if she wins, and making her poorer if she loses her case (because she is liable for her attorney's costs). This disparity in the ability to collect evidence cheaply may also be a hidden factor in the court's decision. As stated by the Colorado Court of Appeals in its opinion in *Jasko*, no one was present when the plaintiff slipped, so the only possible evidence of actual or constructive knowledge would have to come from an employee of the defendant.

When the court reaches its conclusion that the method of selling pizza itself creates a dangerous condition that allows the plaintiff to dispense with evidence of actual or constructive notice, it begins with the statement "extensive selling of slices of pizza on waxed paper to customers who consume it while standing creates the reasonable probability that food will drop to the floor." The court included the facts that the pizza is served on waxed paper and that customers must eat the pizza while standing. Are both conditions necessary to the court's holding? It is useful that the paper is waxed because it means your pizza won't stick to the paper when you try to eat it. But waxed paper may be more slippery than other types of paper, increasing (does someone have to prove this?) the chance that the pizza slice will slip to the ground. Standing means that you can't put the pizza (on the waxed paper) on a table in between bites, a condition that would make pizza less likely to slip to the ground. As between these two facts, it seems that the more important fact is the absence of tables, for surely a seller of pizza is not required to use "sticky" paper on which to sell pizza by the slice. If the pizza sticks to the paper that might lead customers to pull the pizza harder from the paper, causing them to drop the pizza as often as they do from waxed paper. The use of waxed paper might be important not as it relates to the pizza but as it relates to the floor. If customers dropped waxed paper to the floor, that would generally increase the amount of debris on the ground, creating an additional dangerous condition based on the method of sale. If Woolworth's had tables available for use by customers, would the court have applied the "well known rule" of notice? Your professor may ask this question in order to determine how *Jasko* will be applied to other slip-and-fall cases when the method of sale of a different product or in a different setting is claimed to create a dangerous condition. Adding tables takes up space, which means Woolworth would have to reduce the width of the main aisle, or remove shelves where it offered other goods for sale, keeping more inventory in the back of the store. Is the court implicitly suggesting Woolworth should not serve food unless it transforms itself into a type of sit-down restaurant? Or is the holding more simply that Woolworth assumes the risk of liability if it continues to operate in this fashion? The opinion does not offer any suggestions to Woolworth or other companies that operate similarly about how to reduce their liability, in part probably because the court is simply announcing that this type of business activity will increase your possible liability should an injury occur. Your professor, however, may ask precisely that question.

The conclusion about consuming pizza held on waxed paper while standing leads to the next conclusion: "Food on a terrazzo floor will create a dangerous condition." The court does not limit its holding to pizza, or to foods that are similar to pizza. Should it? Would or should this rule apply to the sale of hamburgers? To hot dogs served in a bun? To corndogs (breaded hot dogs skewered with a wooden stick, so the consumer eats the corndog like one would eat a popsicle)? Does it apply to a counter that is selling drinks, because liquids are more slippery than foods? All of these are questions that may be asked of you if you are lucky enough to recite this case. Again, it appears (though this is uncertain) the court is less interested in the type of food served than in the absence of tables. The court mentions the type of floor several times. Terrazzo is a type of tile floor consisting of marble and cement, and is ordinarily polished. Is it important to the court that the flooring is terrazzo because that may be considered more "slippery" than other types of flooring? If so, what constitutes a "non-slippery" (non-skid?) surface? If the flooring was different, would that alter the court's conclusion? The court does not answer these questions. It appears not, for the court seems intent on ending the notice requirement for all similar method of sale cases. Whatever answer one gives to these questions allows the professor to frame the extent of the holding. If *Jasko* is meant to apply to the sale of all food services when tables are not used, it is a broad holding. If it only applies to pizza and pizza-like products and only when tables are not used and only when the flooring is terrazzo or similar to terrazzo, it is a very narrow opinion. The court itself provides few clues about the larger meaning of its decision. This strategy of not committing to a position on the breadth of the rule is regularly employed by common law courts. The common law defines and re-defines the rule of law based on subsequent cases that claim to invoke the rule, or which are claimed to be outside of the rule's ambit. The common law, as we will discuss more below, largely uses *in-ductive* reasoning in framing the extent of a rule, reasoning from the specific (particular cases) to the general (a rule applicable to a set of factual situations).

One possibly confusing aspect of reading cases that are decades old is in understanding the social or economic context that covertly propels the decision. What was the business of the F. W. Woolworth Company? It was the parent company of the Woolworth's chain of stores. These stores were "five and dime" stores (which should give you a sense of when they were created), stores where one could find goods for sale at a relatively cheap price. Woolworth's sold many different types of goods, from clothing to kitchenware to sporting goods. Woolworth's, like its upscale competitor Sears, tried to sell lots of things to lots of people, making it a one-stop shopping experience. Woolworth's heyday was before large shopping malls changed the approach American consumers took to shopping, and Woolworth's broad inventory of a variety of goods is contrary to specialization you find in current "big box" stores. Many

Woolworth's stores offered food service, including either a counter with seats (like an old-fashioned diner) or a stand-up counter, as was the case in *Jasko*, or both. In the late 1960s (the injury occurred in January 1967) selling pizza and hoagies in Denver, while not exotic, was not the run-of-the-mill idea that exists today. Chain restaurants selling pizza were relatively small in the late 1960s, and the sale of pizza slices may have been quite profitable for Woolworth's.

A second difficulty with understanding these cases is the constrained way in which you read them. If you had also read the opinion of the Colorado Court of Appeals in *Jasko* (I do not recommend you do this until you are very comfortable in learning this material you have been assigned to read), you would have noticed that the facts really were viewed "most favorably" to the plaintiff. The plaintiff's testimony as recited by the Colorado Court of Appeals was that she entered the store between 11:00 a.m. and noon in January and slipped as she passed the pizza counter. She "imagined" she slipped on pizza because she found something "red and yellow" on the heel of her shoe. She saw no other debris, and no other customers were in the area in which she fell. Was that material on her heel pizza? No evidence clearly indicates it was; all her testimony indicated was that she had something red and yellow on the heel of her shoe. The absence of other debris also means it was impossible for her to prove actual notice. The Court of Appeals also made two other statements relevant to the discussion: First, it states that the pizza was sold on "paper napkins," and never uses the term waxed paper. Should that matter? Cheese from the pizza can stick to a paper napkin in a way different than waxed paper, but it doesn't appear that the Colorado Supreme Court is focusing on this apparently minor issue. Second, in addition to selling pizza, the Court of Appeals noted, "Other foods were dispensed from adjoining counters to carry out or for consumption in the store." Should that matter in framing the legal rule on the requirement of notice?

Once you know that Woolworth sold a number of foods for carry out, not just pizza, you also know that the decision in *Jasko* will act as an economic constraint on the manner in which Woolworth does business. Because the holding declares the "method" of selling food for "carry around" food creates a dangerous condition that allows the plaintiff to dispense with proving actual or constructive notice, if the decision applies to all foods (and it seems to), then Woolworth will have to make a decision about how to sell food in light of its greater exposure to liability.

One of the great changes to the teaching of the law of torts in the past twenty-five years is the influence of economic thinking in evaluating tort law. After *Jasko*, a merchant selling food over the counter can choose to continue to sell pizza and other foods for "carry out" and "carry around," aware of the possibility of a lawsuit should a customer fall on the merchant's premises. (You will find a food court at many Wal-Mart stores.) The merchant can choose to alter the method by which it sells food. If that change means adding tables, that likely means less profit for the merchant, because the space in which one sells goods has economic value, and a diminishment of space for the sale of goods means a diminishment of sales and thus profits. A second option for Woolworth's and similar merchants is to discontinue the sale of food. This too will have a cost. Are the costs that the *Jasko* rule adds to the business operated by Woolworth less or more than the benefits received by Jasko and similarly-situated injured persons? The Colorado Supreme Court, writing in 1972, spoke not at all about the shift in costs generated by its decision. It concluded that the method of selling food created a dangerous condition, which might result in a person slipping and suffering an injury. When you read the portion of the Court's opinion on the creation of the dangerous condition by the method of its food sales, it may have struck you as a bit abrupt. The Court concludes that the method of selling pizza creates a dangerous condition, thus allowing a dispensation of the notice requirement. What are its reasons for this conclusion?

The Court focuses wholly on the "law" to explain why it reached this conclusion. It declares a dangerous condition is ordinarily an abnormal condition, but when the methods of sale "are such that dangerous conditions are continuous or easily foreseeable, the logical basis for the notice requirement dissolves." The problem with the court's explanation is that it is simply restating the conclusion it has already reached. You will learn much about what is "foreseeable" in the course of your Torts class. For now you should view this as part of the court's after-the-fact legal conclusion. The question is, what makes the sale of pizza for "carry around" dangerous? We are back to asking whether it is the particular food product (the cheese on the pizza melts and falls to the floor, pepperoni slices can fall off the cheese?) that leads the court to this conclusion, or that persons eat while standing and even while walking about the store, thus creating the dangerous condition. Several approaches might help in answering this question: One approach would be an empirical survey of methods of selling food and any incidence in the rise of slip and fall injuries. Courts have neither the time nor the resources to conduct such empirical studies, which may be just as well. Courts often cite to general literature supporting a legal conclusion (literature found either in law journals or in other academic publications), but the *Jasko* Court did not do so. A second approach is to determine on whom the cost of such injuries may best be borne as an economic matter. Another approach is to ask, to what extent do we want the customer to take some care to attempt to avoid injury? Further, should the loss be borne by Woolworth's because it invited customers to its store in the hope of generating profits? In other words, should the law as a moral matter place liability on businesses because they invite people to their place of business in order to make a profit? (If so, should the rule also apply to non-profit businesses? To non-profit businesses if they raise revenue from "customers"? Should it apply only if the plaintiff proves the defendant acted negligently, or should the defendant pay for the harm caused plaintiff as a matter of strict liability?) These and other approaches to justifying the policy of the law are at the heart of the first year learning process, for the questions asked admit of no perfect answer, but some comparative answers about what may be a better approach (either in terms of economics or morals) may be suggested.

How to Read Cases

You will read hundreds of cases in your first year of law school. How well you read those cases will make a huge difference in your academic success. Empirical evidence suggests that the manner in which a student reads correlates with grades. The more effectively a student reads cases, the better the student performs on 1L examinations. Students with similar LSAT and UGPA numbers perform differently in substantial part based on the effectiveness of the student's reading comprehension. Even (or maybe especially) if you are an avid reader, you will need to adjust your approach to reading when reading cases. If you are reading a newspaper (or Internet news site) you are likely to skim through much of the account, possibly reading just the headline or the first paragraph to understand the point of the article. If you are reading a case by skimming its perceived highlights you are not likely to understand its importance, nor are you likely to understand its significance in light of the past cases you have read. Instead, you must read actively. Some research indicates that a student reads more effectively if she puts herself in the position of a lawyer analyzing a case for a client. You may experiment to see whether that aids in your understanding of the case. In addition, you must read the case in light of the material that has come before and, looking at your syllabus, with the material (at least as given in outline form) that will come after. That includes reading the notes following the case in light of the opinion, and re-reading the opinion in light of the notes.

If you are going to realize your abilities in law school you must begin your 1L year by reading each case three times. This is possible if you are spending three hours studying for every hour of class, which should be the norm. If you begin your legal education by reading each case just once, you are either a savant or wasting your time and money. These three readings have very different purposes. The first reading is simply to give you a sense of the spine of the case. Who are the parties? What facts does the court recite? Does the court reverse or affirm? What is its conclusion? In this first reading you should note the procedural and factual background of the case, its conclusion (not necessarily the holding or rule of law) and any difficulties you have in understanding the material. You want a skeletal understanding of the case. One way to make your way through the maze of an opinion is to stop after each paragraph and consider the purpose of the paragraph. Was the judge simply giving the reader the factual or procedural background? Was the judge making an argument in favor of some position and against another? (In *Jasko*, when does the court begin its argument against application of the "well known rule" and in favor of a new rule dispensing with the element of notice?) How are the paragraphs linked? You may decide to underline, circle or note some parts of the opinion, but you should avoid any heavy highlighting during this read. (Highlighting may be effective for some, but it quickly can become a substitute for thinking about how the opinion reasons from the facts to a legal conclusion.) The second read is a contextual reading, allowing you to structure your brief. You may also include comments in the margins of your book, allowing you to consider, this time in writing, what the opinion is attempting to accomplish in any given paragraph. Your third reading is undertaken to make sure your brief is complete as well as interpreted in light of other similar cases, either other principal cases (that is, excerpted in your casebook) or as note cases (discussed in the "Notes" that follow the excerpted principal case). This third reading places the case within the "community" of cases in your 1L class. While doing so re-read your brief, looking for gaps in your brief or in your understanding.

Most cases include one or more confusing or even unintelligible sentences or paragraphs. Do not skip over those parts of the opinion. First, your casebook author has some reason for leaving that material in the edit of the case, even if the reason is to demonstrate how some opinions are confusing or unintelligible. More likely the casebook author left this material in because it was an important part of the court's opinion. You need to re-read those sentences until your confusion has ebbed (not until it has disappeared, for some confusion is normal), for re-reading will generate long-term benefits in your reading comprehension.

Federalism and First Year Substantive Courses

The vast majority of the cases you will read in the first year courses of Torts, Contracts, Property and Criminal Law are written by state appellate courts.

Just a few will be written by a federal district court or a federal circuit court of appeals, and even fewer will be written by the Supreme Court of the United States. This is a consequence of the American constitutional doctrine of federalism. Federalism describes the relationship between the state government and the federal government. In general, the federal government acts pursuant to a specific grant of authority declared in the Constitution. These are called "enumerated" powers. Each state possesses general powers called "police" powers, the authority to protect, as traditionally stated, the health, safety, welfare and morals of its residents. States thus possess the power to determine their own tort, contract and property law, as well as the law of crimes, and different states may choose different approaches to these matters. That is why you will read in the notes following some cases that the primary case (the excerpted case) is an example of the "majority" rule on this topic (that is, a majority of states follow this rule), or an example of the "minority" rule (that is, more states follow a different rule than the rule declared in the excerpted case). As discussed above, casebooks are written with the national legal education market in mind. Consequently, the excerpted cases are usually chosen because they exemplify most articulately the legal issue discussed in that section of the book, and the opinion may come from any state appellate court. Your professor will often inform you what rule has been adopted in the state in which you are studying law.

The doctrine of federalism has become less important in American constitutional law in the past seventy years. The federal government's reach and power has expanded tremendously since the creation of the New Deal in the 1930s. An extensive number of federal crimes now exist, and federal laws that determine civil liability (tort and contract law, in general) will likely be discussed in these otherwise state-law dominated courses. You will, however, largely read cases decided by state courts. The major exceptions to this rule in 1L classes are Civil Procedure, which focuses largely on the Federal Rules of Civil Procedure, and Constitutional Law, which evaluates opinions written by the Supreme Court of the United States.

Federalism also explains why few contracts, property and torts cases are decided by the Supreme Court of the United States. The Supreme Court's jurisdiction to hear cases is, in general, limited to cases that begin in the federal court system (for example, by filing a complaint in the United States District Court for the Eastern District of Wisconsin, one of the ninety-four federal district courts, courts that themselves only have limited jurisdiction to hear cases based on federalism), and have been decided on appeal at the United States Court of Appeals for one of the eleven numbered circuit courts, the circuit court for the District of Columbia, or the Federal Circuit, as appropriate. A party that loses at the federal circuit court level may become a petitioner and peti-tion the Supreme Court requesting it issue a writ of certiorari. The authority to petition the Supreme Court for a writ of certiorari exists only in limited cir-cumstances. If the Supreme Court grants the writ, the case name will be styled *Petitioner v. Respondent.*

If a case begins in a state trial-level court, the judgment of the trial court may be appealed to a state appellate court, and then possibly to the state supreme court (a second appeal will depend on the state's rules of appellate procedure). Most states, like the United States, have a three-tiered system of courts, from trial court to intermediate appellate court to supreme court. Once a case is de-cided by a state supreme court (and also when that court refuses to hear an appeal or petition), the losing party may petition the Supreme Court of the United States for a writ of certiorari. Again, however, the Supreme Court has only limited authority to hear such cases. If the petitioner claims that the state has violated a federal constitutional right held by the petitioner (say, by denying the petitioner the right to free speech), then the Supreme Court may decide to hear the case. In ordinary tort, contract and property cases, a violation of a fed-eral constitutional right is rarely alleged, leaving the Supreme Court without the legal authority to hear and decide the case. In criminal law cases the state usually is requesting that a convicted defendant's liberty and/or property be taken. This triggers more claims by convicted persons of a violation of rights to due process or equal protection of the laws under the Fourteenth Amend-ment. Consequently, more criminal law cases decided by a state supreme court may be subject to possible review by the Supreme Court of the United States. The Supreme Court decides about seventy cases a year, so the odds that the Court will issue a writ of certiorari in any particular case are quite small.

Restatements and Uniform State Laws

Federalism means different state courts can reach contrary conclusions about nonconstitutional legal doctrine, such as the requirement that the defendant have notice of the dangerous condition before being subject to liability in slip-and-fall cases. Although state appellate courts are aware of the decisions of ap-pellate courts in other states, either because the lawyers discussed such cases in the brief to the appellate court or because a legal treatise mentioned the cases, no state supreme court is required to follow the law as declared by an-other state's supreme court. And because the Supreme Court of the United States lacks jurisdiction to make these state appellate decisions uniform among the states, nineteenth century writers of legal treatises often tried to impose some order on the law of torts or criminal law by explaining what those authors believed the law *should be*, not just what it *was*. These treatise writers had no particular authority to impose their view of the law other than their expertise, which was sometimes sufficient for a state appellate court to change its mind about a rule and adopt the conclusion of the treatise writer.

The pressure to harmonize common law subjects grew in the early twentieth century. One response to the growing diversity of common law was the creation of a body of lawyer/legislator-volunteers who joined a private group eventually called the National Conference of Commissioners on Uniform State Laws (NCCUSL). The NCCUSL consisted of commissioners appointed from every state. It drafted model statutes that attempted to make uniform ("harmonize") business and contract law among the states. These laws would encourage trade by ensuring that any breach of such agreements would be handled similarly no matter which state the litigation arose in. The job of the commissioners was to return to their states and convince state legislators to adopt these harmonized or uniform state laws. One of the earliest Uniform State Laws was the Uniform Sales Act. The most famous uniform law is the Uniform Commercial Code (UCC), adopted in every state but Louisiana. You will likely gain some familiarity with the Sales provisions in the Uniform Commercial Code in your Contracts class, and other provisions of the UCC are taught in upper level courses called Secured Transactions and Commercial Paper (also called Payment Systems). UCC subjects are commonly tested on the bar exam.

The Restatement of the Law was a project of a private organization of judges, lawyers and law professors called the American Law Institute (ALI) created in the early 1920s. The initial effort of the ALI was the project of "restating" the common law of Property, Torts, Contracts and other subjects. When published beginning in the 1930s the Restatement included numbered sections in bold print, known as "black-letter law." This was not law in the sense of being declared by a court or legislature. This black-letter statement was intended to provide the predominant or "majority" rule of law on a particular issue (for example, whether contributory negligence was the law of a majority of states) within those common law subjects. The black-letter law was followed by Comments explaining the black-letter law and Illustrations, usually examples from case law (though not formally cited) that demonstrated (or "illustrated") the law as applied. The Restatement of the Law project continued through a Second Restatement (cited Restatement (Second) of the Law of _____, whether Contracts, Torts, Property or other subject). The ALI is now working on a Third Restatement. Again, although the Restatement provisions are not themselves "law," thousands of decisions by appellate courts have cited provisions in the Restatements as support for the conclusion of the court about what the law is. You will find many citations to the Restatement in your 1L courses in Contracts, Property and Torts, and your casebooks may reprint some sections of the Restatement to indicate the state of the law on that particular subject. The Restatement project has been quite successful in harmonizing the common law among the states. Of course, some states will reject particular provisions in the Restatement, and your casebook authors will refer to majority and minority jurisdictions on many issues.

The continued existence of majority and minority jurisdictions re-emphasizes the point about your 1L year: it is important but not sufficient to learn what the law *is* because different state courts disagree on that very point, making it crucial that you learn the reasons *why* the law is a certain way. It is important to keep track of majority and minority rules, but it is more important to learn the reasons why different state courts disagree about legal rules. In other words, part of learning in your 1L classes is understanding how courts adopt or reject particular policies that inform the doctrinal rules. Those explanations and rationales, reached through common types of legal reasoning, provide you with some understanding of what it means to think like a lawyer.

Briefing, Outlining and Study Groups

Views on briefing, outlining and study groups vary tremendously. How you best learn may differ from your classmates, and you should not succumb to peer pressure if you believe you have found an efficient and effective way to study the material. What too many students do not know is how they best learn. You may have succeeded in college by memorizing facts and ideas or by aping the opinions of your professors, but this is unlikely to work in law school. To do well on your law school exams you must know different legal doctrines, so you must memorize many things (especially if your exam is a closed-book exam). However, the greater part of learning law is analysis, not memorization, and analysis requires understanding the reason (policy) for the doctrine and the limitations of the doctrine. Analysis is central to law school exams because the professor will likely ask questions that are similar but not identical to facts found in the cases you studied during the semester. Part of the difficulty in determining whether your study habits are effective is that most law schools test you only after your first semester classes are over. You may believe that you are studying effectively and learn in January (when your grades are posted) that your efforts did not match your grades. This may be the result of a type of overconfidence about your study skills, a difficulty which exists at all levels of education, but from which you likely have not suffered. (What may be even worse in the long-term is when your grades exceed your efforts, for then you are truly at a loss to understand what happened.) The problem of overconfidence that harms law students is a sense that one knows (because one has memorized) the material and does not exert the effort necessary to understand (that is, by demonstrating an ability to analyze hypothetical situations that vary somewhat from the excerpted cases) the importance of analysis in a law school exam. The only solution to this possible problem is doing sample tests, either those on file from the professor (the best option) or those available in a workbook on the subject. A second difficulty is that even if you always brief cases ahead of time and even if you outline regularly, you will find yourself lost during some or most of the discussion during class. At least in the first semester of law school this is intentional. Your professor is taking you deeper and deeper into the intricacies of the making (and unmaking) of doctrine and implementing policy, requiring you to think more cogently about what legally accepted arguments will support and attack the doctrine, and causing you to prioritize the policies that support or undermine the doctrine. If you are never confused in class you aren't trying hard enough.

For many of you the decision to brief your cases will be helpful, a necessary though not sufficient part of your study of law. When you begin the semester, your "briefs" of the assigned cases will be longer, often much longer, than necessary. That problem will remain for some time during the first semester. However, the very act of briefing provides you another opportunity to think about the meaning of the case, for the brief is your initial summary assessment of its "core" or central meaning. As already discussed, you should not write a brief until after your second reading. For some of you, underlining or writing margin notes during either the first or second read provides the chance for you to make an initial assessment about the background and procedural history of the case. The second reading gives the student the chance to look at the meaning of the case. The third reading allows you to look at the case both in isolation and in context. Waiting to write a brief of the case until after a second reading gives the student a better chance to perceive some of the nuances of the case, including implicit policy arguments and the legal reasoning supporting the court's conclusion.

Briefing a case takes time, and part of the learning curve in the first semester of law school is making more efficient use of your limited time. Some students get the hang of briefing a case fairly quickly and stop doing it. Too often this decision is based on a superficial understanding of the case, another form of overconfidence that ensnares students. After some continued practice during your first semester of law school you will likely be able to spot the holding of a case in short order. If you stop writing case briefs too soon you will not attain an important goal of 1L courses: you are learning to "think like a lawyer," not just memorizing rules. Thinking like a lawyer requires a knowledge of doctrine, the ability to understand the policies that justify that doctrine and the limits of that doctrine and the policy that justifies it. Writing briefs creates the best opportunity to reaching those particular and more abstract goals.

The briefing compromise many students adopt is to quit writing briefs of cases in favor of "book briefing." A book brief, as its name suggests, is a summary of the case written at the beginning or end of the case, or more usually, in the margins next to the opinion in your casebook. Book briefing is the rule by the second year of law school. It should remain the rare exception in the first semester of law school, and should be used with caution during the second semester of a student's first year of law school (or, if you are in a quarter system, the third quarter), for continued briefing can provide surprising and valuable insights once you have some experience doing it.

Law school publishers print standardized outlines for all 1L classes. These outlines are well written, and you must be wary of relying too heavily on them, of avoiding the hard work of learning this material in favor of having a supplement do it for you. This is particularly so because most 1L exams will not allow you to bring in the supplement to the final exam. During your first semester of law school you are likely to enhance your learning curve by generating your own outlines. Do not begin working on an outline less than three weeks from the beginning of class, for you don't know enough to know what should be excluded from your outline at the beginning of the semester. That will give you plenty of time to think about what is important enough to include in the outline. You should consider working on your outlines in some general order on the weekends, but on no account should you try to work on more than two subjects during any weekend until the last month of the semester. Using a published supplemental outline is a good check on your work, but must remain your secondary outline.

When your professor provides a syllabus of the course, she is giving you a skeletal version of an outline of the material. You should use the syllabus as an opening in constructing an outline. In addition, the table of contents of your casebook also presents a skeletal outline. Use it to complement the syllabus, giving you two sources to construct an outline. Finally, one important reason to write an outline rather than adopt another's is that the act of writing down the material is another way to learn the material. It is the doing of the act that may provide that "aha" moment in reaching an understanding of a particularly confusing area of doctrine or in understanding why policies are in conflict.

The traditional reason to join a formal study group is premised on the idea that students must be active learners to best understand law. Nearly all professors assume you have read and tried to understand the material before class. The primary purpose of class is to delve more deeply into the meaning and application of the material to a host of related legal problems. It is not to teach you the material you were required to read before class. A study group can help assist you in getting beyond what the case *says* to what the case *means*. You will find, however, that as you become more comfortable with your classmates, you will discuss your assignments with them informally and at length. These informal discussions may be more valuable than anything you could take from a formal study group. Whether you join a study group or not, continue to work on actively learning the material assigned for each class.

Learning Styles and 1L Study

Learning theory lists four distinct types of learning styles, and though many students may have a dominant learning style, most will have some combination of learning styles. These styles are known by the acronym KARV.

K stands for Kinesthetic learner, someone who learns best from experience, as well as from activity, action and tactile sensations. A stands for Aural or Auditory learner, someone who learns best by listening, including reading aloud. R stands for Read/write learner, someone who learns from reading. V stands for Visual learner. This is someone who learns best through pictures, charts, graphs and the like. The last three types of learners are dominant in law schools.

Law school demands you read a significant amount. A read/write learner has something of an advantage in the 1L year, for that learning style fits much of what a student must do competently to successfully complete the 1L year. However, law school also demands that you listen well in class, including listening well to statements made by your classmates, who in the socratic method are teaching you by their responses to the professor's questions. Even if you dislike listening to your classmates, writing down some of what they say may be helpful for you better to understand the material. Law school professors may use flowcharts, decision trees and other visual media to reflect, for example, how the elements of a tort work. You certainly may brief your cases in a visual way if that best suits your learning style, for rules of law can regularly be translated from words into pictures, charts and graphs. In your 1L year you may have a few simulations or assignments that attempt to have you act in the role of lawyer (for example, giving an oral argument in a 1L legal research and writing class), but kinesthetic learning will be the exception in your 1L classes. That learning by doing, by experience, will await upper level simulation and clinical courses. Most of us, as stated above, use several learning styles, even if one is dominant.

If you do not enjoy close reading of material (that is, it's not the length of the material you need to read, it's the density of the material assigned), you will struggle to find a pleasant manner in which to complete your assignments. Many successful lawyers read relatively little after law school; they synthesize through conversations with others, and they focus on areas of law in which close reading is not central to their work. If you believe you may fit that bill, you will need to find an approach to reading the material that will get you through the 1L year. Most universities have a counseling and testing center that can assist you in ascertaining your learning style and how to adapt that style to your 1L classes. If you believe you are struggling during the first several weeks of class, do not delay your trip to the counseling and testing center. The idea that a law student has to tough it out is long gone. Take advantage of the resources available to you.

If you have been diagnosed with a learning disability, the federal Americans with Disabilities Act (ADA) prohibits law schools and other educational entities from discriminating against you. If you need extra time, separate space or some other accommodation for your exams, you can obtain that accommodation if you comply with the law school's (or University's, if the law school is part of a University) ADA guidelines for obtaining accommodations. Do not decide that you will avoid obtaining an ADA accommodation to see if you can pass your exams without an accommodation. That is a recipe for disaster, and may strangle your law career in its infancy. You may have greater difficulty in obtaining ADA accommodations when taking the bar exam, but worry about that later. Your present goal is to succeed in your 1L year.

Sections and Silence

Nearly all law schools will assign you to one section for your first year classes (this does not apply to any elective available in your first year). These sections will range from 50–100 persons. Some schools will break out one class as a small section (legal research and writing is common, but some schools will take a course such as contracts and create as many sections of twenty-five students as necessary), but most courses will be taken with the same group of students during your 1L year. As a result you will get to know most members of your section by the end of your first year. This also means that you will not become acquainted with most of those students in another section. Each section will have its own culture, developed in part by the faculty assigned to teach that section (some professors work well together, others don't) and in greater part by the students themselves.

Most students who attend law school are competitive, and have succeeded in the competition for grades at the high school, university and graduate school levels. Most law schools grade on a mandatory curve (check the school's website for information about that school's 1L curve), and it is difficult for many law students to accept being average. The negative aspect of law school competitiveness is often found in the hostility of some students to questions asked by other students. Law professors will often declare "no question is a stupid question." Saying it in that way may reinforce the unwillingness of students to speak up voluntarily, for they may think that *this* question will be viewed as stupid by the student's classmates. Because legal education promotes active learning, questions are a crucial element in teaching students how to think clearly and how to articulate those thoughts. Law teachers want questions because questions give them a sense of what students might not understand or misapprehend. Students dislike questions because they believe they don't learn from another student's question. After all, the student is not the expert, but is just like them. This belief is a residue of undergraduate learning, a belief that only the "expert" (professor) should speak and the expert's views are what a student needs to learn. This learning style is one that law education abhors. This student antipathy to questions is why you will learn some students will play "turkey bingo" in class, even occasionally saying it out loud. Peer pressure may be used to silence those students who speak in class; if successful, this silencing will inhibit the learning curve for all to learn to think like a lawyer. Silencing and ostracism are unfortunately common maladies at too many law schools.

Many professors, aware of the silencing of students, use alternate fora for students to communicate. A student's e-mail to a professor will usually be answered quickly. Many professors post messages on Blackboard or TWEN (The West Education Network) and encourage students to post responses or their own messages. Some use an instant polling device that allows a professor to ask a question and obtain immediate and anonymous responses from the class. Some professors jealously husband their time, but many are willing to speak with any student about the course subject and related topics as long as it is not shortly before the professor is to teach.

Take advantage of the opportunities you have to communicate with your professors. Your willingness to risk looking foolish may lead to work as a research assistant to the professor or a willingness by the professor to serve as a reference to legal employers. You are paying too much money not to take advantage of everything the school offers you.

The rise of wireless Internet access has led many professors to ban laptops in 1L classes. This is usually not because of the harm a distracted student may cause himself. Instead, it is the distraction that this student causes others that leads many professors to ban laptops. If you have become enamored of note taking (or brief writing) on your laptop, make sure you learn quickly whether you will be able to do so in your 1L classes.

Legal Reasoning and "Thinking Like a Lawyer"

To learn to think like a lawyer is to take you from beginner to expert (or at least move you in that direction) during your law school experience, particularly in your 1L year. As is true with most learning, you will be expected to possess and be able to recall a great deal of factual information, factual in the sense of knowing the structure of the legal system (what kinds of cases are heard in what kinds of courts?), the ideas that generate doctrine (to what extent should economic efficiency be a goal of law? To what extent should claims of moral right be protected?) and a large number of legal rules. This mass of data must be organized conceptually. What are the goals of the law of contracts? Of civil procedure? How do the doctrines you have studied work together to make the subject something whole and not just a collection of scattered rules? Finally, can you take the concepts and doctrine learned in one factual setting and show that you understand them by applying those concepts and doctrine in another factual setting?

As is discussed in much detail in the next chapter, your essay examinations will test your ability to remember doctrine. You will not, however, be asked to disgorge on your examination bluebook (sixteen lined pages, the cover of which is a light blue) everything you remember. You will instead be tested largely on how well you can apply that remembered doctrine to different (possibly even new) factual situations. Applying doctrine (or determining which of two competing doctrines applies) certainly requires that you know and remember many doctrinal rules. However, a good examination will not ask you to define the rule applicable to the tort of false imprisonment. It will test you on whether the facts as stated constitute false imprisonment, and ask you to analyze the facts to argue for opposing conclusions. Your task on most essay examinations, then, is a twofold task: know the relevant rule(s), and then articulate whether and how this rule is applicable to the facts as written by the professor.

The ability to analyze the applicability of legal rules to factual situations is learned and honed by repeated use of several types of reasoning, reasoning that is at the heart of legal analysis and thinking like a lawyer and thus called "legal reasoning." This reasoning is not peculiar to law, for it is reasoning used in every day interactions. These forms of reasoning have also been described in Chapter 2 when discussing the LSAT. All persons use these forms of reasoning to some extent, even though they may not be able to articulate their reasoning process. Naming and explaining the commonly recurring types of reasoning used in law allows a student to better see how they are used by judges and lawyers.

Lawyers use both *deductive* and *inductive* forms of reasoning. Deductive reasoning takes a person from a general proposition or premise to a specific conclusion. Inductive reasoning begins with a specific conclusion or specific premise and ends with a general proposition. The common law shifts back and forth between deductive and inductive forms of reasoning depending on what task is given the lawyers and judges. In general, when a doctrine or legal rule is being shaped or created, inductive reasoning is used, for the specific cases are melded after the fact (that is, after the decisions have been rendered in several cases) to fashion a general rule. Conversely, once a legal rule is settled, deductive reasoning is used, for the issue is whether the general rule applies to this new, specific case. As new rules are generated from old rules (as is demonstrated in *Jasko*) this inductive and deductive process continues.

The most common form of deductive reasoning is the *syllogism*. A syllogism consists of a major premise, a minor premise and a conclusion. The conclusion, because it follows from the premises, is unassailable as a *logical* matter (you can, of course, disagree with the conclusion as a *policy* matter, but that attack is simply an argument that the syllogism is inapt, not that it is a faulty syllogism). To attack a syllogism directly requires the person attack either the major or minor premise.

One common way in which a syllogism is used in law (and legal education) is in moving from an existing rule to its application in a current case. The major premise is the rule of law and the minor premise is the current case or issue. Using the rule modified in *Jasko*, the following syllogism can be constructed:

Major Premise: In a premises liability (slip-and-fall) case the plaintiff must offer evidence in her case-in-chief that the defendant possessed actual or constructive notice of a dangerous condition or the plaintiff's case will be dismissed;

Minor Premise: The plaintiff offered no evidence in her case-in-chief that defendant had actual or constructive notice of a dangerous condition that plaintiff claims caused her to fall and injure herself;

Conclusion: The plaintiff's case must be dismissed.

The trial court and the Colorado Court of Appeals adopted this syllogism in *Jasko*. The Colorado Supreme Court disagreed with the conclusion reached by the lower courts. The only way to reach a contrary conclusion was to reject the Major Premise. The Court abandoned the pre-existing requirement that the defendant have actual or constructive knowledge before it owed a duty of care to the injured plaintiff in cases in which the method of selling created a dangerous condition. The Major Premise could then be restated: In a premises liability (slip-and-fall) case the plaintiff must offer evidence in her case-in-chief that the defendant possessed actual or constructive notice of a dangerous condition or the plaintiff's case will be dismissed *except when the defendant's method of selling creates a dangerous condition.*

These exceptions may begin to pile up as the previous rule is whittled down. Once a number of exceptions have been created, the court is faced with deciding whether to abandon the "well known rule of law" or to limit its application to a few types of premises liability cases. Occasionally, the court will modify this whittling process by creating an exception to the exception.

Courts use deductive logic when looking to place a current case within the framework of an existing rule. Stating the rule in major premise form, and stating the current case as falling within the class of cases for which the rule is adopted (the minor premise), the conclusion will be that the current case must be treated as within the rule. For example, if the major premise is "The government may not ban political speech unless it proves it has acted in the least restrictive way to promote a compelling governmental interest," and the minor premise is, "The government banned the plaintiff's political speech for a trivial reason," the conclusion follows that the government's action is impermissible (that is, unconstitutional), for the case as described in the minor premise (political speech banned for a trivial reason) does not fit within the "unless" clause as stated in the major premise.

The above-stated premises in the major and minor premises above include particular facts, that the speech of the plaintiff was "political" speech and that the reason for the ban was "trivial." The government could attack the premises made by the plaintiff by alleging that the speech is something other than political speech or that, even if the speech was political, the reasons for the ban were compelling and the least restrictive alternative available to the government. In addition, the major premise includes a statement of law, that political speech may be banned only if the government acts in the least restrictive manner to promote a compelling governmental interest and that the government has the burden of proving these two elements. This is a correct statement of law. If, however, the major premise invokes an invalid or partially valid statement of law, another attack on the major premise is an attack on the rule of law as declared in the premise.

The common law system in American law has today been joined by the relatively deductive nature of statutes. Statutes are general rules, and one question for lawyers is whether the general statute applies to the specific facts in the matter. Thus, like a general rule created by case law, a general rule created by statute forms the major premise in a syllogism. The deductive question (the minor premise) is whether the rule or some exception to the rule applies in a particular matter. Consequently, lawyers regularly toggle back and forth between deductive reasoning (say, looking at a general rule and applying it to a particular case) and inductive reasoning (looking at the facts of a particular case to reach a general rule).

The most common form of inductive reasoning you will use is *analogical* reasoning. Reasoning by analogy requires you to group like things together, and to separate "unlike" things from "like" things. As noted in Chapter 2, the Sesame Street skit and song "one of these things is not like the others, [which] one of these things just doesn't belong," is a type of reasoning by analogy. The point was reinforced by another lyric in the same song that "three of these things belong together, three of these things are kind of the same." Reasoning by analogy requires you to think how legally relevant facts are "kind of the same," meaning those type of factual events that should probably be treated the same way. In order to make a proper analogy, you must learn, through trial and error, what facts are legally relevant. Your reference point is to a particular case or statute. A new set of factual events arise that are not identical (if they are then your need to reason by analogy is absent) to the facts found (or implied) in your reference point. Can those two sets of factual events be grouped together? A demonstration of expertise in law is the ability to articulate clearly how two sets of legally relevant facts are "alike," and how they are "unalike." When one can argue a set of facts is both alike and unalike a stated precedential set of facts, you have found an ability to think like a lawyer (and that ability is one reason why the public distrusts lawyers, because they believe a lawyer can argue in favor of or against any proposition, making it appear lawyers are both amoral and powerful). Your ability to argue how cases are alike or unalike is a necessary but not sufficient stage in becoming a good lawyer. However, this facility to reason by analogy as a 1L student marks a jumping off point in the making of one "lawyerly" trait.

We can use *Jasko* to demonstrate how lawyers and judges reason by analogy. *Jasko* allowed a plaintiff to dispense with proof of the defendant's actual or constructive knowledge of a dangerous condition when the method of sale created a dangerous condition. Eight years after *Jasko* was decided, the Idaho Supreme Court heard an appeal of a verdict in favor of the defendant store in *Tommerup v. Albertson's, Inc.*, 607 P.2d 1055 (Idaho 1980). The plaintiff was walking in the defendant's parking lot when she slipped and fell on a cupcake wrapper. The defendant, a grocery store, made and sold cupcakes in the store. No evidence was offered indicating that this cupcake wrapper came from the defendant's store, and the plaintiff failed to offer evidence that the defendant possessed actual or constructive notice of a dangerous condition in its parking lot. The trial court instructed the jury that proof of the defendant's actual or constructive notice was necessary to return a verdict in favor of the plaintiff. That, you may recall, is the "well known rule of law" that was modified by *Jasko*. The jury returned a verdict in favor of the defendant. On appeal, the plaintiff asked the Idaho Supreme Court to hold the trial court's instruction was erroneous and to adopt the modified rule as declared in *Jasko*. The court affirmed, rejecting *Jasko*.

The Idaho court reacted to the plaintiff's claim that the *Jasko* rule should be applied by stating, "That case, however, is readily distinguished on its facts." *Jasko* was distinguishable from *Tommerup* because, unlike *Jasko*, the accident suffered by the plaintiff Tommerup was "an isolated incident." But was it true in *Jasko* that accidents were not isolated? It doesn't appear from the facts in *Jasko* as stated in either the Colorado Supreme Court's opinion or in the opinion of the Colorado Court of Appeals that accidents regularly occurred. No other accident involving slipping on pizza at the Woolworth's store was ever mentioned in any appellate court decision in *Jasko*. What the Colorado Supreme Court focused on in *Jasko* was that porters constantly swept up debris, not that accidents were common. In *Tommerup*, the plaintiff failed to offer evidence of a substantial number of daily sales of cupcakes reaching the amount of slices of pizza (500–1,000) sold in *Jasko*, or evidence that customers were eating cupcakes while shopping. Those facts distinguished *Jasko* and *Tommerup*, but the policy question is whether it is the number of sales (modest) or the method of sale (selling food that is "carry around") that drives the decision whether to eliminate the requirement of notice on the part of the defendant? Finally, no evidence was offered that porters were constantly cleaning up debris in *Tommerup*. Thus, the Idaho court concluded, *Tommerup* was not similar to *Jasko*. This is known as "dis-analogizing," showing that two cases (or two sets of facts) are unalike.

The *Tommerup* case offers two additional insights that provide a policy reason for its refusal to adopt the rule in *Jasko*. First, the Idaho court accepted the plaintiff's contention that "plaintiff is in a very difficult position to carry the burden of proof on the issue because he usually has no prior knowledge of the condition, is surprised and upset by the accident, and therefore unable to gather evidence to prove how long the condition existed, does not know of the proof requirement at the time when evidence could best be gathered, and most of the people who are best able to supply the evidence are employees of the proprietor with an interest adverse to the plaintiff." The court concluded that plaintiff's difficulty in obtaining proof was irrelevant to its decision because the defendant was not an "insurer" of those it invited to the store. The conclusion that the defendant is not the insurer of those it invites into its store is a policy argument. Remember that the policy favored by the *Jasko* court was that if the dangerous condition was "foreseeable" by the defendant, which seems to mean not exceptional, then the reason for the requirement of notice disappeared. The *Jasko* conclusion did not make the defendant an "insurer," but it placed some greater responsibility on the defendant to avoid creating the possibility of debris that might cause a customer ("invitee" in the language of the law) to fall and suffer an injury.

Second, the *Tommerup* court concluded that defendants were placed in a very difficult situation by the *Jasko* rule: "[L]iability could be imposed upon a defendant storeowner if a customer, shopping in its store, discarded a piece of litter in an aisle upon which a second customer slipped and fell five seconds later.... We decline appellants' invitation to foster such an unreasonable result." The *Tommerup* court's conclusion appears driven by another policy: that adoption of the *Jasko* rule was wrong as a moral matter, because it placed liability on a party that, in its hypothetical, could not have fixed the problem before the injury occurred.

Finally, you should be aware that a common law decision of state supreme court is not inalterable. A future Idaho court could have decided that the holding (that is, the legal conclusion) in *Tommerup* was no longer viable as a result of changing societal conditions (say, the manner in which people buy food and other products). Further, a state legislature has the authority to override common law decisions by statute. The law adopted by the Idaho Supreme Court in *Tommerup* was eventually overturned by statute. This is one crucial way in which the common law differs from constitutional law. A decision by the Supreme Court of the United States declaring unconstitutional some action by the government can be overturned only by constitutional amendment, which has happened just four times in over 200 years, or by a decision of the Supreme Court reversing itself.

The applicability of *Jasko* to other, arguably analogous factual situation was the subject of other appellate court decisions. A result contrary to *Tommerup* was reached in *Smith v. Safeway Stores, Inc.*, 636 P.2d 1310 (Colo. App. 1981). The Colorado Court of Appeals found *Jasko* analogous in the following case. The plaintiff was shopping at defendant's "self-service" grocery store. While walking down an aisle between two rows of shelves, the plaintiff slipped and fell on what appeared to be hand lotion. The trial court did not require the plaintiff to prove the defendant had actual or constructive notice that hand lotion was on the floor, and the jury found in favor of the plaintiff. The defendant appealed, claiming the *Jasko* rule (that is, an exception to the rule of notice) did not apply under these circumstances. The court of appeals affirmed. It noted that the facts in *Jasko* did not involve a grocery store, but proof of notice was excused because the method of selling pizzas created a "continuous" dangerous condition. In *Smith*, the method of selling (allowing customers to pick their own grocery products and put them in a grocery cart and then go to a checkout lane) also created a continuous dangerous condition, making the rule of notice inapplicable. In support of its conclusion, the court of appeals noted that several of the cases cited as in "accord" in *Jasko* were actually cases that decided the rule of notice was inapplicable in any self-service grocery store. This allowed the court of appeals to apply the *Jasko* rule beyond "carry around" food sales to the sale of any food. This is "analogizing" from one case (*Jasko*) to the present case.

In both *Tommerup* and *Smith* the question whether the *Jasko* rule applies is a question of both reasoning by analogy and a question of the nature of precedent, of following the holdings issued in past cases. Precedent is not immutable (as shown indirectly by *Jasko*), but courts are expected to articulate clear reasons when precedent is not followed. *Jasko* does not eliminate that "well known rule" of actual or constructive notice; it simply dispenses with that requirement in a particular kind of case, a case in which the method of food sales creates, in the opinion of the court, a dangerous condition. Although *Jasko* creates an exception to the well known rule, part of the subsequent history of slip and fall cases is whether the "exception" ends up swallowing the "rule." Part of the social value of precedent is stability, or settled expectations. If legal rules change all the time, not only will that create economic and social havoc, it will bring into disrepute the common law legal system. Another value of precedent is its efficiency. The common law system believes it is simpler to build on prior case decisions than in receiving each case as if it is one of first impression. Without a sense of precedent, of course, reasoning by analogy becomes much less important, for the precedential case serves as a comparison or reference point for all subsequent cases someone alleges as similar, as analogous.

The courts deciding *Tommerup* and *Smith* use *Jasko* as a settled point of reference. Both also use the well known rule of notice as an additional settled point of reference. The question is, which particular point of reference is closer to the facts in the current (that is, either the *Tommerup* or *Smith*) case? The question for the law student is always whether the set of facts in the current case are "like" or "unlike" the set of facts in the precedential case or rule.

One more case may be helpful in understanding how courts analogize, and how lawyers hedge their bets in an adversary system of law. In *McDonald v.*

Safeway Stores, Inc., 707 P.2d 416 (Idaho 1985), the plaintiff entered a Safeway grocery store at 1:00 p.m. Walking down an aisle, she fell. The store had conducted three promotions for ice cream at 10:00 a.m., promotions that included handing out samples as well as napkins. Those samples, the court noted, were given to anyone who asked, including "infants," meaning children. As stated by the Idaho Supreme Court, "The substance that Mrs. McDonald slipped on was cream colored and appeared to be melted ice cream." Mrs. McDonald and her husband sued, alleging two theories of liability on Safeway's part. First, Safeway was liable in negligence because it had actual or constructive knowledge of the dangerous condition and failed to eliminate that dangerous condition. Second, Safeway was negligent because it held its ice cream demonstrations on Good Friday, a busy day at the store, and gave samples to infants, thus creating a foreseeable risk of harm to its customers. The first theory of liability invokes the well known rule. The second theory of liability follows the *Jasko* modification of the well known rule. This is how a plaintiff's attorney will hedge the claims of liability when the law is slightly in flux. The lawyer will offer as many theories of liability (a defense lawyer will offer a similar number of defenses) as may be necessary in order to obtain a favorable judgment.

Safeway moved for summary judgment (a ruling that the case created no factual disputes that could lead to any conclusion in favor of the plaintiff, so as a legal matter the court must rule in the defendant's favor without any jury decision), which the trial court denied. The McDonalds won a large verdict concerning damages and Safeway appealed. The Idaho Supreme Court noted the decisions in both *Tommerup* and *Jasko*. The former favored the arguments of Safeway, while the latter favored the position of the McDonalds. The court concluded that "[t]he facts of the instant case more closely approximate those of *Jasko*, than those of *Tommerup*." Why? Because "the trial court could not have concluded *as a matter of law* that the presence of the ice cream on the floor was merely an isolated incident." Therefore, the case involved a factual dispute (was the presence of ice cream an isolated incident?) that could be solved only by a trial by jury, and the jury found in favor of the plaintiffs.

What *McDonald* reminds us is that the rules of law serve largely as a skeletal framework in the American common law, and within the rules of law a number of factual disputes (did the defendant possess actual notice of the dangerous condition?) can be decided for either party, for the jury decides which version of the facts it believes is more true. It also reminds us that rules of law can change dramatically, as occurred in *Jasko*, or more slowly, as occurs in *McDonald*. By comparing both *Jasko* and *Tommerup*, and by siding with the *Jasko* conclusion in *McDonald*, the Idaho Supreme Court is suggesting, in a very indirect manner, that *Tommerup* will not always be the rule in slip-and-fall cases

arising in Idaho. Instead, the decisions of the jury will be given great deference if the dispute between the parties can be defined as a dispute about the
facts rather than a dispute about the law.

Courts regularly use two other types of tools related to legal reasoning:
first, courts assess problems at varying *levels of generality*. A level of generality argument is one that narrows or broadens a rule of law. For example, does
the *Jasko* rule apply to any method of operation or sale that may foreseeably
place the customer in possible danger? Does the *Jasko* rule apply to the sale
of any goods may make a dangerous condition foreseeable? Should *Jasko* be
applied only where food sales (Woolworth's, gas station convenience stores,
grocery stores, restaurants) take place? Or only where food/drink sales take
place where customers stand or "carry around" the food or drink? Levels of
generality argument are a type of analogical argument relating to the proper
application of the legal doctrine. In other words, whether a rule should be applied broadly or narrowly requires that you think about how the referenced
case (*Jasko*) is best interpreted. It is also a consequentialist argument. A consequentialist argument attempts to foresee the consequences that may flow
from a particular precedential case, and devise a rule that avoids pernicious
consequences.

A second tool used in legal arguments and opinions are arguments of *rhetoric*. These are arguments that focus on suggested justifications for one's argument
or conclusion. These arguments can be both accepted and lead to fallacies in
thinking. A significant number of rhetorical arguments are found in law. However, a few recur regularly in legal argument. They include 1) the *appeal to authority*, 2) the claim of speculation, also known as the *slippery slope* or "*parade
of horribles*" argument, 3) the *appeal to passion*, and 4) arguing by "*flipping*" the
adversary's argument.

The appeal to authority can be as simple as an appeal to a precedential case.
Counsel analogizes the current case to a previous (and favorable) decision of
the court and argues that the court should just follow the result in that previous case. This was what the lawyers for Woolworth attempted to do when they
argued *Jasko* at the Colorado Supreme Court. The Court refashioned the case
to state that the precedents were not applicable to method of sales cases, thus
narrowing the level of generality of the "well known rule of law." The appeal
to authority argument can also turn into what is colloquially called the "famous dead person" argument. The lawyer or judge may justify a conclusion
by declaring that this same conclusion was also reached by a famous dead judge.
The judge has to be famous because if he (often he) isn't, the judge won't be
considered an authority. The judge has to be dead (well, not always, but it
helps) because then the judge can't declare that he changed his mind and no

longer agrees with his earlier views. The appeal to authority will often invoke Supreme Court Justices such as John Marshall, Joseph Story, Oliver Wendell Holmes, Benjamin N. Cardozo and others. One problem with the appeal to authority is that it is likely that none of the judges cited as authority was faced with precisely this problem. That's why this problem is before the court. A second problem is that one can easily engage in a battle of authorities who reach contrary conclusions. As noted by Justice Robert H. Jackson in *The Steel Seizure Case* (*Youngstown Sheet and Tube Co. v. Sawyer*) (1952), a case discussing the extent of presidential powers, "A Hamilton may be matched against a Madison. Professor [William Howard] Taft is counterbalanced by Theodore Roosevelt.... It even seems that President Taft cancels out Professor Taft." Alexander Hamilton and James Madison, of course, were the two most prominent authors of *The Federalist Papers*, which provided an initial understanding of the Constitution, and both were prominent government officials (Madison was our fourth President as well) in the early Republic. Taft was Roosevelt's Vice-President and succeeded him as President. Jackson is noting that the authorities themselves are in conflict, making the appeal to authority irrelevant. You may find both a majority and dissenting opinion in the same case appealing to the same famous dead person as justifying contrary conclusions. In *Texas v. Johnson* (1989), the flag-burning case, both the majority and dissenting opinions in the Supreme Court cite to statements made by the Oliver Wendell Holmes, one of the most famous Supreme Court justices in American history, in support of their opposing conclusions.

The claim of speculation is a variant of a consequentialist argument and a type of if-then argument, for the lawyer or judge declares that if this case is resolved in a certain way, then all kinds of similar cases will have to be resolved in the same way. For example, if the Constitution created a requirement that the government show a "compelling interest" if it wanted to apply its illegal narcotics laws to religious believers who ingested an illegal narcotic (say, peyote) for a religious reason, the argument is this would "open the prospect of constitutionally required religious exemptions from civic obligations of almost every conceivable kind," from the military draft, to taxes, to child neglect laws and so on. This argument is also known as the slippery slope or parade of horribles argument because the person advocating the argument may list a series of consequential difficulties caused as a result of a ruling. The argument contrary to the claim of speculation or "parade of horribles" is to explicitly state the decision in the current case is only about the current case and not about a hypothetical future case or set of cases. In other words, the claim of speculation should be rejected precisely because it is speculative, a guess about the future that may or may not come true.

The appeal to passion is, of course, an attempt to justify a legal conclusion based on an emotional appeal. Although you are trained in your 1L year to avoid relying on emotional appeals in assessing the legal claims made by parties, human tragedies that find their way into legal decisions inevitably create difficult assessments. For example, appellate court opinions will justify their conclusion in part based on emotional appeals, not just rational appeals. One of the most famous appeals to passion is found in the dissenting opinion of Justice Harry Blackmun in *DeShaney v. Winnebago County Dep't of Social Servs.* (1989). Joshua DeShaney was brutally beaten by his father, eventually causing Joshua brain damage. Joshua's mother had asked government officials to remove Joshua from his father's care. Despite some knowledge that Joshua was being battered by his father, government officials failed to remove him from his father's home. Joshua then suffered the beating that led to brain damage. Through his mother Joshua sued, claiming that the failures of government agents violated his constitutional right to liberty found in the due process clause of the 14th amendment. The Supreme Court held Joshua did not have a legitimate legal claim. In dissent Justice Blackmun wrote, "Poor Joshua! Victim of repeated attacks by an irresponsible, bullying, cowardly, and intemperate father, and abandoned by respondents who placed him in a dangerous predicament and who knew or learned what was going on, and yet did essentially nothing except, as the Court revealingly observes, 'dutifully recorded these incidents in [their] files.'" Justice Blackmun's appeal to passion is quite effective, from naming the victim to characterizing his violent father and the feckless government officials who did nothing but "record" the incidents of abuse. The general approach to counter an appeal to passion is not to deny its existence in law but to acknowledge it and limit its reach. A lawyer or judge may do this by quoting Aristotle (another famous dead person) that "The law is reason, free from passion." Law, at least American law, is not reason free from passion. But laws and legal decisions are best made in the dominant light of reason, not passion, for appeals to passion raise fears of populism that may be contrary to the rule of law. In *DeShaney*, the majority accepted the emotional appeal of Joshua's claim, but concluded that its "natural sympathy" to find a way for Joshua to obtain compensation for his injuries did not create a *legal* duty on the part of the state to pay damages for Joshua's injuries.

Finally, the argument of "flipping" is the attempt to take your opponent's argument and use it to justify your contrary conclusion. When a judge or lawyer accepts the predicates of another's argument, and then states that this still results in a conclusion contrary to the argument of the opposing side, that is "flipping" an opponent's argument. In *Marbury v. Madison* (1803), a foundational Constitutional Law case, the Supreme Court, in an opinion by Chief

Justice John Marshall, held unconstitutional § 13 of the Judiciary Act of 1789. One justification for the Court's conclusion that it had the power to declare Acts of Congress unconstitutional (known as the power of judicial review) was that the members of the Court swore an oath to uphold the Constitution. A decade later the Virginia Court of Appeals was ordered by the Supreme Court to enter judgment in favor of a party whose interests were anathema to Virginians. The Virginia court refused to do so, claiming that § 25 of the Judiciary Act of 1789 (through which the Supreme Court issued its order to the Virginia Court of Appeals) was unconstitutional. It justified its conclusion on the ground that the members of that court also swore an oath to uphold the Constitution. This is taking an argument made by your "opponents" to use in your favor, or "flipping" an argument. A related example is found in another part of Justice Jackson's concurring opinion in *The Steel Seizure Case*. When Jackson served as a lawyer for President Franklin D. Roosevelt he argued for a very broad interpretation of presidential power. After President Truman's authority to seize privately-owned steel mills on broad claims of presidential power was challenged his lawyers used Jackson's earlier argument to support the constitutionality of Truman's action. In response, now-Associate Justice Jackson wrote, "a judge cannot accept self-serving press statements of the attorney for one of the interested parties as authority in answering a constitutional question, even if the advocate was himself." Jackson thus refused to accept this attempt to flip Jackson's argument by noting the difference between a lawyer's role as advocate for his client and a judge's role as neutral arbiter of the meaning of the law.

Several other arguments of rhetoric are used to justify legal conclusions. One is the *appeal to consensus*. The appeal to consensus takes two forms: 1) the appeal to *popular consensus*, a claim that the people (and occasionally states) accept a particular view of law; and 2) the appeal to *intellectual consensus*, a claim that most lawyers (usually law professors) or other judges accept a particular interpretation of the law. A second additional argument of rhetoric is the appeal based on a *straw man argument* (allowing the lawyer easily to knock down the straw man, leaving, the lawyer will argue, her correct interpretation as the only available and correct interpretation). The straw man argument sets up a false choice by creating a choice between the straw man argument and the contrary argument made by the lawyer for one side, not the choice between the arguments made by the lawyers for both sides. Occasionally one will also read cases in which the lawyer or judge fails to distinguish between *correlation and causation*, interpreting a connection between two events as actually meaning that one event caused the other. High LSAT scores are correlated with good 1L grades, but a high LSAT score doesn't cause one to get good 1L grades. The difference between correlation and causation is also found in part in the fallacy known in Latin as *post hoc ergo propter hoc* (after the fact, therefore because of the fact).

These types of justifications will become more visible to you as you read more cases. Most importantly, you need to be aware of how to use both inductive analogical reasoning and deductive syllogistic reasoning. That takes practice and time.

Eras of Legal Thought

Lawyers and judges have understood the nature of law and the nature of judging very differently in different periods of American history. These different eras of legal thought have been based in part on different ways about thinking of the sources of the common law, which you will study extensively in Contracts, Property and Torts. Legal thinkers in different eras have also thought differently about the value and interpretation of statutes, which affected beliefs about interpretation of the criminal law and, to a lesser extent, the rules of civil procedure (which were also drafted within a specific jurisprudential framework). Your common law courses will include cases from these different eras, and you will learn how different understandings of law affect how judges reason. You will see that particular legal conclusions accepted by nearly all legal thinkers in one era are rejected by later courts or state legislatures using different starting premises. The following is a brief guide to those different eras of American legal thought.

American legal thought can generally be divided into four eras: 1) the period between 1800 (when case opinions were first published and sold to lawyers) and 1860 (all dates are rough estimates) is called the era of Grand Theory, in which judges such as John Marshall, Joseph Story and others created a distinctively American law, both common law and constitutional law; 2) from 1870–1918 or 1870–1937 (the ending date depends on your view of the Supreme Court) is known as the era of Legal Formalism, in which judges looked at the internal logic of the law to decide cases, an internal logic that may have ignored external (social) needs, and an era in which judges occasionally elevated the form of law over its substance; 3) 1906–1946, or 1930–Present (again, you will find a great deal of argument about the proper time frame) is known as the era of Legal Realism, in which judges were expected to make contextual decisions based explicitly on a balancing of the interests of the parties as well as the public, a use of standards (guidelines) rather than concrete or formal rules. Legal Realism is viewed as a response to Legal Formalism, and these two types of jurisprudential approaches are regularly compared; and 4) the Post-Realist era, in which judges used a number of "tools," from economics to sociology, psychology, statistics and philosophy, recognizing that legal decisions are often decisions of public policy. The extent to which one considers judging a form of "politics" is one highly contested idea in post-Realist legal thought. Similarly, the use of "law and" (law and economics, law and society, law and philosophy) ideas to construct approaches to law are regularly defended and attacked. The tools of reasoning can also include using both legal formalist and legal realist (sometimes with a "neo" attached to the beginning of formalist and realist) ideas. The diversity of current American legal thought makes law and legal education both more chaotic and more exciting.

Whether your 1L professors speak explicitly about the different eras of legal thought or only allude to them implicitly, you should be aware that ideas about the nature of law and the nature of judging have differed over time, and those different beliefs have led to very different approaches to law.

A Word about Constitutional Law

Courses in Constitutional Law often straddle the 1L and 2L years. Like Criminal Law, a course in Constitutional Law is a public law course, focused on the proper exercise of power by the federal and state governments. Unlike your other 1L substantive law courses, nearly all cases discussed in Constitutional Law are decisions of the Supreme Court of the United States. Further, the cases in Constitutional Law will be longer and include many more dissenting opinions than you will find in your other 1L courses. This should be expected, for the Court regularly decides difficult cases, and the different premises adopted by the Justices to constitutional decisionmaking nearly ensure different conclusions. Unlike the cases studied in your common law courses, the names of the judges writing the opinions in the cases are important. You will learn why it is important to remember whether the decision was written by Justice William Brennan or Justice Antonin Scalia. You will also learn that different periods of American legal thought have led to very different understandings and interpretations of the Constitution. Finally, you will learn that lawyers and judges have very different approaches to the manner in which the specific language of the Constitution should be interpreted, whether in light of its meaning at the time the language became part of the Constitution, or as adapted to changing historical circumstances. The debates between originalism and non-originalism or between textualism and historicism provide some insight into why the Court is often divided in its interpretation of the Constitution.

Academic Support

Some students take easily and quickly to the study of law. Most do not. Many of those who struggle early in their legal studies have never faced academic difficulty. The result is a reluctance to acknowledge that one may need academic assistance. DO NOT MAKE THIS MISTAKE. The examination structure at most law schools, one final examination testing you on the material learned during the entire semester, largely leaves you uncertain about your understanding of the material and your ability to communicate that knowledge. Do not wait until after your first semester grades are released to do something about your confusion. A student who performs poorly during the first semester of law school has created a deficit that will take the remaining five semesters to overcome. Some schools exclude students with poor grades after the first year of law school. If you don't know whether your understanding is incomplete until mid-January, when most schools release first semester grades, you are going to have a more difficult time fixing your problems in time. Even if your law school has a policy of near-zero academic attrition, finding yourself at or near the bottom of the class after the first semester will have dramatic consequences on your search for a job.

Offices of Academic Support began to spring up in the mid-1990s, when a number of law schools saw a steep decline in the bar exam passing rates of their graduates. In addition, law schools and the ABA concluded that a "sink or swim" approach to learning law was wasteful and harmful both institutionally and individually. A good office of academic support can provide you with a better sense of how *you* study more effectively, in light of your learning style and your personality type. Visiting the office of academic support is not a substitute for studying or attending class, nor is it a substitute for continuing to work on active learning, on reading the material before class in the expectation (not fear) of being called on. Learning how to learn can be taught, and the office of academic support can assist you in better understanding how you best learn.

One approach some academic support offices will take is to evaluate your "style" of learning, using the KARV approach discussed earlier. Are you dominantly a kinesthetic learner, an auditory learner, a read/write learner or a visual learner? Again, legal education means a great deal of reading, even when the assignments are just ten pages in length. Classes involve a great deal of listening and little speaking. Writing a brief or an outline can be a kinesthetic experience, but your practice and development of legal skills will largely be deferred until after completion of your first year of law school. Understand how you best learn. It may be the case that sketching out the case as you read it allows you to learn it better. It may be that you learn better by visualizing a case while listening to your professor or a classmate describe it. No matter what learning style you predominantly use you are likely to use each to move from novice to expert.

What the science of learning has found valuable to students is a "metacognitive" approach to learning. This approach requires students constantly to evaluate their learning. This requires you to adopt a self-critical stance. What do you understand? What do you not understand? What do you think you understand, and how can you test that perception? The manner in which law is taught provides students with a sound template for self-assessment. What did you think you understood about the cases, doctrine and legal policy before class? What did you fail to note and better appreciate once class was finished? Was it specific material, general concepts, the contextual relationship among the cases? A self-assessment protects a student from overconfidence, especially after the student has some facility in writing briefs.

Chapter 5

Exams

The American Bar Association (ABA) has been gently pressing law schools to expand their "assessment" tools of law students. The traditional 1L examination (that is, "assessment") structure was limited to a final examination given at the end of the academic year. Any examination given shortly before or after the Christmas holidays was not formally graded. Today most schools give 1L students fall semester exams that are graded. It is common that this "end of the semester" examination is the only assessment tool for 1L students, although some professors now use weekly or monthly multiple choice or true/false exams to ensure students are keeping up with the reading. Other professors have taken the step of giving students graded midterms examinations or graded take-home assignments in addition to the final examination, but this appears presently to be more the exception than the rule in 1L classes. Within five years the ABA will likely mandate more than one assessment tool in 1L classes, but inertia (also called tradition) is quite powerful in law schools.

The benefit of the single "end of the semester" examination is that you can catch up. Even if your legal learning curve is flat longer than some of your classmates, any penalty for that delay in understanding the material may be minimal if you can bend the learning curve quickly upward toward the end of the semester. The costs of giving just one examination to assess students include the time delay, that is, not having an external reason to force yourself to understand the material more quickly (as well as the concomitant possible cost of false confidence that your understanding of the material is correct) and the higher stakes of one examination. You will find yourself stressed during the examination period, and legal education is designed in part to exacerbate stress, in the apparent belief that this will make you a better professional for your clients. As written the prior sentence demonstrates how troublesome the "one exam" perspective is, but again inertia makes change difficult. One simple and important way to combat stress and test anxiety is to maintain some type of regular exercise regime, whether lifting weights or running, cycling or walking. If your test anxiety becomes acute, you must see the law school's Associate Dean for Student Affairs and/or the counseling office at your university before the exam takes place.

Final examinations are usually given over a two-week examination period, often following several "reading" days in which no classes are held. (These reading days are a trap if you think you can learn the material during that time.) A 1L student taking five 1L classes will take three exams one week and two the other. The length of the examination usually equals one hour per credit, so you will likely take a three hour exam for a three-credit course.

Preparing for Your Exams

It cannot be stressed enough that preparing for your exams should be a semester-long process. You may early on decide that your classes are uninteresting, or that some of your professors are incredibly boring. If you attend an elite law school, your absence from classes will not matter. Even if you miss all your 1L classes at an elite law school you will likely not fail because those schools have nonexistent academic attrition. The ABA requires all law schools to have an attendance policy. Some enforce that policy more vigorously than others. Some allow a professor to reduce a student's grade if the student misses more than a minimal number of classes. Whether you attend classes due to this negative incentive or otherwise, you will learn much about what the professor is likely to test. More importantly, you are being acculturated into professional norms, and doing things you'd rather not (like attending class) is part of becoming a professional.

As stated in Chapter 4 you need to attend class having already spent a considerable amount of time reading and re-reading the assignment. You do not attend class in order to obtain the received wisdom about the meaning of the assigned cases from the professor. Instead, you attend class to learn how to analyze the reasoning in the opinions from different perspectives. What you take from class should be added to the briefs and notes created in preparation for class. Your class notes should focus on how the professor assesses the material, for your professor is the person who writes and grades the exam. In order to obtain a good grade, however, merely parroting what the professor stated in class about a set of cases or some doctrine is an exercise in futility. You want to take what the professor has said and, using the analytical tools described in Chapter 4, offer a thorough analysis.

You should begin your exam study schedule about two weeks before the end of the semester. You should have a fairly complete outline as of that time. By the time finals arrive you should have attempted to answer all available past exam questions written by the professor to prepare for this final exam (discussed below). As you finish the course, make sure you have re-read your initial outline and begin summarizing it into a condensed form (the length of this condensed form is less important than the act of condensing your initial outline). The acts of writing your own outline and then summarizing it work quite well in gaining a more complete understanding of the material. One approach to consider in allocating exam study time is to study first the course that will be tested last. This can work particularly well if you must take five exams, for you may have little energy to study for the last test, or lack the intensity you mustered for the first several exams. Having gone through that exam first means you will not have to study quite as much for it after your penultimate exam. It also may reduce your stress level because you are studying for a test that is, in the scheme of things, distant. If you are taking four exams or fewer you should have plenty of time during the two weeks plus reading period to whittle down your outline, generate hypothetical problems with classmates or a study group, and reassess your answers to previous exam questions. In addition, not all of your courses will have the same value. A two-credit course is worth half a four-credit course. It should be evident that you need to spend twice as much time studying for an exam for a four-credit course than an exam for a two-credit course.

Practice Exams and Exam Instructions

Most professors will place one or more past examinations on reserve in the library or post them online to show students what an examination from this professor may look like. The ABA does not require professors to disclose their past exams. However, some law schools mandate the publication of past examinations as a matter of school policy. Particularly when speaking of essay questions, such a policy poses little if any threat to the ability of the professor to draft another exam. The number of doctrines and policies are more than sufficient to give the professor a plethora of options in crafting an essay examination. This open-exam policy presents more difficulties for a professor when speaking of multiple-choice exams. In terms of workload, essay exams are back-loaded, while multiple-choice questions are front-loaded. The professor's work in an essay exam is largely found in the grading of each individual essay; the work in multiple-choice exams is in crafting a well written question, not in the grading.

Past exams are valuable tools for purposes of practice, for professors find little need to reinvent the wheel in constructing essay questions. Although the particular legal rules the professor may ask about will differ, most professors use the same style of question year after year. Occasionally this is due to laziness, but ordinarily stylistic similarities are due to a belief that this is the best way to assess students. You should thus have a good idea of the type of essay examination your professor is likely to ask. Follow the instructions given for that past examination and attempt to answer it in the time given. Some professors will either post a model answer or provide some modest feedback if you get to the professor at least two weeks before the end of the semester. If your professor provides neither written nor oral advice, compare exam answers with a few fellow students. Although it is possible that all of you are misguided, the wisdom of crowds will likely give you a sense of your strengths and weaknesses in answering the questions asked in the past examinations.

Examination instructions may also provide some initial insight into the type of exam questions your professor will ask. Examination instructions will ordinarily tell the student the number of pages in the examination, the number of questions that follow the instructions, and the value accorded each question. If you are given a six page examination consisting of three questions, each equally valued, you are likely to be asked similar issue-spotter questions requiring you to identify a number of issues. If you are given a two page examination consisting of three questions, at least one and likely two of those questions are going to be policy questions. The length of an essay examination will thus suggest the type of essay examination you will face. This may make some difference to your strategy of answering questions if the examination is open book, partially open book, or a closed book examination, which your professor will make clear to you early in the semester. In an open book examination, one in which you are permitted to bring your notes, your casebook, a code or statutory book and other materials, your professor has little hesitancy in asking questions about doctrines both large and small. In a closed book examination your professor may be reluctant to ask a question that focuses on a relatively minor topic, in large part because in grading such a question it is possible that too many students 1) failed to perceive the issue (because they don't remember this minor doctrine), 2) perceived the issue incorrectly, or 3) perceived the issue correctly but then had difficulty in analyzing the problem. If too many students fall into one of these three categories of error, the question has created the likelihood of a "bunched" group of exams, a body of answers that works poorly in forming a bell curve, which makes the assessment less reliable and thus less accurate.

The exams in your first-year classes will largely be of three types: essay examinations, which are further divided into issue-spotting essay questions and policy essay questions, multiple-choice questions, or a combination of both.

The focus of this chapter is to give you a sense of how to perform well on your essay and multiple choice examinations.

Essay Examinations

The essay question is a staple of 1L and upper level examinations. The essay may be divided into two types: First, a question consisting of a long series of events that leads to an injury (or more than one injury), to a claim of breach of contract, to a contest of ownership of land or other property or to a claim of invasion of a constitutional right. This "issue-spotter" essay is usually structured in one of two ways: The first type of "issue-spotter" question will, in one or two pages of facts, offer a detailed series of events. Those events will raise anywhere from six to fifteen legal issues which must be addressed ("spotted") and then analyzed. Even if you are given an hour to answer this type of question, you will have between four (if fifteen issues) and ten (if six issues) minutes to craft a response to each issue. Whether you have four minutes or ten to address and analyze an issue, you have relatively little time to engage in any thorough analysis of each issue. The goal in such a case is to state, in legally accurate terms, the precise issue raised. You then will offer a brief analysis of each issue and then move on to the next issue. The major goal of this type of essay examination is a demonstration of the student's knowledge of law, and more specifically, a demonstration that the student can elucidate clearly how the facts may raise particular legal issues. The minor goal is analysis. Though the minor goal, the student who best analyzes the impact of the facts on the presented legal issues will get the best grade. The second type of essay question is a "honed issue-spotter" examination. This type of question offers a page or so of factual events, and the goal of the professor is for the student 1) to correctly state the three to five issues of law presented by these facts, 2) to read the question closely so that the student understands that the facts raise Issue A and not Issue B, or that the facts may raise Issue A *and* Issue B depending in part on how the facts are understood or interpreted, 3) to assess what legal rule or policy may apply (often you have your choice between two versions of a rule, such as in *Jasko* (discussed in chapter 4), which may lead to different legal results. The major goal in this type of issue spotter is analysis.

The second kind of essay question is one that asks you to evaluate competing legal policies. This can be accomplished in one of two ways: first, you may be given a one or two paragraphs that offer some facts. The "call of the question" may be something like, "Discuss how this case will be decided in a com-

mon law jurisdiction and in a UCC jurisdiction." The question might include
a statute and ask how it should be interpreted in light of the tools of statutory
interpretation, including the impact of the statutes on common law. A second
way of asking this type of question is to ask the student to assess a particular
legal policy. For example, you may be asked, "Compare the benefits and costs
of modified comparative negligence and pure comparative negligence." This
fairly simple statement requires you 1) to define accurately the difference between two legal policies (both constitute a shift from the doctrine of contributory negligence in tort law, which barred a plaintiff from recovering any
damages if the jury found the plaintiff's negligence caused his or her injuries,
even if that negligence was just 1% and the defendant was 99% responsible for
plaintiff's injuries. Modified comparative negligence allowed a plaintiff to recover that percentage of damages caused by the defendant, as long as the plaintiff's negligence was less as a percentage than the defendant's negligence. Some
modified comparative negligence rules altered that by allowing the plaintiff to
recover the defendant's portion of the damages if the plaintiff's negligence was
equal to or less than the defendant's negligence. That meant that if the plaintiff and defendant were each 50% responsible for the plaintiff's injuries, and
the jury found the plaintiff's damages were $100,000, the plaintiff would re-
cover $50,000, 50% of $100,000. This became more complicated when more
than two or more defendants were sued by plaintiff. Pure comparative negligence awarded a plaintiff that percentage of damages caused by the defendant
even if the plaintiff was more responsible for the injuries than the defendant.
Thus, if the jury found the plaintiff 80% responsible and the defendant 20%
responsible, and awarded $100,000 in damages, the plaintiff received an award
of $20,000, 20% of $100,000.), and 2) to evaluate the justifications for each
policy in light of the goals of tort law (is it to make the plaintiff whole? To encourage economic efficiency and growth? To limit the redistribution of property (that is, money) only upon a showing of fault? To shift costs to those best
able to bear them? To encourage individual responsibility?) and the particular
justifications for pure and modified comparative negligence. One benefit of
the legal policy question is that it expands the level of generality, requiring the
student to be ready to shift gears in answering a question. A policy question
requires knowledge of particular and competing policies, and also requires the
student to compare the various and possibly conflicting goals of tort law. A
system of tort law that focuses on shifting costs to those who are best able to
bear them (however one defines "best able to bear") may differ markedly from
one that limits the redistribution of property based on ideas of individual responsibility. The answers given by judges and legislators to these broader questions will inform the law of torts for the next several decades.

IRAC and Essay Questions

You will likely learn about an approach to answering issue spotter essay questions called IRAC early in your first semester of law school. IRAC stands for Issue, Rule, Application/Analysis and Conclusion. The idea of IRAC is that the exam taker spots the Issue, states the legal Rule applicable to that Issue, Applies that Rule to the Issue (that is, Analyzes the Issue in light of the facts given you, facts that will affect which of several possible Rules applies), and then Concludes.

Consider the following question: "A woman named Sally Davidson was hospitalized for acute stomach pain. Doctors and staff at the local charitable hospital released Davidson after she underwent surgery, and four weeks after her release, Davidson reported no stomach pain. At some point after she returned home she called the director of the hospital, telling him, 'I was cured due to the fine work of the staff, and I want to give the hospital some money to show my gratitude. So I can keep things straight for financial and tax purposes, please send me a written request for a donation.' The director immediately did so. Davidson replied with her own letter, which stated in part, 'I pledge to pay the hospital $5,000,000, to be paid within five years in deepest gratitude for the work of the hospital in saving my life. I ask that this money be used solely in the battle against cancer, and ask that no more than $100,000 be used in any year for the first ten years by the hospital so that the fight against all cancers may continue for decades. I also enclose a check for $500,000 as my first payment.' The hospital director immediately wrote back, 'We are all delighted at your generosity and we agree that we will spend no more than $100,000 in each year for the first ten years and will spend this money solely in the quest to cure stomach and other cancers. Because your contributions will generate a significant amount of money, we have created the Sally Davidson endowment in which to place the funds given by you. We are happy to have you join us in the fight against the scourge of cancer.' Later in the year, Davidson revokes her agreement to pay the remainder. The hospital sues for breach of contract. Discuss all relevant issues."

Using IRAC a student might write, "The *Issue* is whether Davidson's request that no more than $100,000 of the sums given by her be used in any year for the first ten years of the existence of the monies and used solely to fight cancer creates a binding agreement subject to judicial enforcement. [*Rules*] In general, an agreement will be held a binding contract only if consideration exists for both parties to the agreement. A gift is a voluntary exchange for which no consideration is given. Consideration is defined as something bargained for and given in exchange for a promise or act. A promise given after the other party has performed an act is held past consideration and past consideration is not legally consideration. However, even if no consideration exists, a promise by one party (Davidson) that should reasonably expect to induce action on the part of the other party (hospital) which does induce such action is binding necessary to avoid injustice, and charitable subscriptions are binding even without proof that the promise induced action. [*Analysis*] If Davidson's promise of $5,000,000 and initial payment were given for the services performed in the past by the hospital, this past consideration would be insufficient to create a binding contract. In the past consideration case of *Mills v. Wyman*, the court held that a father's agreement to reimburse a Good Samaritan for the costs involved in taking care of the father's adult son was a mere moral obligation and was not sufficient consideration to enforce a contract. Davidson indicates she is giving this payment and pledge in gratitude because she believes the hospital saved her life. [*Conclusion One:*] This speaks somewhat in the language of past consideration. [*Back to Analysis:*] Though Davidson initiated the request by the hospital based on her belief that the hospital saved her life, Davidson's promise and initial payment were given in response to a request for a contribution. [*Conclusion Two:*] This appears to be a promise and partial payment that would constitute a gift, for Davidson gave her promise and made her initial payment on the promise without any evidence that she received something given in exchange for her promise. [*Back to Analysis:*] However, if Davidson's promise and payment were given in exchange for the hospital's promise to limit the spending from this money and to use this money solely to cure cancer, then [*Conclusion Three:*] her promise and payment were bargained for and given in exchange for a promise. In such a case, consideration would exist and Johnston's refusal to continue paying would constitute a breach of contract. [*Back to Analysis:*] The promise made by Davidson appears similar to the promise made by Mary Yates Johnston in the *Allegheny College* case, which the NY Court of Appeals held was consideration and not a gift. In *Allegheny College* Johnston wrote she was pledging $5,000 "in consideration" of the school's creation of an endowment in her name as well as because of her interest in Christian education. Davidson did not declare she was making the promise in light of some "consideration" and the first mention of an "endowment" was made by the hospital, not Davidson. She did request that only some of the monies pledged by used during the first ten years it was available to the hospital, creating some conditions on its use. In both *Allegheny College* and this case the recipients (the College and here, the hospital) were given a pledge and some money and asked to do something, a something that both agreed to, which sounds in consideration. [*Conclusion Four:*] Even if the court holds no consideration exists for Davidson's pledge, the plaintiff-hospital may be able to recover under the doctrine of promissory estoppel, which enforces a promise not supported by consideration if [*Back to Rule:*] Davidson should reasonably have expected her promise to induce action by the hospital, the hospital acted in reliance on that promise and enforcing the promise is necessary to avoid injustice. the party to whom the promise the made. [*Conclusion Five:*] A reasonable person in Davidson's position who pledged the considerable amount of $5,000,000 should have known that her promise requesting a restriction on spending for ten years and limited use of her contributions would be viewed as a demand, not just a request, for she had paid a substantial amount ($500,000), which constituted just 10% of the pledge. The defendant created an endowment and agreed to limit the spending of her money and limited that spending to a single purpose. Whether this constitutes "injustice" is unclear. [*Back to Rule/Analysis:*] Another provision of Restatement (Second) § 90 of the Law of Contracts states that a court may uphold a charitable subscription even if no action on the part of the hospital was induced. [*Conclusion Six:*] If Davidson's contribution is held a charitable subscription because the hospital is a local charitable hospital and thus likely a non-profit corporation then Davidson's promise may also be enforceable. [*Continuing Conclusions:*] It appears from the facts that although Davidson initially may have contemplated a gift, which was revocable at any time, or a payment for past consideration, she placed conditions on her promise and payment, conditions that the hospital agreed to. This makes Davidson's case like *Allegheny College* because Davidson should have known that her request would induce reliance on her pledge by the hospital, and it did induce reliance making Davidson's promise enforceable. [*Contrary Conclusion Seven:*] However, nothing in the pledge by Davidson created any undue reliance, for the hospital made no investments in either people (by employing new cancer researchers) or in projects, such as in building a new cancer wing for the hospital, possibly making Davidson's promise unenforceable."

As you will learn in your Contracts class, one of the traditional elements of a contract is "bargained-for" consideration. You will also learn that courts may hold a promise is enforceable even when bargained-for consideration is lacking under the concept of promissory estoppel. The question sets forth in fairly brief form a few events: Sally Davidson received excellent medical care which she believed saved her life. She invites a request for a monetary contribution. After receiving a request from the director of the hospital, she sends a check for $500,000, and pledges a total contribution of $5,000,000, with a written request setting forth what appear to be conditions to her pledge, conditions agreed to by the hospital director and even added to (creating an endowment in Davidson's name). These facts give rise to several possibilities of applicable Rules: 1) the pledge is for "past consideration," that is, given after the act was completed for which the pledge was promised (*Mills v. Wyman*, a famous 1825 Massachusetts case, is taught to inform students that past consideration may constitute a moral consideration but does not constitute a binding legal consideration); 2) a gift, which is revocable unless some particular reliance on the promised gift makes it enforceable under the doctrine of promissory estoppel; or 3) is an enforceable contract similar to the case of *Allegheny College v. National Chautauqua County Bank*, (1927), a famous case in which Benjamin N. Cardozo (one of the most famous judges in American legal history), then a judge in the New York Court of Appeals, held the "gift" was actually a contract because Mary Yates Johnston received consideration for her promise of money to the College in the form of an endowment named after her.

As you can tell by this hypothetical essay question and possible answer, what your professors are likely to ask are questions that generate several legal possibilities (does consideration exist? If not, does some other doctrine allow enforcement of the promise?), possibilities that differ depending on how the facts are analyzed. Law school essay exams are generally based on finding "boundaries" and "gaps" in law. A "boundary" question is one in which the student can look at two or more legal possibilities, depending on how the facts are understood and interpreted. The keys to answering a "boundary" question are 1) can you provide a correct statement of the Rules that may apply to this question, and 2) can you analyze how the facts, as presented by the question, may affect the applicability of one or more Rules? Students too often avoid these two key aspects of answering essay questions and thus perform poorly. For example, instead of providing a correct statement of the Rules that apply, students often begin writing down all that they know about this doctrine, providing chapter and verse on how the doctrine of consideration came to be. The apparent hope is that one or more statements will eventually reach the answer sought by the question. This is "circling," a type of avoidance common in law school exams. This is also a type of "expurgation" answer, an answer that spills everything one knows about the topic on to the bluebook. This approach may have worked in college. In law school this answer is disastrous. You are not being tested on the amount of knowledge you have accumulated. Yes, you must know a great deal of doctrine and legal policy. However, you are likely to be tested only on a modest amount of the doctrine studied during the semester; the greater goal of the exam is to test you on how well you can articulate and analyze different and occasionally conflicting rules and policies in light of the facts given. This leads to the second key to performing well, a key that students also often avoid. Students regularly "fight the facts." That is, instead of using the facts given, students will add additional facts, or write, "If the facts were like this, then this would be a case of past consideration. Past consideration means...." If the facts don't raise the issue of past consideration, why is the student offering an exegesis on past consideration? Too often this error is a result of entering the exam room bound and determined to discuss some particular doctrines, believing that because the professor emphasized some doctrine in class it must be on the exam. This can be a result of seeing a "pattern" in past examinations and trying to outguess the professor. The fact that the professor has failed to ask about those doctrines is not going to stop that determined student. Professors may stress some doctrine or policy because they believe it is complex and needs more attention, because the class thinks it is an easier subject than it is and the professor wishes to disabuse the students of that belief, or because the doctrine may offer some insight into the mechanics of the legal system. The second classic stylistic essay is the "gap" question. In this case there is no answer to a particular question, possibly because the issue is new (What privacy rights does one have on the Internet? What jurisdictional rules apply to claims of libel on the Internet?) or may be an extension of a related and relatively new rule. The response to this type of stylistic question is to use your thoughts concerning both policy and concepts in that area of law.

Correctly state applicable legal doctrines. Students often make a basic mistake by misstating doctrine in a rush either to analyze or worse, conclude. As you can see in the above answer, a host of conclusions are made, many of which do not materially advance the student's answer. You must know the legal doctrines taught by your professors, or your performance will leave you lagging well behind your classmates. Second, once you correctly state the applicable legal doctrines, you must offer more than a superficial analysis of the relation between the facts and the possible applicable rules. In general, professors are less interested in your legal conclusions than in your analysis of the relation of facts and law. (On the contrary, bar examiners ordinarily ask for and expect the examinee to state a conclusion.) This limited interest in conclusions exists for at least two reasons: 1) you are a 1L being trained to analyze issues, not issue legal conclusions, for that is what judges do; and 2) the issues you are asked to analyze are intended to be boundary or gap issues, not issues for which there is or should be a clear answer. If your professor demands an answer, provide one, but the conclusion need only be one sentence only, and your analysis will take you to that conclusion, making it the crucial aspect of writing an answer to an issue-spotter essay question. Additionally, your answer may end up couched in the language of "possibly," for the arguments available to both parties may suggest you hedge any conclusion you reach.

IRAC has a valuable but limited use. It makes excellent sense to use IRAC when annotating the essay question on the margins of the exam. However, analyzing an essay question ordinarily requires that you blend the issue, rule(s) and analysis. Separating your answer into four distinct parts on each issue eats into your limited time with limited appreciable gain in productivity.

Suggestions on Answering Essay Questions

While reading any issue-spotting essay question, consider underlining or briefly annotating each paragraph of the essay, noting legal issues that may arise as a result of the facts stated in the essay. THE FACTS DRIVE THE IS-SUES, SO CAREFULLY READ THE FACTS. Although some professors will include a number of irrelevant facts that may serve to distract the student, this is more the exception than the rule. Unless you have seen in prior examinations that the professor regularly includes facts in order to distract the student, you should assume that any facts included are present because they mean something. In a contracts exam it may be crucial that the alleged agreement was in writing (because an issue concerning the statute of frauds will be an issue for you to spot), or between merchants (giving rise to certain duties under the Uniform Commercial Code).

Second, if the question is two single-spaced pages in length, consider first looking at the call of the question. Does the professor conclude with the vague and general "Discuss all legally relevant issues," or does the professor conclude with a more specific call, such as "Discuss plaintiff's three best causes of action?" The professor's past exams may provide insight into the type of call the professor prefers to ask. The more general the call, the more emphasis the professor is likely giving to issue spotting (exceptions exist to this assertion, so be wary).

Do you read the question once or twice before you begin writing? The answer depends on how quickly and thoroughly you read. If you plan to read the question twice, read initially for a sense of the participants and the number of issues asked. The second reading then becomes an annotated reading, using IRAC or a brief outline. Should you draft an outline before you begin writing your answer? An outline's value is in ensuring that you 1) do not skip particular issues in your haste to complete your answer, and 2) organize for yourself (and your professor, the grader) the issues from greatest to least importance. Outlining is not necessary for all or even most students, for annotating the question may serve the same purpose, and writing the outline can take too much time from the limited time available to write in your bluebook or laptop. Please be aware that an issue-spotting essay answer is not judged based on the number of words you can fit into the time allotted for the answer. A cogent and shorter answer is always better than a long-winded answer. Begin by analyzing how the facts generate possible legal doctrines, and how those doctrines may result in different legal answers. Not only do the statements of the Rules and the statements of Analysis blend together, but a good issue-spotter question is designed to state facts that give rise to boundary issues, forcing you to assess distinct and often contrary legal rules (such as "no consideration means no enforceable contract" and "promises that are reasonably expected to induce reliance and in fact induce reliance must be legally enforced to avoid injustice even absent consideration").

It is possible that the professor has made an error in drafting the exam. At some law schools faculty proctor their own exams, and if you believe an error has been made you can ask the professor if you are correct in your assessment. In general, however, professors do not proctor their own exams, which means your best option is to write a quick two sentences offering legal options depending on whether this fact is part of the problem or was inadvertently introduced. This is different from creating facts, an act that professors strongly dislike.

A Torts Essay Question

Pamela Parsons was driving home when she realized she needed gas. She stopped at the nearby Dawson's Pump-n-Go. Her six-year-old son Andrew asked for something to drink. After filling the gas tank, Pamela took Andrew inside Dawson's. She went to a self-service machine dispensing soft drinks and filled a cup for Andrew. Pamela then remembered she needed to purchase a few other items available for sale at Dawson's. Telling Andrew to remain close to the soda-dispensing machine, Pamela spent about "three to five minutes" gathering up her items. She then returned to the spot where she had left Andrew. As she neared him, she noticed that Andrew was drinking his soft drink and was "pawing" through a bin containing a number of small items. She began walking quickly toward Andrew, told him stop, and then slipped, hitting her head on the floor. Pamela lost consciousness for several minutes, during which time an ambulance was called and arrived at Dawson's. When the EMTs arrived, they found the clerk, Andrew and another customer hovering near Pamela. As the EMTs approached Pamela opened her eyes and moaned, "I should have gotten new shoes." She also asked the other customer, Willa Sinton, "Did you see the liquid on the floor where I fell?" They noticed that she was wearing a "flip-flop" type of sandal. Sinton later testified at her deposition, "I saw this kid spill some soda and then refill his cup after he moved a stool to the machine. I told the clerk what happened and he just shrugged his shoulders and did nothing." The clerk, William Rawson, testified, "Right after the lady slipped I saw her child holding a soft drink cup and he had a wet soda stain on his shirt. I also heard the child say to his mom, 'I'm sorry I made a mess but I wanted to slide on the floor.'" Rawson denies Sinton mentioned the spill to him. Andrew was also deposed but remembers nothing other than his mother falling and injuring herself.

Dawson's Pump-n-Go sells a number of convenience foods, including cupcakes, ice cream bars, food that may be heated in the store's microwave oven and soft drinks from a self-service machine. Approximately 20% of its total sales are from food and drinks.

The accident occurred in the state of Mariana, which has adopted the following statutes, which declare in part: 1) "no person shall be held negligent as a matter of law if the person is under the age of seven years"; 2) "contributory negligence is abolished, and a person may recover damages based on a percentage of the liability of the defendant or defendants if the plaintiff's negligence is no greater than 50%"; 3) "joint and several liability will apply to each and every responsible party in a negligence matter but no responsible party shall be jointly liable if that party's allocation of negligence is less than the negligence allocated to the injured party"; and 4) "a parent may be held liable for the willful and malicious acts of a child."

Pamela sued alleging Dawson's was negligent. Dawson's denied liability. Assume at trial the court agreed to the request of Dawson's that the jury assess the extent to which Andrew Parsons was negligent. In addition to discussing all relevant legal issues that may arise at trial, assume that the jury's verdict declares the damages to Pamela were $100,000 and that Pamela Parsons was 45% negligent, Dawson's was 40% negligent and Andrew Parsons was 15% negligent.

An answer to this question requires that you address the following: 1) Can Pamela show a breach of duty by Dawson's in this premises liability case by showing notice or through the method of sale exception to notice?; 2) Can Dawson's defend by showing a lack of proximate cause, either a) due to the "flip-flops" worn by Pamela or b) by arguing that Andrew's actions were the cause-in-fact of Pamela's injuries despite the statute that declares children under the age of seven incapable of negligence?; 3) Is there a conflict between the first and fourth statutes and, if so, how should that conflict be analyzed, particularly in light of the jury's verdict?; and 4) how should this verdict be analyzed given the existence of comparative negligence and a joint and several liability statute?

A Constitutional Law Essay Question

In 2010 Congress adopted a law which states in part: "Human papillomavirus (HPV) is the most common sexually transmitted infection in the United States. The spread of HPV has created a national crisis. It affects millions of women, many of whom are unaware they carry this disease. The rise in HPV cases creates a tremendous burden on the business of medicine throughout the United States. It causes many to miss work and school due to illness, resulting in economic loss. These harms substantially affect the national economy. HPV may cause serious physical and mental harm to persons, including a shorter life span and greater pain and suffering. Therefore, each public school district or other educational institution that directly or indirectly receives federal funds in which students have attained the age of 12 shall be required to implement a plan to inoculate all students ages 12 or older who may be at risk of contracting HPV. Failure to implement such a plan shall result in the loss of any federal funds awarded those schools. Any student who refuses to show proof of inoculation against HPV shall be banned from registering at any educational institution that receives federal funds directly or indirectly until receiving an inoculation. A person is exempt from this requirement if provided treatment by spiritual means alone in accordance with the tenets and practice of a recognized church or religious denomination."

After the law was passed, the school board of the public Carrington Independent School District in Texas sued for a declaratory judgment in federal court claiming the law is unconstitutional. Additionally, Melissa Hardeman, a 20-year-old college sophomore at the University of Carson, a state-supported university, refused to be inoculated and was not permitted to register for classes. She sued in federal district court alleging the law is unconstitutional. Hardeman argues that she refused to be inoculated because, as stated in her complaint, "Complainant believes as a matter of her moral beliefs and conscience that no government should be permitted to force a person to take any medicine, for that violates the person's bodily integrity, and in her moral view and conscience, the mind, body and spirit are connected to a greater force, a one-ness with others on the earth that otherwise will be trampled upon by an intrusive government."

The cases have been consolidated and assigned to a federal district judge. You are the law clerk to that judge. The judge has asked you to discuss all relevant constitutional issues in these two cases.

These facts require the student to consider issues of 1) standing, 2) commerce clause power, 3) spending power, 4) free exercise and 5) establishment clause.

(Equal protection is a distractor because the statute does not speak in the language of gender discrimination even though only females are given the HPV vaccination. If it were used, one would use the equal protection component of the due process clause of the 5th amendment because this is an act of Congress not a state law.) If you were given 40 minutes to complete your answer, you have less than eight minutes to discuss each issue. The standing question requires some application to the interest of Carrington ISD in challenging the law, and whether Melissa Hardeman has standing with respect to the establishment clause question. The commerce clause analysis applies to both cases, and requires you to assess the general breadth of that power in light of both *United States v. Lopez* (1995) and *Gonzales v. Raich* (2005). The spending power issue affects the analysis only in the Carrington ISD matter. The free exercise and establishment clause issues apply to Hardeman's case. Is the statutory exemption constitutionally permissible given the broad level of generality used by the Court in interpreting the establishment clause? Must a limited statutory exemption for free exercise be broadened as a constitutional matter to encompass similarly situated females whose request for an exemption is arguably non-religious in light of *Employment Div. v. Smith* (1990)? When answering constitutional law essays your reference points (precedential cases) should be fairly clear. A Constitutional Law problem will likely give rise to facts that bring to mind some relatively well known cases with which to compare the facts given in the problem. Your analysis will require evaluating those facts in light of precedential cases. Whether those facts are analogous must be the focus of your answer.

Multiple Choice Examinations

The multiple choice examination for 1L students is a development of the past twenty years. In the mid-1990s the overall bar examination passing rates fell substantially. It is unclear why this occurred, but one response to this increased failure rate was for law schools to replicate part of the bar examination experience. The Multistate Bar Examination (MBE) has been adopted by a majority of states. It consists of 200 multiple choice questions, each of which has four possible answers, tested over a six hour period (with a one hour lunch break after completion of the first 100 questions during a three hour period) on the following six subjects: Constitutional Law, Contracts, Criminal Law, Evidence, Property and Torts. Contracts, Criminal Law, Property and Torts are all traditional 1L subjects. In about half of all law schools Constitutional Law is also a 1L subject. Only Evidence is traditionally an upper level course, and a significant minority of law schools require their students to take Evidence as a condition of graduating. Because the MBE tests on 1L subjects in multiple choice format, a number of law professors have begun testing in the same fashion.

Several keys exist to answering correctly multiple choice questions. They are: 1) a little knowledge is a dangerous thing; 2) understand how to categorize multiple-choice questions; 3) understand the different styles of multiple-choice questions; 4) learn what distractors exist and how to ignore them; 5) how to improve your odds by quickly eliminating some answers; 6) standards v. rules; and 7) how to pace yourself.

In addition to the discussion in that follows, you may wish to look at the explanations of the MBE found in Chapter 7, which discusses and offers examples about how to answer multiple-choice bar exam questions.

A Little Knowledge Is a Dangerous Thing

You must know a great deal of doctrine in order to do well on a multiple-choice examination. Most multiple-choice examinations will be closed book examinations, or, if open book, will be structured in such a way as to limit your opportunities to look at your outline or other available material. Multiple-choice exams are time-sensitive in part to replicate the MBE and in part to see how well you know the material under the constraints of time.

Knowing the material includes reviewing your outline and re-writing it in summary form. It is also crucial, however, for you to practice taking multiple-choice questions under the same time constraints as your professor gives (a common rule of thumb is two (2) minutes per question). Most professors, intentionally or not, model the MBE format, which includes four answers per question, and which does not include the answers "none of the above" or "all of the above." Some professors will use those answers and provide five possible answers for each question. Ask about the format well before the exam takes place. As a general rule professors don't "hide the ball" on their approach to multiple-choice questions.

Categorizing Multiple-Choice Questions

Three types of multiple-choice questions exist: 1) the "definitional" question; 2) the "multi-definitional" question; and 3) the "application" or "analysis" question.

The *definitional* question is the simplest type of multiple-choice question. It merely asks you to define a rule of law in light of the facts given in the question. The following is a definitional question that might be used in a Constitutional Law examination.

> Congress adopted a law barring the publication of any materials declared "highly confidential" without first obtaining approval from the Confidential Clearinghouse Commission of the Department of Defense. If a party fails to obtain such approval, it may appeal to the court of appeals. However, the party is prohibited from publishing such material before obtaining judicial permission to do so. The law is
>
> A) unconstitutional on its face.
> B) unconstitutional unless the government can show the law is the least restrictive means to effectuating a compelling state interest.
> C) constitutional on its face.
> D) constitutional if the plaintiff does not show the law violates the first amendment.

The best answer is B. A is wrong because prior restraints are presumptively unconstitutional but not always so, C is completely wrong on the law (prior restraints cannot be constitutional on their face), and D is wrong because the government has the burden of proof in prior restraint cases, not the party wishing to print. That leaves B, which is a correct statement of the law regarding the laws that infringe fundamental rights, in this case, freedom of speech.

The definitional question above asks whether you know what the doctrine is concerning prior restraints of speech. Now, like most definitional questions, you must also have some understanding of a "subsidiary" or latent legal doctrine, and in this example that is the doctrine of "facial invalidity" of legislation.

The *multi-definitional* question, as its name suggests, asks you to define two or more legal doctrines. The multi-definitional question is designed to force you to understand how the facts stated in the question may raise different (indeed, possibly conflicting) doctrines. The following is an example of a multi-definitional question, again based on Constitutional Law.

> Congress passes a law creating a moratorium on the taking of any person's private property by any government for a period of six months in order to study the empirical consequences of takings. The law is

A) unconstitutional, because it violates separation of powers.
B) unconstitutional, because it violates the doctrine of federalism.
C) constitutional, because it is passed pursuant to Congress's power under Section 5 of the 14th amendment to enforce the substantive provisions of the 14th amendment.
D) constitutional, because Congress adopted the law pursuant to the takings clause of the 5th amendment.

This question requires you to think about more than one doctrine in order to answer correctly. You are required to know the definitions of separation of powers, federalism, Congress's power under Section 5 of the Fourteenth Amendment and the meaning of the takings clause. The best (and "best" is used intentionally, because none of the possible answers may be "correct" as a matter of law) answer is B. A incorrectly offers as its justification separation of powers, which concerns the division of federal (legislative, executive, judicial) power, and the question concerns Congress's power to restrict the actions of "any government," which includes states governments. A moratorium on the exercise of eminent domain has nothing to do with the judiciary and only a little to do with the executive. C is incorrect because Congress's power under Section 5 of the Fourteenth Amendment only applies to the power of Congress to enforce the substantive clauses found in that amendment, and this law is irrelevant to that exercise of power. D is wrong because Congress does not derive any power to pass laws from the takings clause; that clause is a restriction on the exercise of power by the government in favor of the individual. B is the best answer not only because it the last option standing but also because the law passed by Congress is a law directed at state and local governments telling them (commanding them) they cannot do something, which is constitutionally impermissible. Now, it would be possible for a lawyer representing Congress to justify its constitutionality by claiming Congress acted pursuant to its authority to regulate commerce (I still think it would lose, but ...), but that was not included as an answer. Look for the best available answer.

The third and most difficult multiple-choice question is the *application or analysis* question. It is also the most common. The analysis question requires that you undertake two steps. First, you must know the doctrine applicable to the question. Second, after locating the correct doctrine you must analyze the facts in light of the applicable law and choose the correct legal answer. As discussed above in the section on essay examinations, the key to doing well in law school is analyzing. Too often students believe that analysis is confined to essay questions and is absent in multiple-choice questions. That belief leads to poor results. The following is an analysis question, once again from the subject of Constitutional Law.

> Texas adopts a law regulating hunting leases by making all Texas commercial hunting licenses six month licenses. These licenses cost $500. This leads to a drop in the number of hunters who arrive from outside the state of Texas to hunt for a week or less, due allegedly to the cost of the license. Owners of property available for lease by hunters sue the head of the state department regulating hunting, alleging that the law is unconstitutional. The law is likely
>
> A) constitutional because the privileges or immunities clause of the 14th amendment is not applicable to licensing of leisure rather than work activities.
> B) constitutional because the privileges and immunities clause of Article IV, section 2 is inapplicable to the complaint of the lease owners.
> C) unconstitutional because the equal protection clause of the 14th amendment requires more than substantial equality when offering licenses of any type.
> D) unconstitutional because the privileges and immunities clause of Article IV, § 2 applies to hunting licenses as well as other activities.

The best answer is B. First, you have to determine the correct doctrine given the facts. (What is the difference between privileges or immunities clause of the Fourteenth Amendment and privileges and immunities clause of Article IV, § 2? What is the difference between privileges and immunities and equal protection?) The privileges or immunities clause of the Fourteenth Amendment largely applies as stated in *The Slaughterhouse Cases* (1873), which means hardly at all. The Supreme Court did offer a possible revival to the clause in *Saenz v. Roe* (1999), which included the right to travel as a privilege or immunity found in the Fourteenth Amendment, but the Supreme Court has not developed this clause in any subsequent case. The equal protection clause of the Fourteenth Amendment requires equality of treatment among those who are affected by the law, but this clause does not focus on any different treatment between those affected by the law who are located in the state and those who citizens or residents of another state. The privileges and immunities clause of Art. IV, § 2 requires a state to treat a nonresident similarly to a residents with regard to things that are categorized as "privileges and immunities" protected by Article IV. An individual hunting license may be a privilege and immunity (which is why the question calls it a commercial hunting license, eliminating that possibility), the law is adopted by a state, not the federal government (this clause does not apply to federal laws, only state laws), and it affects persons residing outside of Texas (nonresidents) so the correct legal doctrine that may apply is the privileges and immunities clause of Art. IV. This makes choices A and C incorrect doctrines for this question. Then to step 2: We have a pair of opposites. As a legal matter, does the privileges and immunities clause of Article IV apply to these facts? The facts indicate that no disparity exists in the cost of the hunting license between Texans and non-Texans. All persons, no matter where they reside, are charged $500 for a commercial hunting license. Therefore, because the privileges and immunities clause of Article IV is intended to prevent disparate treatment of persons residing outside the state that enacted the law (here, anyone not a resident of Texas), and no disparate treatment of non-Texans exists, the law cannot be unconstitutional on privileges and immunities clause grounds, making D incorrect. That leaves B as the last standing answer.

Understanding the Different Styles of Multiple-Choice Questions

Three general styles of multiple-choice questions exist: 1) the "two-and-two" and its variant the "three and one"; 2) the "complete the sentence"; and 3) the "multiple options" question.

The "two and two" is when you are asked a question that divides the answers into two possibilities, each of which also has two possibilities. The questions above are all stated in "two-and-two" terms. In Constitutional Law the "two-and-two" offers two answers that begin "constitutional, because" and two answers that begin "unconstitutional, because." Consequently, your first approach may be to determine whether the law is constitutional. After you decide that the law is "constitutional," your second step is to choose the correct legal justification for the constitutionality of the law. In your common law courses, the answers in a "two and two" are couched in terms of whether the plaintiff will or will not prevail, giving two "yes, because" and two "no, because" options. In Criminal Law, of course, the questions often are based on correct categorizations of the action in terms of the law of crimes.

The cousin of the two and two is the "three and one." This variant may provide two "yes" and two "no" answers, but one of the yes or no answers is followed by "unless." That means that three of the answers fall into one category (either yes or no), with just one answer in the other category. For example:

Palko is treated by a medical doctor for asbestosis, caused by her on-the-job handling of materials containing asbestos. Palko's doctor has told her that the asbestosis is not presently cancerous, but that it considerably increases the risk that she will ultimately develop lung cancer. Palko brought an action for damages, based on strict product liability, against the supplier of the materials that contained asbestos. The highest appellate court in this state has barred recovery of damages for negligent infliction of emotional distress without proof of physical harm. If the supplier is subject to liability to Palko for damages, should the damages award include damages for any emotional distress Palko suffered arising from her knowledge of the increased risk that she will develop lung cancer?

A) No, because Palko's emotional distress did not cause her physical condition.

B) No, unless the court in this jurisdiction recognizes a cause of action for an increased risk of cancer.

C) Yes, because the supplier of a dangerous product is strictly liable for the harm it causes.

D) Yes, because Palko's emotional distress arises from bodily harm caused by her exposure to asbestosis.

Option B, "no, unless" is actually a "yes, because" or "yes, if" answer. That makes this question a "three and one" question. Thus, only A in effect allows for a "no" answer. In this question the best answer is D. You must read the facts carefully, for the facts in this case also tell you the state of the law ("highest appellate court in this state has barred recovery of damages for negligent infliction of emotional distress without proof of physical harm.") you must apply. A misstates the law, and C merely restates the law of strict product liability without applying the specific facts to this matter. B focuses on the requirement of a separate "cause of action," a distractor that attempts to take the reader from the call of the question, which concerns the "damages award," not whether a separate cause of action exists. D fits law (damages law) with the facts. Palko did suffer bodily harm caused by exposure to asbestosis according to the facts. Emotional distress can result from bodily harm, and the legal doctrine only barred recovery in the absence of proof of physical harm, which the first sentence told us existed.

A "complete the sentence" question requires you to finish the call of the question, ordinarily by selecting the correct statement of law. For example,

Palmco owns and operates a beachfront hotel. Under a contract with City to restore a public beach, Dredgeco placed a large and unavoidably dangerous stone-crushing machine on City land near Palmco's hotel. The machine creates a continuous and significant noise so disturbing to the hotel guests many have canceled their hotel reservations, causing a substantial loss to Palmco. Palmco's best chance to recover damages for its financial losses from Dredgeco is under the theory that the operation of the stone-crushing machine constitutes

A) an abnormally dangerous activity.
B) a private nuisance.
C) negligence.
D) a trespass.

You are to choose the most correct legal answer in completing the question. In this example the best answer is B, a private nuisance. The hotel's interest in its land is affected by the stone-crushing machine, and the "continuous and significant" noise is a common illustration of the difference between a nuisance and a trespass (answer D). The machine is necessary to "restore" the public beach, making negligence an incorrect answer, and nothing in the facts indicates that the stone-crushing machine, though "unavoidably dangerous," caused an abnormally dangerous activity, such as a flood caused by the machine.

The "multiple options" approach is a devilish type of multiple choice question, for it requires the examinee to look at two sets of answers, a set within a grouping (usually three) listed by Roman numerals, and then the conventional four options A–D. The multiple options question should be taken in reverse order. First, look at the answers given in A–D. Based on those answers, try to eliminate or isolate one of the three Roman numeral possibilities. The following is one type of multiple options question.

Purcell bought a used car from Dale, a used car dealer. Knowing them to be false, Dale made the following statements to Purcell before the sale:

I. This car has never been involved in an accident.
II. This car gets 25 miles to the gallon on the open highway.
III. This is as smooth-riding a car as you can get.

If Purcell asserts a claim against Dale based on misrepresentation, which of the false statements made by Dale would support Purcell's claim?

A) I only.
B) II only.
C) I and II only.
D) II and III only.

The best way to answer this question in a timely fashion is to try to eliminate two possibilities with one assessment. First, ignore the three Roman numerals and begin with options A–D, counting how many times each Roman numeral is used. In this example, Roman numeral I is used twice, Roman numeral II is used three times, and Roman numeral III is used once. That means that if you eliminate Roman numeral I, you are down to two answers. If you can eliminate Roman numeral II you can eliminate three answers, leaving you with the correct answer. If you eliminate Roman numeral III you only eliminate one answer, making this your least efficient option. The problem with starting by looking at Roman numeral II is that it is highly likely to be accurate, for if not, it would be too easy to answer this question (if II is incorrect then the answer must be A), for you would only have to look at one answer! Your examiners likely want you to peruse at least two of the three Roman numerals, so your most efficient option for dealing with this type of question quickly is to always look at the option that eliminates two possible answers. If you look at Roman numeral I first, it is either correct (in which case answers B and D are thrown out), or it is incorrect (in which case answers A and C are thrown out). Roman numeral I is not an example of permissible "puffery" or opinion, but a factual claim that, if false, allows one to sue for misrepresentation. Thus, answers B and D cannot be correct, leaving us with just A and C as our possibilities. To choose between those remaining options requires us to read II. Like Roman numeral I, II also is a statement of fact, not an opinion. If false, that statement also supports Purcell's claim. Thus, C is the correct answer. Note that we answered this question without ever looking at III.

With one exception, you can usually answer a "multiple options" question by looking at just two of the three Roman numerals. The one exception to this rule is the following grouping:

A) I and II only.
B) II and III only.
C) I and III only.
D) I, II and III.

If you are given a question with these options, you'll note that each Roman numeral is listed three times, including an "all of the above" answer in D. If this is the case you will have to look at each of the three options. You are unlikely to eliminate more one answer at a time. In this case if you look at option I and it is true, then you have only eliminated B. If you then go to II and find it is accurate, then you have only eliminated C. You will then have to look at III to determine whether the answer is A or D.

Multiple option questions are much less daunting than initially perceived as long as you have practiced how to eliminate two possibilities by looking at just one Roman numeral. If your professor uses this option, find which option is used twice. After that you can choose which remaining option to look at.

What Are Distractors and How Do You Spot (and Ignore) Them

Each subject tested in multiple-choice format will include some "distractor" answers. These are answers that are rarely right but which appear facially plausible, often causing the examinee to doubt his initial response to the question. Raising some doubt leads the examinee to spend more time on a problem than otherwise would be the case, which may cause the examinee to rush through some other questions in order to complete the multiple-choice exam on time, increasing the likelihood of further errors. The reason distractors can raise doubt in an examinee's mind is because distractors tug at the gnawing fear that the examinee hasn't studied enough, and somehow missed a doctrine, at least the doctrine as stated by the distractor answer. The two most common types of distractors are 1) the "Portentous but Nonsensical or Meaningless Legalese" distractor, and 2) the "There's Some Rule about This, but This isn't that Kind of Case" distractor.

An example of the Portentous but Nonsensical or Meaningless Legalese distractor follows, based on Evidence law:

> Plaintiff sued Defendant for breach of a commercial contract in which Defendant had agreed to sell Plaintiff all of Plaintiff's requirements for widgets. Plaintiff called Expert Witness to testify as to damages. Defendant seeks to show that Expert Witness had provided false testimony as a witness in his own divorce proceedings.
> This evidence should be
>
> A) admitted only if elicited from Expert Witness on cross-examination.
> B) admitted only if the false testimony is established by clear and convincing extrinsic evidence.
> C) excluded, because it is impeachment on a collateral issue.
> D) excluded, because it is improper character evidence.

Answer B states, "admitted only if the false testimony is established by clear and convincing extrinsic evidence." That sounds so inviting. But it's wrong, and you can understand this in part because this nonsensical legalese has two false aspects to it. First, under the law of evidence extrinsic evidence is never admissible when impeaching a witness based on nonconviction misconduct. Second, the answer offers an enticing burden of proof: a "clear and convincing" standard sounds good, but that is a standard rarely used in evidence law. The actual standard is a "good faith" basis for asking the question. C is wrong because impeachment about lying that did not result in a conviction is admissible and is not collateral, and D is wrong because the issue is not about character but about credibility. Thus, A is correct. It states correctly that this evidence is admissible only if the Witness admits it on cross-examination. That is, Defendant is not permitted to call the Witness's former wife to testify about the lie (that's what is called collateral).

A similar example is found in Criminal Law:

> Davis is charged with robbery. Waller testified that the robber walked favoring his left leg, and Davis walks favoring his left leg. When the prosecution asked the court to order Davis to walk from his courtroom seat to the jury box and back to enable the jury could determine whether Davis was the person Waller saw, Davis's lawyer objected. The objection will most likely be
>
> A) sustained, because the order requested by the state violates Davis's constitutional right to avoid an illegal search and seizure.
> B) sustained, because the order requested by the state violates Davis's constitutional privilege against self-incrimination.
> C) denied, unless the order requested by the state violates Davis's right to privacy.
> D) denied, because the order requested by the state is a permissible part of the courtroom identification process.

The first three answers all invoke an individual constitutional right, each of which applies to both the state and federal governments. Answer C raises the scope of an invasion of privacy, which certainly sounds portentous. It is, however, meaningless legalese, for although each person has a right to privacy, that right is inapplicable in terms of issues arising at a criminal trial. But the right to privacy is alluring, and it may get you to stop and think about it more than you should, about three seconds. Answers A and B also sound good, but both are wrong because requiring a defendant to take a walk is neither a search or a seizure nor is it "testimony" that is protected by the privilege against self-incrimination.

The second common distractor, the "There's Some Rule about This, but This isn't that Kind of Case" distractor, preys on the examinee's lack of confidence of his or her knowledge of the law. The following is an example from Constitutional Law.

> Petersen operates a small "adult entertainment" store, part of which is dedicated to "viewing booths," where customers can rent videos and watch them onsite. The Dawsonville city council recently adopted an ordinance that bans "the operation of any video facility in a location at which other goods and products are sold." Petersen has sued the city in federal court for a declaratory judgment. The district court will declare the ordinance
>
> A) unconstitutional, if the Dawsonville city council was motivated by a desire to lessen pornographic speech in the city.
> B) unconstitutional, if Congress has adopted a law awarding cities and states grant monies to "clean up the problem of pornography and the destruction of city life."
> C) constitutional, if the ordinance is intended to curb the secondary effects of sexually explicit speech.
> D) constitutional, because the ordinance is merely a time, place or manner regulation.

Answers A, B and D are all distractors. Unlike obscene speech, pornographic speech cannot be regulated by the government (you will learn the difference between the two in your Constitutional Law class, or, "I know it when I see it" in the famous words of Justice Potter Stewart regarding the difference). Motivation is rarely an issue in constitutional law cases and the constitutionality of this ordinance will not depend on the city council's motivation. Answer B offers some meaningless issue that raises the issue of Congress's spending power to eliminate pornography and aid in building cities. Whatever the extent of Congress's spending power, it has no relevance to the constitutionality of this city ordinance. Finally, you also learn that regulations that affect only the time, place and manner of speech may be constitutional, and you will learn rules on how governments may constitutionally regulate the time, place and manner of speech. But the ordinance does not speak of a regulation of the time, place or manner of pornographic speech, so D is inapt in these circumstances. That leaves C.

A second example is based on the law of Evidence:

> Plaintiff sued Defendant for money owed on a cost-plus contract. The contract required that Defendant receive notice of any proposed additional expenditures by Plaintiff before Plaintiff could act. Defendant claims it did not receive the required notice. Plaintiff calls Witness, its financial director, to testify it is Plaintiff's routine practice to send cost overrun notices as required by this contract. Plaintiff offers through

Witness a copy of the cost overrun notice letter to Defendant on which Plaintiff is relying, which Witness has taken from Plaintiff's regular business files.

On the issue of giving notice, the copy of the letter is

A) admissible under the business record exception to hearsay.
B) admissible, because it is a routine practice of the company.
C) inadmissible, because it is hearsay not within any exception.
D) inadmissible, because it is not the best evidence of the notice.

Answer D states, "inadmissible, because it is not the best evidence of the notice." The "best evidence" rule of evidence applies to "writings." A letter (and any copy of it) is a writing. Is D correct? No, because the call of the question is, "on the issue of giving "*notice*...." This is not "On the issue of the admissibility of the copy to prove D is in breach." Answer D is inapt, but works well as a distractor if the examinee doesn't read the call of the question closely. You may end up thinking about the best evidence rule rather than the rule of habit ("routine practices") because the case involves a copy offered as evidence. This is not that kind of case. The correct answer is B.

The only sound way to learn how to spot and ignore distractor answers is to practice multiple-choice examination questions. Distractors become much more apparent the more questions you answer, and the more apparent they become the easier they are to ignore. If your professor plans on making multiple-choice questions a significant (one-quarter or more) part of your grade, you need to begin practicing taking multiple-choice questions no later than the middle of the semester. A number of books now exist that offer several hundred examples, broken down by area of law, allowing you to test yourself on subjects you have already covered in class. In addition, published MBE questions are available at most law school libraries and for purchase from the National Conference of Bar Examiners at ncbex.org.

Standards v. Rules

One of the topics you will be exposed to on a regular basis in your 1L classes is the longstanding debate between standards and rules. Standards are general guidelines that provide the trial and appellate courts with a modicum of discretion in interpretation. The doctrine of "unjust enrichment" in contracts is one example of a standard. A rule, by contrast, applies to a particular event or situation with little (or no) discretion available to the judge. An example of a rule would be the "general rule" discussed (and avoided) in the *Jasko* case, discussed in the previous chapter. The general rule in a premises liability case is that the owner of the premises cannot be held liable for injuries suffered by another unless the owner knew or should have known of the dangerous condition of the premises. (The exception to this rule, as declared in *Jasko*, was that this "notice" provision was inapt if the method of sale created a foreseeably dangerous condition.)

When a legal doctrine is framed in terms of standards or in multi-pronged tests (replete in Constitutional Law), it becomes very difficult for the person drafting the exam to write a question that requires the examinee to apply or analyze the law in such a case. That difficulty arises because different appellate courts may reach different results given alternate understandings of the discretion available to the court. The result, then, is that questions in which a standard will apply will usually be phrased as definitional or multi-definitional questions rather than as application or analysis questions. Although you will find many rules are also less clear than they appear upon first glance, a rules question in multiple-choice form can be asked both in terms of defining a rule (that is, can the examinee define the general rule concerning premises liability) and in terms of applying or analyzing that rule in light of the particular facts given in the question.

The long-term trend in law has been toward standards and away from rules, a consequence of the influence of legal realism at the expense of legal formalism. A recent reaction to this long-term trend has resulted in the creation of some rules designed to constrain the discretion accorded judges through standards. Essay questions that focus on standards are common, for they require analysis of the provisions of the standards in light of the facts generated by the professor. This creates a generous flexibility in framing the facts (and thus the legal issues) when drafting an essay. At the same time, testing on legal standards in multiple-choice questions is more difficult than testing on rules. If your professor creates an exam that uses both methods of assessment, be aware of this difference when preparing for your exam.

How to Improve Your Odds

You can improve the odds of answering more questions correctly through two broad strategies and three particular tactics. The strategies have been discussed above, and are rooted in how one should engage the law school experience: First, study throughout the semester even (especially) if you have just one end-of-the-semester assessment. Intelligence helps law students perform well, as do a prodigious memory and a facility for writing clearly. Studying the material effectively and efficiently are crucial to performing to the best of your ability. Second, practice taking exams under the time constraints given you. Even if you know the material you must be able 1) to correctly state the law applicable to the fact pattern and 2) analyze the law in light of the facts stated by the professor (not the facts you would like to add). This is a skill that can be learned. You learn how to analyze not only in your classes but in your conversations with your classmates. Exam taking is also a skill, and practicing taking exams is the best way to master that skill.

Three tactical approaches may provide the best insulation against the stress created in a multiple-choice examination, for one goal of a multiple-choice examination is to see how well a student performs under stressful conditions. First, read the facts of each question closely. Your professor will differentiate among students by providing answers that are similar, and choosing well between these two answers requires you to read closely and comprehensively. Skimming or reading sloppily will lead you to the similar but incorrect answer. Close reading is particularly helpful on "application" questions, for the facts stated in the question will provide both a strong hint of the correct answer and help you quickly eliminate choices that do not fit the facts. Second, if the facts of the question are substantially longer than other questions, begin by looking at the call of the question, giving you a clearer sense of what you are being asked. By beginning with the call of the question you may be able to ignore some interesting but irrelevant facts designed to distract you. If reading the call is unhelpful, consider trading time for an incorrect answer. Going into a multiple-choice exam you should have a default letter if you are pressed for time. A student will not be penalized for guessing incorrectly on a multiple-choice exam (which may not be the case on an essay question), and you may guess correctly on one or more questions, so make sure you answer every multiple-choice question. You are unlikely to get every question right, and, if a question has you stumped or frustrated, it may be most efficient for you to guess and move on. You must guess rather than leave the question for later because you want to ensure you continue to circle answers to the correct questions, and having a default answer (C seems too pat, but just choose one) allows you to do so quickly. Third, know what answers pair off. One key to answering questions quickly and accurately is to look at correlative pairs. Consider the following Evidence question:

> Plaintiff sued Defendant for personal injuries suffered when a branch from a tree fell and struck Plaintiff. Defendant claims the tree is not on her property but is located on the city's property. In his case-in-chief the Plaintiff offers evidence that Defendant cut down the tree two weeks after Plaintiff suffered his injuries. The evidence is
>
> A) admissible to prove the tree was located on Defendant's property.

B) admissible because the probative value of Defendant's action is not substantially outweighed by its prejudicial effect.
C) inadmissible, because the probative value of Defendant's action is substantially outweighed by its prejudicial effect.
D) inadmissible, because of the evidence policy encourage safety measures.

This question has two sets of paired answers. Answers A and D are paired off, as are answers B and C. Answer D accurately states the rule of what is called subsequent remedial measures, found in Federal Rules of Evidence (FRE) 407. Answer A states an exception to that rule. Answers B and C and correlative opposites. Two problems exist with answers B and C: First, although both correctly state the standard to balance the probative value and prejudicial effect of relevant evidence (this rule is found in Rule 403), both ask for a conclusion, which is nearly impossible in a standards-type question, making either answer highly unlikely; second, answers B and C are "residual" answers, answers that we choose only if no other answer is possible. Neither seems specifically applicable to the facts, which again makes both unlikely. This seems to leave the examinee with either A or D, which requires one to know whether the rule or the exception applies to the facts. In this case, because Defendant denies owning the land on which the tree was located, her decision to cut down the tree may be offered as evidence of her ownership of the land and the tree. Thus, the exception (answer A) applies.

How Do You Correctly Pace Yourself?

Pacing is about practice. Those of you who participated in a sport that involves timing, such as track or swimming, learned how to pace your times through practice. The same is true for learning how to complete a multiple-choice exam within the stated time constraints. Use a professor's past exams, published MBE questions, and multiple-choice questions available from law publishers to practice answering questions at the correct pace.

Chapter 6

Your Upper-Level Years

Two generations ago law students were told that "they work you to death" in your second year of law school and "they bore you to death" in your third year of law school. Neither is likely true today. Some students find themselves bored to death at the beginning of their second year of law school. Others find they were never worked to death at any time during law school. What you will find in your 2L and 3L years of law school is that law school is what you make of it. Many law schools offer a panoply of courses on legal subjects that did not exist two generations ago. Those courses are taught using a variety of approaches that go beyond the doctrinal. Law schools regularly offer a number of "law and" courses (law and economics, law and literature, law and psychology, etc.) and courses looking at law from various jurisprudential perspectives. Most law schools offer students one or more opportunities to learn law by doing, by taking a legal clinic in which students offer legal assistance to actual clients. Vast new areas of legal specialization have been created in the past quarter-century. The explosion of new areas of legal practice has led to an expansion in the number of advanced courses on such subjects as ERISA, consumer bankruptcy and elder law, as well as corporate transactions and civil litigation. If you are worried about knowing enough law to pass the bar examination in your state, you will find plenty of courses that cover those subjects.

All ABA-approved law schools are required to teach a course in Professional Responsibility (sometimes called Legal Profession or Legal Ethics) or teach legal ethics "pervasively." Most choose the former option, so you are likely to be required to take this course. Because nearly all jurisdictions now require you to take and pass the Multistate Professional Responsibility Exam (MPRE), discussed in Chapter 8, this should not inconvenience you in your course scheduling decisions. All ABA-approved law schools are also required to provide students with an upper-level writing opportunity. Most schools provide a number of writing seminars on topics chosen by faculty members. Many will also allow students to fulfill this requirement through an independent study, in which a student works with a faculty member on a topic of interest to both.

Once you have decided on your class schedule, you need to decide what other opportunities to take advantage of during your final two years of law school. The remainder of this chapter discusses upper level course offerings, co-curricular and extracurricular options, the advantages and disadvantages of taking a legal clinic, organizing and completing your upper-level writing requirement, joint degrees and other topics.

Bar Courses v. "This Is What I'm Interested In"

Fortunately, this is a false choice. You will find some bar courses, that is, subject matter that is likely to be tested on a state's bar exam, very interesting. Even if you feel obliged to take an extensive number of bar courses you will find time to take other courses in subjects in which you are interested. One important decision to make is when to take bar courses and when to take other courses. Bar courses such as Evidence are taught regularly, often once per semester, meaning you can take them at any time during your last two years. Any course that is a prerequisite to advanced courses on a subject of interest to you should be taken in the first semester of your 2L year. Some courses not tested on the bar may be taught by just one professor at your school. If that class (say, Entertainment Law) if offered in your 2L year, and you are not sure whether to take it then or in your 3L year, ask the professor who teaches it when you should take it. Fear not approaching a professor you do not know; he or she will be happy to see someone else interested in a subject that clearly is of deep interest to the professor. Two reasons you need to ask the professor when to take the course are because the course may be offered alternate years and because the professor may be planning a sabbatical or visit and be unavailable to teach the course in the following year.

If you decide that you need to make the choice stated in the heading, to what extent should you take courses on subjects tested on the bar examination? How should such bar courses be prioritized? First, a definition of "bar courses." The basic courses taught in the 1L year of law school, Contracts, Criminal Law, Property, Torts and possibly Constitutional Law, are all tested on the Multistate Bar Examination (MBE), a multiple-choice examination used by the board of law examiners of most states. The sixth subject tested on the MBE is Evidence, which many states also test on the essay section of the bar exam. The Multistate Essay Examination (MEE) has been adopted by twenty-six jurisdictions as of 2010. The list of subjects that may be tested on the MEE constitutes a fairly standard list: "Business Associations (Agency and Partnership; Corporations and Limited Liability Companies), Conflict of Laws, Constitutional Law, Contracts, Criminal Law and Procedure, Evidence, Family Law, Federal Civil Procedure, Real Property, Torts, Trusts and Estates (Decedents' Estates; Trusts and Future Interests), and Uniform Commercial Code (Negotiable Instruments (Commercial Paper); Secured Transactions)." As you can tell, a number of first-year subjects tested on the MBE are also tested in essay form on the MEE. The key upper level courses that form the "core" of the bar exam include Business Associations, Evidence, Trusts and Estates, the Uniform Commercial Code (UCC), Family Law and, to a lesser extent, Conflict of Laws and Constitutional Criminal Procedure. Your state may test other subjects, such as Tax Law or Administrative Law. The subjects specifically tested in the state in which you plan to take the bar will be listed on the website for the board of law examiners of your state.

The lower your 1L GPA, the more you should consider taking more rather than fewer bar courses, even or especially in subjects about which you have little interest. Bar examination passing rates correlate with law school rank, both rank after the 1L year and rank at graduation. Your professor is not teaching this "bar" course so that you can pass the bar; she is teaching you this material for the practice of law. One of the most difficult aspects of the bar exam is studying material about which you have little interest, for example, studying an area of law from which you plan to stay far away. If you have had difficulty in understanding some subjects during your first year of law school, you will have even greater difficulty attempting to learn a subject for the first time while studying for the bar exam. For those in the top half of their law school class after the 1L year, taking bar courses for the sake of taking bar courses is useless. An occasional student in the top half of a graduating class will fail the bar, an event unusual enough that it is worthy of mention. Those students are at a minuscule risk of failing the bar exam. Take a bar course because you are interested in the topic. Students in the bottom quartile of their class are at risk of failing the bar exam (this, of course, will differ depending on what school and what bar examination we are speaking of). Those students should consider taking "core" bar courses even if they are uninterested in that area of law. Those students in the third quartile after their 1L year need to obtain counsel from the Office of Academic Support or a trusted professor to discuss what courses they should consider taking in their 2L year.

No one wants to take the bar examination more than once, and law schools are required by the ABA to assess and publish the first-time bar passage rate of their students. A number of studies have been done on bar passage, and law grade point average correlates most strongly with success or failure on first time bar exam attempts. That correlation is significant but not conclusive, for much of the reason(s) why a person fails the bar examination is unknown. Those who do very well in law school rarely fail the bar exam (note the "rarely," so it does happen). Most of those students who perform in the broad middle of the pack at any law school pass the bar exam, though there may be a few outliers in a state such as California, with its relatively modest overall bar exam passage rate. At stated above, those who graduate in the bottom quarter of their class struggle more with first-time bar examination success than those in the top three-quarters of the class (this differs also by state and particular law school, so please use just as a rule of thumb). If you find yourself in this position, you need to consider carefully how to manage your course work in the last two years of law school. Most law schools do not have formal advising systems for students. At the very least you should speak with either the Associate Dean for Student Affairs (or Associate Dean for Academic Affairs, for the naming of the position differs among law schools) or a trusted professor from your 1L year. When asked, faculty will give frank and (usually) sound advice about courses (and sometimes professors) to take, to avoid, to consider.

Several years ago the ABA permitted law schools to offer bar preparation courses for credit. For most students this course is unnecessary. Those who have struggled in law school should take such a class if offered. This is not, of course, a substitute for a formal bar preparation course. It can, however, give the student some insight into the student's strengths and weaknesses in studying and exam taking. Most such courses require students to complete weekly or biweekly assignments, so one should not take this course assuming you will learn passively.

Foundation and Capstone Courses

Some law schools divide their upper level curriculum into foundation (basic) and capstone (advanced or final) courses. Foundation courses include Business Associations (or Corporations and Partnerships), Uniform Commercial Code courses (Commercial Paper/Payment Systems, Secured Transactions, Sales), Evidence, Family Law, Constitutional Criminal Procedure, Professional Responsibility, Federal Income Tax and Administrative Law, nearly all of which are also bar courses. Whether a law school requires its students to take Evidence or any other upper level course other than Professional Responsibility is entirely up to the law school. Schools differ markedly in the extent to which they will require students to take upper level courses. Capstone courses, for which you may be eligible only upon completion of a foundation course in the subject, may include courses such as Advanced Federal Criminal Procedure, Estate and Gift Tax, Scientific and Expert Evidence and similar courses. The extent to which you follow the broad path of taking foundation courses in your second year and then selected capstone courses in your third year will depend on what upper level courses your law school requires, your level of concern about the bar exam (the greater your level of concern, the more you should take courses that are likely to be tested on the bar exam, many of which are foundation courses), and your interest in a particular field of law (for example, an intense interest in practicing environmental law may leave you fewer opportunities to take some foundation courses). In making your decision about which courses to take, your level of concern about the bar exam must be weighed carefully against your interest in a particular field of law. For example, if you have a deep interest in water law, its absence from the list of subjects tested on the bar exam should not affect your decision to take the course. In other words, do not let the specter of the bar exam cause you to avoid non-bar courses in which you are interested.

One value in taking most of the available foundation courses in your 2L year is the surprising interest you may find in subjects that appeared boring or unduly complex. A course in Constitutional Criminal Procedure may awaken an interest in litigation, criminal defense or white collar crime. A course in Federal Income Tax may generate an interest in administrative law or transactional work. Taking these foundational courses early will allow you to pursue some advanced courses in those areas in your 3L year.

If you have a sound idea of what you want to do in the practice of law after the completion of your 1L year, you are a member of a happy minority. You can look closely at the structure of course offerings in that area and related areas, and consider how these courses will assist you in gaining the skills and knowledge necessary to practice.

Upper Level Writing

ABA-approved law schools are required to provide students with an upper level writing opportunity. The ABA does not specify the type of writing other than it must a "rigorous" writing experience. Most schools have adopted some form of research paper as the paradigmatic upper level writing experience. The research paper requires a student to evaluate some aspect of law (doctrine, policy or history), necessitating the student's discovery and evaluation of numerous sources. In most research papers, some of the sources found by the student are likely to conflict. The following offers some thoughts on how to organize and structure such a paper.

Your first decision is to find a topic about which to research and write. Occasionally your interest in a topic may result from a brief comment in an excerpted case discussed in your first year, or as a result of reading a footnote in a law review article. You may even want to learn more about a doctrine or policy after thinking about it. As a general matter, begin broadly and work your way more narrowly to your topic. Three ways to avoid writing a "survey" of your topic, which will either be completely derivative or fail to scratch beyond the surface of the topic, are 1) limit the specific issue discussed (that is, move from a study of negligence to a study of accidents to a study of accidents of airplanes to a study of private airplane crashes to a study of the economic impact, if any, of negligence law on private airplane manufacturing), 2) limit the geographic scope of your study, by focusing on the law in one state or region, or comparing the law in two different states, and 3) limit the time frame of your study, avoiding a recitation of the origins of the doctrine or policy in favor of stating the issue in the present.

Once you decide on a topic, you need to research that topic thoroughly. Some students believe that once they find a book or article relevant to their topic, they are finished researching in that area. That is never the case. Different books and law review articles have very different emphases, and parroting the conclusion (or premises) of one book makes it appear that you are simply putting into your relatively short research paper what the author needed an entire book or long law review article to do. Professors grade research papers in part by assessing the depth of research undertaken by the student. An overabundant use of one book or a few law review articles as your complete sources for any particular part of your paper exhibits poor research. The result of such use is a succession of "Id." citations. Occasionally a student will look at the cascade of "Id." citations and decide to throw in the complete citation to the work instead of using "Id." This "trick" is not only incorrect as a matter of proper citation form, but your professor will notice it and become very annoyed. One way to avoid this problem is to demand of yourself that you have a minimum of twenty-five sources, of which 50% must be primary sources (cases, statutes, administrative regulations).

After you have enmeshed yourself in your research you can begin thinking about how to construct your paper. You do not have to complete your research in order to begin writing, or complete an outline before you begin writing. For some, writing focuses the student more clearly on the goal of the paper, giving the student a better sense of what research is incomplete. For others an outline is not only inconvenient but unhelpful. For most, however, an outline provides the student with a way to chart the path your research paper will take. That outline will evolve as you begin to write and complete your research, but should work as a blueprint for your paper. When you begin writing you should consider using headings and subheadings (either with or without titles as you prefer) in the paper, headings based on your outline. The advantage of using section and subsection headings within a paper is that it forces you to make sure you take each step in its proper order. This should provide greater coherence, consistency and clarity to your paper.

Include in your introduction some detail explaining the goals and theme(s) of your paper. For example, "The goal of this paper is to assess the development of products liability law in Texas from 1970–2000. Part II of this paper evaluates the general origins of tort law in American jurisprudence since 1945. Part III examines how changes in civil procedure affected the development of theories of negligence, and then discusses how changes in the legal profession in the last third of the twentieth century drove the expansion in products liability lawsuits. Part IV specifically addresses the development of products liability law in Texas, and compares Texas law with products liability law in the rest of the United States during the last three decades of the twentieth century. Part V suggests why Texas law differed in several respects from the law extant in most of the rest of the states, and Part VI offers a brief conclusion."

A paper should go through at least two drafts before it is turned in. The first draft may be a partial draft, one that sketches the argument made in the paper but which is incompletely researched or organized. The second draft should be the student's best effort, one ready for the faculty member to provide an initial assessment. Unless you are uncommonly thorough in your research aided by a facility with the written word, it is likely that this second draft will be lacking in some fashion. The value of having your professor comment on this draft is for you to become more self-critical, a necessary trait for one to succeed in the practice of law.

Use a topic sentence introducing the subject of the paragraph at the beginning of each paragraph. This will aid you in organizing each paragraph. Short, tightly worded sentences are better than long, meandering sentences. If the topic of the paragraph is complex or complicated, you will find it easy to continue that paragraph for a page or more. Try to avoid this problem, largely by thinking closely about the most important point of the paragraph. Once that point is made, move on to a new paragraph, which may continue to discuss another aspect of the broader topic.

In writing a legal research paper, you should be aware of and follow the conventions of this type of paper. For example, when the full name of a case is mentioned in the text the first time, it must be footnoted by the end of the sentence and the citation to the case (but not the name of the case) is placed in the footnote. No citation of a case is ever put in the text of a research paper. This differs from an appellate brief, in which the full citation to a case or article is given in the body of the paper. You should also italicize the case name in the body of the paper.

When completing a quotation at the end of a sentence, put the close quotation mark after the period in the sentence, not before (thus, "... date." And not "… date".) The same is generally true of quotations and commas (first comma, then close quotation mark). Footnotes are also placed after a period or comma, not before, and there is no space between the period and the footnote number.

If you are quoting something that is more than fifty (50) words in length, the quote must be placed in a separate paragraph and indented on both left and right sides. This is called a block quote.

When you have cited a case, and cite it again in the next footnote, law school research papers use "Id." for that second citation, not "Ibid.", which is commonly used in the social science field. Thus, if the first footnote reads, "*Stein*, 435 F. Supp. 2d at 336–37," the following footnote, which also cites *United States v. Stein*, should read "*Id.* at 338."

Know the difference between plural and possessive. "Many Americans think" (plural), "One American's view" (possessive). Know what plural possessive is ("The professors' argument concerned …").

When speaking of persons, use "who" or "whom," not "that." When speaking of things or ideas, use "that" or "which" (or occasionally "whose") as appropriate.

Never use "feel" as a verb. Use "believe," "think," "conclude," or other similar word. Never use "impact" as a verb. Use "affect." Don't write, "The decision impacted a wide range of concerns." Write either "The decision affected a wide range of concerns," or "The decision had a tremendous impact."

Know the difference between "imply" and "infer." The party that implies is the speaker. The party that infers is the listener. Thus, "The professor implied that the exam would test only material discussed in the last half of the semester," and "The student inferred the exam would test material discussed during the entire semester," not "The professor inferred" or "The student implied."

Avoid passive voice (*e.g.*, "It is said" or "an idea believed to be important"). Use active verbs and active voice (*e.g.* "Several scholars argue" or "I believe"). Use "The court concluded," not "The court came to the conclusion that".

Avoid redundancy, saying the same thing over and over. If you repeat yourself, simply by writing the same thing you've already written, you're saying it over and over. Avoid redundancy.

Avoid run on sentences, which go on and on, using commas, semi-colons, and other signaling devices, but which refuse to use a period, which would end the sentence, and which would make the sentence much clearer and more powerful, and would allow the writer to move on to another sentence.

Avoid trite comments, such as "*Brown v. Board of Education* was an important case if ever there was one."

Avoid surplus clauses in sentences, such as "*Brown v. Board of Education*, which was a civil rights case that ended 'separate but equal,' but which did not have an immediate impact, and which applied only in *de jure* segregated states, was the biggest case decided by the Supreme Court in years."

When using two or more verbs in a sentence, keep those verbs parallel in tense (e.g., "I *swam*, and then *ran* home," not "I *swam*, and then *was running* home.")

When using the words "it" or "they," make sure you have a clear antecedent to which "it" or "they" applies. For example, "The institute concluded that welfare policy remains unsettled. It worked to support changes in culture as well as income." Does "it" in the second sentence refer to the "institute" or to "welfare policy"? It's unclear.

Avoid "utilize." Use "use."

Avoid "in that," a form of classic lawyer jargon (along with "party of the first part"). Use "because." Do not write, "The constitutional crisis of 1937 remains important less in that what really happened and more because the subsequent explanations and analyses of the crisis tell us much about our desire to shape the past for use in the present." Use "The constitutional crisis of 1937 remains important less because of what really happened and more because the subsequent explanations and analyses of the crisis tell us much about our desire to shape the past for use in the present." Relatedly and technically, if you are speaking in the context of a subsequent time frame, use "since" rather than because. For example, "The Model Rules have since been amended as a result of the work of the ABA's Ethics 2000 Commission."

"Where" concerns a geographical location, not a situation. When discussing an event or situation, use "which" or "in which." "Courts were faced with a situation which required immediate action." Do not write, "Courts were faced with a situation where it was required to take immediate action."

In the text, never use "U.S." Always write "United States," or use "America" or "American."

"Between" means 2 persons or things; "among" is used when speaking of 3 or more.

"Further" means additionally or also. "Farther" means a distance away from someone or something.

"Find" is the verb usually used to describe court decisions concerning facts. "Hold" is used in regard to determinations of law by a court. "The court held the first amendment inapplicable." "The court found the statement was not directed toward the plaintiff."

Never begin a sentence with "Also." And, unless you are a very good writer, never begin a sentence with "And."

When discussing a court, it is never capitalized unless 1) you are speaking of the Supreme Court of the United States, or 2) you are using the full name of a court (*e.g.*, Supreme Court of Texas, United States District Court for the

Western District of Wisconsin). The correct phrasing is "Supreme Court of the United States," not "United States Supreme Court." If you use the shorthand phrase "Supreme Court" without any antecedent, that means you are referring to the Supreme Court of the United States, not the Supreme Court of a state.

"Congress," "court," "United States," and "corporation," are all singular, so use "it," not "they." "They" is reserved for more than one entity.

The words "more" and "less" are comparative, so if you use them, you have to compare the "more" or "less" with something else. For example, "The cases were more about policy disagreements than about the parties themselves," not "It is more difficult to win such cases in Wisconsin." (You need to add something like, "than in Texas.")

In general, avoid Latin words or phrases when English words will do. Avoid "via." Use "through" or "because" or "due to." Also avoid "per." Unless you are using it in conjunction with "de jure" (usually when discussing issues of racial discrimination), avoid using "de facto." Avoid "ipso facto." Use "therefore" or "thus" or "consequently." Also avoid "i.e." ("in other words"), "e.g." ("for example") in the text (you can use "e.g." in footnotes or parentheticals, e.g., "See, e.g.," as a signal stating, "see, for example,"). Phrases such as *res ipsa loquitur*, on the other hand, have a clear meaning in law, and using the Latin phrase is not only permissible but expected.

Use "it's" only as a contraction of "it is." Use "its" for all other cases. Correct: "It's about time I graduated." Incorrect: "The school was pleased with it's graduates." (Should be "its.")

Avoid "etc." in papers.

Make sure you use "like," "including" and "such as" correctly. Do not use "like" as a substitute for the other two. "Like" means similar to but not the same as something. "Such as" is an example of a certain type or kind. "Including" is an example of one of a type, as part of the event or action described. So, "the development of contract law was like the development of tort law." So, "the development of tort law, including the development of negligence law, followed an instrumentalist trend." So, "the development of tort law created a need for professionals such as doctors to testify as experts."

Know the difference between "enormity" and "enormous," "infamous" and "famous" and "notorious" and "well known." To be called the former in each pairing is really bad (enormity usually refers to events rather than people, but you get the idea). Too often writers use enormity when they mean "immensity." Use "The immensity of the damage caused by the flood astonished later visitors to the area," not "The enormity of the changes to his life that occurred after the divorce astonished him." "Carl was a well known businessman," not

"Carl was a notorious businessman" (unless Carl was defrauding those with whom he did business).

Know the difference between "uninterested" and "disinterested." Disinterested means neutral or impartial. A good judge is disinterested. Uninterested means you don't care about the difference between uninterested and disinterested. An uninterested judge is a bad judge.

Understand the difference between "flout" and "flaunt." To flout is to disregard, and is often used in conjunction with "rules." "Dave flouted the rules of etiquette," or "Dave flouted the rules of advocacy in the courtroom." To flaunt is to show off something.

The words "mete" and "metes" are used in law in two very different senses. "Mete" is ordinarily used accompanying the words "out" and "punishment." It is ordinarily used in the criminal law context, and means issued or undertaken. "The jury decided to mete out punishment to those ringleaders of the conspiracy." The word "metes" is ordinarily used in property law and is part of the phrase "metes and bounds." "Metes and bounds" refers to boundary lines of real property and is a type of measurement.

The following words are often used in legal writing. Know the difference between:

"affect" and "effect"
"allude" and "elude"
"canon" and "cannon"
"cite," "site" and "sight"
"complement" and "compliment"
"counsel" and "council"
"disperse" and "disburse"
"dissent" and "descent"
"eminent," "imminent" and "immanent"
"hale" and "hail"
"imprudent" and "impudent"
"peak" and "pique"
"phase" and "faze"
"precedent" or "precedents" and "precedence" (and not "presidents")
"principle" and "principal"
"rational" and "rationale"
"reign", "rein," and "rain"
"role" and "roll"
"staunch" and "stanch"
"tenet" and "tenant"

"then" and "than"
"there," "their" and "they're"
"versus" and "verses"
"wary" and "weary"

If you're not sure which word is correct, look it up, or use another word.

Clinic

A substantial majority of law schools host one or more legal clinics in which students perform legal work for clients under the supervision of a clinical professor for which they receive academic credit. Clinical professors are full-time professors who teach students the basics of the practice of law. Most clinics exist to serve the legal needs of the poor, both because that is a worthy cause and because law school clinics do not want to be perceived as taking business from the practicing bar. Clinics are both litigation-based and transactional, and may be divided by subject (civil, criminal, immigration) or by focus (litigation or transactional). Many state bars have created a student bar card available to law students who have completed two years of law school. Those students who have obtained a student bar card are permitted to act as counsel in court as long as they are supervised by an attorney licensed in the state. When the student serves as counsel, the job of the attorney-supervisor is usually to ensure the students avoid committing legal malpractice. Interviewing the client, investigating the claim, preparing the case and advocating in court for the client are the responsibilities of clinic students. If the state in which your law school is located has a student bar card program, it will make much more sense to take clinic in your 3L year than in your 2L year. Because the cost of clinic classes is much higher than the cost of classroom classes (the student-teacher ratio in clinics is much lower than it is for most upper level classes, thus costing more), most schools will limit students to one clinic experience. Consider carefully what your goals are in clinic. Is it to learn how to interview a client, how to prepare legal documents, how to examine witnesses in court, or how to construct a case file or document file? Who are the clients served by the clinic? How many hours are you expected to spend at the offices of the clinic each week? How are students assigned matters? How often do you work alone or with another student with clients? Finally, how are students graded?

A student who takes a clinic course will usually gain tremendous experience. Of course, the student interested in trying cases may learn that, despite his or her best efforts, the cases assigned to the student settled. Clients may disappear, postponements may mean next semester's clinic students will finish the work you began, and despite your best efforts you may not be able to assist a client with real legal needs. As a small slice of the practice of law, clinic offers those students who learn best by doing a dramatic change from the classroom. Clinic experiences are usually quite demanding, and most students will take a slightly lesser course load when they are in the clinic than in other semesters. Clinic work will also limit the student's ability to work part-time or to engage in law review or other co-curricular activities, so consider your interest in other aspects of law school when deciding whether to take a clinic course.

Overall, the benefits gained from clinic experience substantially outweigh its costs. Even if you are uninterested in litigation you may find a litigation clinic experience valuable, if only to reassure yourself that this career path is not for you. Taking a clinic course may give you the rare opportunity to both give and receive, to serve others who would not otherwise have access to legal counsel while learning how to practice law. Few opportunities are better for law students than clinic.

Concentration

ABA-approved law schools are not permitted to create "majors" for their J.D. law students. (If you take an LL.M. degree after your J.D., it usually is a degree in a specialized area such as tax.) Schools are, however, permitted to create areas of "concentration," and a student may be awarded a certificate of concentration in addition to a diploma. Should you consider a concentration?

For most students the answer is no. A formal concentration has little value in the job market. You can signal your interest in a particular area of law by taking several courses in that subject; a formal concentration is not necessary to demonstrate your interest to possible employers. If you are considering sole practice or work in a small (2–10 persons) firm, a concentration may be helpful but is certainly not necessary for you to understand some of the intricacies of that line of work. Further, a concentration may hem you in should you later decide to move to another area of practice. Finally, no matter how well prepared you may be through your class work, you will find you have much still to learn about this practice area.

For a few students a concentration makes sense. Second-career students may have definite ideas about what law they wish to practice. Others may use the concentration as a substitute for the LL.M., giving the student the opportunity to delve into the specialized area without paying the opportunity cost of an additional year in law school. Finally, the law school may have established a sufficient reputation in this field to make a concentration from that school valued in the legal community.

Joint Degree Programs

Should you obtain two degrees while in law school, a master's and a law degree? For most law students the answer is no. However, a substantial minority of law students may find entering a joint degree program makes great sense. Most universities require the law student to apply separately to the master's degree program and most law schools require the joint degree student to complete his or her first year of law school before beginning the master's program. The advantage of a joint degree is its efficiency. For example, instead of spending two years in a graduate M.B.A. program and three years in law school, a student obtaining a J.D./M.B.A. will usually spend just four years to receive both degrees. Further, instead of taking all the hours required if the student took the degrees separately, some hours in the graduate program will count as law school credit hours and vice versa, reducing the overall cost of the degrees.

From a financial standpoint the best choice is taking an M.B.A. in addition to a J.D. A master's in business administration allows you the opportunity to understand more fully the needs of future business clients should you practice law. It will give you a different lens through which you can assess how the legal interests of a business fit its business needs. It may lead you to decide to use your joint degrees in business rather than in the private practice of law. The "case method" or "case studies" approach found in many business schools, in which students learn how past events or crises were handled by business executives in order to consider how to manage similar crises in the future, will appear familiar to anyone who has spent a year in law school. In most schools obtaining an M.B.A. will add a year to your professional schooling, so you need to evaluate whether this additional time in school is more valuable than beginning your career as a lawyer.

The increased importance in health law may make it useful to enroll in a master's in public health program, and globalization may make taking a master's degree in international relations valuable. Some law schools offer law students the chance to earn a master's in government or public policy, and a few offer a master's in engineering. Each of these degrees can be very useful in gaining additional knowledge and enhancing the student's marketability, whether the student practices law or enters the field in which the master's is received.

Some students enter a joint degree program not for its financial value but because it is important to their own development. Some schools offer joint degree programs in theology, philosophy, history or literature. Most who take a master's in the humanities (or theology) will not improve their financial prospects. It may, however, allow them to avoid the ennui or cynicism found in some who practice law. Such joint degree graduates may use their "other" degree to invest themselves in the practice of law with a commitment and understanding that will make their work enjoyable and fulfilling.

If obtaining a master's degree is for a limited subset of students, obtaining a Ph.D. should be undertaken only by a very few law students. Only those students who are interested in research and teaching, either in law schools, the university or in a think tank that works on public policy matters, should consider enrolling in a joint J.D./Ph.D. program. The length of time to complete most Ph.D. programs makes it likely you will spend somewhere between six and ten years obtaining both degrees. If a joint degree program consistently takes just five years the investment in time and money may be worthwhile. Once the student is at seven or more years to obtain both degrees the costs seem to outweigh the benefits.

Law Review

One co-curricular opportunity for law students that many outside the legal profession have heard about is law review. When law review was invitation-only to the highest ranking students in the 1L class, membership on the law review connoted status, which often resulted in more employment options for one's future legal career. Law review membership is today gained less often from invitations based on solely on 1L grades than from invitations based on successful completion of a writing competition open to all rising 2L students, or an invitation based on a writing competition combined with 1L grades. Few law reviews invite students based solely on grades. The writing competition often takes place immediately after the conclusion of the 1L exam schedule. You are likely to be tired of law study. You may be working. You may think the subject of the writing competition is stupid and you may ask, is law review worth it? For most students the answer is still yes, but the reasons for its value will differ among students.

Membership in law review still connotes a favored status distinguishing you from your classmates who are not members of the law review. It is a signal to law firms of student success and, just as importantly, student ambition. Membership in a law review will not make up for modest grades, particularly if the law review does not have a stringent selection policy. However, membership in a selective law review is the next best thing to excellent grades in signaling your talent to hiring law firms.

Should you choose (or be invited) to join the law review, you will learn in your 2L year how to choose a topic on which to write, how to write a law review note or comment (a note and a comment can technically differ, but in most law reviews the title is interchangeable), and how to become self-critical in editing your own writing. You will learn how to meet deadlines, sometimes arbitrary deadlines, on your note or other assignment you've been given. You will learn how to cite authorities (cases, books, other law review articles) correctly according the Blue Book (most law reviews) or the Maroon Book (some law reviews). You will learn how to assess the structure of someone else's paper. You will learn many formal rules concerning law review writing, some of which will have little or no perceptible value. You will add your membership on law review to your resume, and use it to your benefit in interviewing for summer work in between your 2L and 3L years and afterward. And you will have to learn how to play with others, including 3L editors whose assignments for you may seem (and actually be) silly, and 2Ls who may be jockeying with you for a position the following year on the editorial board.

Around February of your 2L year the editorial board for the next volume of the law review is named. If you are selected as an editor, you will further distinguish yourself to future employers. Whether you are an editor-in-chief or notes and comments editor makes little difference to employers. An editor-in-chief and executive editor have the most extensive managerial tasks, and usually the fewest editing tasks. Note and comment editors have both editorial responsibilities, particularly for those notes and comments chosen for publication, and managerial responsibilities, supervising the production process for the 2L students writing notes and comments. Those editors will also supervise the work of associate editors who have the responsibility of shepherding notes and comments and recent developments to completion.

It is a coup to have your note or comment (or recent development, if such exist at your school's law review) published. This accomplishment should not, however, be overstated. Employers are unlikely to make any distinction among candidates based on whether one was published. This reticence among employers may be a result of the fact that American law reviews are largely student-edited. The editors are indeed bright persons, but no employer is likely to defer to the publishing decisions of student editors in determining which applicants will be hired. Traditionally the early hiring season (fall of the 2L year for summer jobs that may lead to permanent positions) and the later publication decision period (usually late in the fall or early in the spring semester) meant law firms hired students for summer work (which might be parlayed into an offer for a permanent position) without knowing whether the person's note or comment would be published.

"Primary" and "Secondary" Law Reviews

Most law schools have an eponymously named law review, the first law review published by the law school. This "first in time" law review is often known as the "primary" law review. Most law schools now publish more than one law review. The "other" law reviews published are sometimes grouped as "secondary" law reviews. Is there a significant difference in the respect accorded to membership on the different law reviews? Some difference exists in the prestige attached to different law reviews. The extent of that difference is difficult to judge, but it may relate in part to 1) the manner in which membership is attained in the secondary review, including its selectivity, 2) the impact of the secondary review in the relevant legal community, and 3) the purpose of the secondary law review.

Membership in a secondary law review is often much less stringent than membership in the primary law review. The looser or less selective the membership requirements, the less prestigious the secondary law review will be perceived by most private law firm employers. The impact of a secondary law review can often be quite substantial, which will enhance its reputation, which has a positive cascading effect on those students who are members of that law review. Impact is assessed by citation counts, both citation counts in courts and citation counts in other law reviews. That is, the more times the appellate courts or other law reviews cite an article published in the secondary law review, the more impact it is perceived as having. Several law reviews regularly publish these citation numbers, giving interested employers a simple though not necessarily accurate way of assigning a value to your participation in this journal. Finally, most secondary law reviews have a specific purpose or justification, unlike the primary law review, which ostensibly publishes articles on all types of legal topics. That specific purpose may be international law, criminal law or dispute resolution. The better the reputation of the secondary journal within that specialized field of law, including its reputation among legal academics who specialize in those areas, the more valuable your membership will be from an employment standpoint.

From the standpoint of experience, no difference is likely to exist in the management and operation of any student-edited law review. You will still learn much about how to organize your thoughts coherently in written form, how to read your prose critically (in part by reading the prose of others), and how to play well with others, an important feature of any good law firm. Consequently, if your desire to work on the primary law review at your law school will not be fulfilled, you should join the secondary law review.

Moot Court/Mock Trial

You likely had some experience in moot court as a 1L as part of your legal research and writing experience. If you find this of interest, you will find an entire world of moot court and mock trial competitions that take place regionally and nationally. Some law schools take very seriously their moot court and mock trial programs as exemplifying the litigation focus in the curriculum. Should you consider competing for a spot on the moot court or mock trial teams?

First, definitions. Moot court concerns appellate arguments. Lawyers regularly "moot" their appellate arguments before groups of lawyers who act as judges, and lawyers always do so if they will be arguing before the Supreme Court of the United States. To "moot" in this context is to practice, and moot court began as a type of practice for law students in making legal arguments based on hypothetical cases. These practice sessions were organized by clubs within the schools, and, as you might expect, the competitive urges of the mostly male student body led to competitions between the clubs. These intra-school competitions eventually became inter-law school competitions. In moot court competitions two lawyers argue for each side. The hypothetical case is usually divided into two legal issues, giving each student a chance to argue. The teams will be randomly assigned their client, so in a competition they will represent both the appellant/petitioner and appellee/respondent. Moot court competitions may in preliminary rounds use one judge, but the preference is for three judges to hear the arguments (one acting as chief judge), who then vote on which team has presented the best argument (ostensibly without regard to the substantive legal issues, though that is easier said than done), and which advocate is the "best advocate." In moot court competitions the team also drafts a brief that is separately submitted and judged. A third member of the team is usually responsible for the bulk of the appellate brief, and a "best brief" award is also given at most competitions.

"Mock trial" concerns trials, from opening statement through closing argument. The "mock" part of mock trial is the formal and highly stylized nature of this trial. Two students represent each party. Two witnesses are called by each side, including the party, giving each lawyer one opportunity to engage in a direct examination and one chance to cross-examine a witness. One of the two lawyers gives the opening statement and the other gives the closing argument. The students are judged on their presentation skills, including their use of the rules of evidence and procedure. Again, the competition is judged on the skills of the students, not the substantive case, and a best advocate is usually named at the close of the tournament.

Moot court is considered more cerebral than mock trial, while in the latter lawyers use emotional appeals as well as rational arguments based on the rules of evidence and procedure. A number of law schools and legal organizations sponsor moot court and mock trial competitions, some of which are national in scope. National competitions require teams to qualify in regional competitions.

Should you join a moot court or mock trial team and, if so, which one? In short, yes, though not at the expense of law review and not if you have no desire to litigate. Further, if you must choose between moot court/mock trial and clinic experience, choose the latter, for the clients are actual persons with actual legal problems that you must attempt to resolve. The benefit of these competitions is actually doing the legal work you have looked at through the appellate opinion lens during your first year of law school. For those who wish to become litigators, the experience you gain in moot court or mock trial can be helpful in thinking about how litigation is conducted, though it is unlikely that you will be arguing before an appellate court immediately after law school. If you are considering working as a public defender or as an assistant district attorney, you may get to make a closing argument (probably in a misdemeanor case, not a felony) in your first year or two of practice, and your experience in mock trial may give you the confidence in your ability to question a witness during a deposition, argue a motion before trial and even try a case. Neither moot court nor mock trial is a substitute for experience, and the stylized nature of these competitions makes the analogy to the practice of law strained. But those competitions can have a value that makes them worthwhile.

Part-Time Work

Should you work at a law firm or government agency during your 2L and 3L years? For most students at most schools, work experience benefits students in several ways. First, it gives students a sense of the work this lawyer (and this type of lawyer) does on a daily basis. This experience, for good or ill, gives the student some insight into some law work. If the experience is good, the student can use what he or she has learned in subsequent work. If the experience is poor, the student has learned what (or who) to avoid in the practice of law. Second, it may lead to permanent employment. Smaller firms do not have the resources to interview students at law schools. More importantly, smaller law firms are quite cautious about new hires, and having a familiarity with the student who worked as a part-time law clerk makes it much easier for those lawyers to take the large step of hiring a new associate. In some places students with experience will be given preference for any open assistant district attorney positions. Third, part-time work forces you to use your time more wisely. As a 1L you may have been overwhelmed by the assignments given you. As a 2L or 3L those assignments have become much less daunting, especially if your teachers no longer call on students randomly to recite in class. If you are spending a considerable amount of time on law review or moot court/mock trial, part-time work may not be an option, but most students will find that they have sufficient time to take on some part-time work. Fourth, part-time work provides students with some slight financial cushion, making the cost of legal education slightly more bearable.

If you are going to work, how many hours a week should you work? Some part-time or evening division students work forty hours a week and take ten credit hours each semester. Such a schedule is not recommended. Even working twenty hours a week is a substantial commitment. It means working four hours per day for each work day, which means 8–noon or 1–5 p.m. Including commuting time, that means something around twenty-two to twenty-five hours per week. For full-time students the ABA limits part-time work to a maximum of twenty hours per week (how the ABA enforces this rule through law schools is another question). If you are working twenty hours a week (plus commuting time), taking fifteen credit hours each semester (or about ten hours per quarter), and spending just one hour to prepare for each hour of class (and that's not very much), that means you are committed for about fifty-five hours (15 plus 15 plus 25) each week. This is not unreasonable, but it requires a maturity and focus to accomplish. Further, studying just one hour for each hour of class is, for most students, insufficient. It makes little sense to sacrifice your grades in pursuit of your first job, for most graduates will not make a career at their first job outside of law school. Organize your schedule before you begin to work part-time.

A second option for part-time work is as a research assistant or tutor for a professor. Research assistants typically work between ten and fifteen hours per week, and no commuting is required. The job varies by professor, but many will want their research cite checked, somewhat tedious work that is not likely to be of great interest. Others may want the research assistant to create a compendium of sources on the subject the professor is researching. Finally, some may ask that you undertake some specific research projects and write memoranda regarding those assignments, something that may be of great interest and long-term value in honing your writing skills. If you do your job well you will gain an academic reference who will know you outside of the confines of a class. This academic reference will likely serve you well not only for your first job but for subsequent employment.

Many schools now hire 2L and 3L students to serve as tutors for 1L students. These tutors usually attend each meeting of the course in, for example, contracts, and then meet one hour per week with a group of students (usually self-selected but not always) who have some need or desire for additional information on the material. The tutor will work with the professor on how this weekly session with students should be structured (after all, neither the professor nor the tutor has any interest in having the tutor re-teach the material), whether that means using additional hypotheticals, helping students organize an outline, or having students evaluate sample responses to possible exam questions. The student not only makes some money and gets to know the professor, but learns the 1L course material much more thoroughly the second time around, material will be tested on the bar exam.

Transferring?

The decision regarding which law school to attend was once final as soon as the student entered law school. Very few students were permitted to transfer to another law school after their first year. One of the most well-known cases in which a student transferred is the case of Supreme Court Justice Ruth Bader Ginsburg. Justice Ginsburg spent her first two years at Harvard Law School. Her husband graduated before her from Harvard. He took a job in New York City. She transferred to Columbia Law School for her third year. Despite having matriculated at Columbia for just one year, Justice Ginsburg received her law degree from Columbia.

The case of Ruth Bader Ginsburg was and is quite unusual. Occasionally law schools would allow a student to spend a year away for family reasons as a "transient" student, but the host law school ordinarily had no interest in taking the visiting student as a transfer student. The visiting student would still receive his or her degree from the law school at which that student spent two years.

About fifteen years ago, the reticence among law schools to accept transfer students began to change. The reason for this change appears linked almost wholly to the *Annual Guide to American Law Schools* published by *U.S. News*

& World Report. One of the ways in which *U.S. News* ranked law schools was by the median LSAT score of the schools entering students. This emphasis on LSAT score made some law schools lean even more heavily on LSAT scores in admitting students, even at the expense of undergraduate grade point average. As you might expect with a tool as blunt as the LSAT, a number of law students with good but not excellent LSAT scores achieved superb grades during their 1L year. Some law schools listed in the first-tier of *U.S. News Annual Guide* tried to "game" the system by reducing the number of students admitted to the 1L class, thus possibly increasing its median LSAT score (later the *Annual Guide* went to LSAT scores at the 75th/25th percentiles because law schools gamed the median LSAT score). The lost revenue from these "missing" 1L students was made up by accepting as transfer students those students (who often spent their first year at law schools ranked in the second or lower tier by *U.S. News*) who performed very well in terms of grades but who did not have high LSAT scores. Those accepted transfer students did not count in the calculation of median LSAT scores given to *U.S. News* because they were not 1L students but 2L students. However, their initial success in law school made them very good bets to become good lawyers (and certainly highly likely to pass any bar exam), so the risk of admitting the student as a transfer was minimal, while the reward to the law school (admitting students who were talented, usually hard-working, grateful to be allowed to transfer to first tier law school and thus maybe a future donor?) was great.

A number of law schools now allow students to transfer in after the completion of their first year of law school. If you performed well at a "lower" tier law school, should you transfer to a first-tier law school after your 1L year? The answer depends on how you evaluate the opportunity costs that exist if you make such a move. First, if you are performing very well at your current school, you may have the opportunity to receive scholarship awards that may cover most or all of your tuition. Any school to which you may transfer will not give you any scholarship monies. They are giving you the opportunity to use the "brand" value of the school (especially in comparison with your current law school) to enhance your employment chances with a large law firm. Thus the difference in tuition may be considerable. Second, you are unlikely to be allowed to join the primary law review at the recipient school. At your current law school you are likely a shoo-in for membership. You may be able to join a secondary law review at the school to which you transfer (find out before you move), and that secondary journal may be very good. Third, when interviewing season arrives, you may be slightly disadvantaged compared with your fellow 2L students at the new school. You will have no grades from the school to which you have transferred. You will have excellent grades from your 1L school, but whether that will be sufficient for employers visiting your new law school to interview you is unclear. At your current law school, you will be eligible to interview with any employer. Fourth, if your current school and the one to which you may transfer are distant, you have to decide, does geography matter? If the school to which you may transfer is a national law school, then one reason to transfer is to assess the possibilities of moving to very different locations within the United States. Fifth, if you are interested in a judicial clerkship, you will have one semester's worth of grades at your new school to show any judge who may interview you, for most judges interview and hire in the spring. (Efforts are underway to change the interviewing and hiring process to some time in the 3L year, but you should not count on that happening.) Will that be enough? If your grades are very good, probably. If they are average for the school, probably not. Sixth, if you transfer will you be able to enroll in the courses that interest you? Registration for courses takes place each spring for the following fall semester. You will be admitted sometime during the summer, so you will need to find out how registration will work for transfer students. Seventh, you will lose a set of friends with whom you had in common your 1L experience and make a new set of friends with whom you have no experience.

For students interested in entering law teaching, transferring to a higher ranked law school (that is, in the upper half of the first tier) makes sense. Law school hiring is elitist (this is a descriptive statement, not a prescriptive statement), and the higher the "rank" or reputation of the law school from which you received a J.D., the better your chances of obtaining a teaching job. You may be able to "wash" your J.D. degree by obtaining an LL.M. from an elite law school, but that means spending another year and a significant amount of money (both in tuition and in lost income) in legal education. It is possible to obtain a tenure-track teaching if you finish in the top 5% (or better) at most law schools, but if you are from a regional law school you will have the burden of proving your competence (for example, by writing law review articles after graduation and by obtaining a prestigious judicial clerkship). A graduate of an elite law school is presumed to be competent to teach and research even if that graduate has not written law review articles since graduation and has not distinguished himself in any other way. None of the above is offered to suggest that elite law school graduates make better teachers and scholars than those who graduated from non-elite law schools. Too many examples exist that prove otherwise. But this perception, fueled by the fact that a significant number of current law professors graduated from a tiny sliver of law schools, often displaces the reality that judging the aptitude of an applicant for a teaching position is quite complex, certainly more complex than simply looking at the applicant's J.D. degree.

Part III

Getting On

Chapter 7

Studying For and
Passing the Bar Exam

You've graduated from law school![1] Now, on to the bar examination. The bar examination is a two- or three-day examination, depending on which state's exam you take. The bar examination passing rate varies widely among the states, from slightly under 50% in California to over 85% in Utah. Despite this apparent difference, you will find that the bar examination passing rate for first-time examinees is relatively high if you are a graduate of an ABA-approved law school. Further, nearly all graduates of an ABA-approved law school will pass a bar exam at some point, even if that test taker fails on the first attempt. As a general rule, passing the bar examination is not a test of intellectual talent. It is a test of endurance, in terms of the time spent sitting for the exam itself, but more importantly, in terms of the time spent preparing to take the bar exam. You should view the bar exam as an endurance event, training as you would for a physically exhausting event such as a marathon.

As stated above, the vast majority of bar exam applicants who graduated from an ABA-approved law school eventually pass the bar exam. If 80% of first-time test takers pass the bar on the first attempt, and the passing rate for repeat examinees is just 50%, then 90% (.5 multiplied by the remaining 20% equals 10%) will have passed by the second administration, and 95% (.5 multiplied by the remaining 10% equals 5%) by the third administration. But those who pass the bar exam on the second, third or later attempt have cost themselves a great deal of time in the practice of law, will have given themselves too

---

1. A few states permit students to take the bar exam before graduating. See Texas Board of Law Examiners, Rule III (a)(3), allowing students "in an approved law school" to take the Texas bar examination if the applicant has "satisf[ied] all requirements for graduation with a J.D. degree or its equivalent, except for not more than four semester hours or its equivalent in quarter hours; provided, however, that no person shall be licensed to practice law until graduation or satisfaction of all requirements for graduation, unless specifically excepted hereunder."

many anxious moments and will have foreclosed other work opportunities during this time. Further, the sheer tedium and terror in having to prepare for and take the bar exam a second or third time is not conducive to maximizing the applicant's chances of doing well on the exam. That is one reason why the passing rate of re-takers is substantially below the passing rate of those taking the examination for the first time. Thus, when looking at bar examination passing rates, it is important to differentiate between the overall passing rate (everyone), first-time passing rate and repeat test taker passing rate.

The key bar examination statistic is the percentage of *first-time* applicants who pass the bar examination. In the combined results for the February and July 2009 California bar examination, the overall percentage of applicants passing the bar was 49%. But first-time test takers taking the general bar examination passed at a combined rate of 66%, while repeat takers of the general bar exam passed at a rate of just 22.4%. First-time examinees who graduated from an ABA-approved school from California passed the July 2009 bar exam at a rate of 79.3%, while those who graduated from an ABA-approved law school from *outside* California passed at a 69.4% rate. Overall, 73.2% of the graduates of an ABA-approved law school passed the 2009 California bar on the first attempt, about a three in four rate of success, even though the overall passing rate for examinees in 2009 was below 50%. California's overall passing rate is lower than that of most states because California, unlike nearly any other state, permits graduates of law schools not approved by the ABA to take its bar exam. If you are a graduate of an ABA-approved law school, the likelihood is that the state in which you plan to take the bar exam will have a minimum first-time passing rate of 70%, and most states will have a higher first-time passing rate. In the July 2009 New York bar exam, the overall passing rate was 72%. But 80% of first-time test takers passed, and when the New York Board of Law Examiners looked only at graduates of ABA-approved law schools (thus excluding graduates of foreign law schools who are eligible to take the New York bar exam under certain conditions), the success rate of first-time examinees was 88.2%.

Consequently, for the vast majority of test takers, the bar examination is an annoying but modest and surmountable hurdle on your way to obtaining a license to practice law. This chapter shows you how to organize your time in studying for the bar exam. It also discusses by example how to succeed on the objective multiple choice exams, the Multistate Professional Responsibility Examination (MPRE) and the Multistate Bar Examination (MBE), discusses ways to draft answers to essay questions, and analyzes how to answer the assignment given in a Multistate Performance Test (MPT). It also offers suggestions about bar examination prep courses and some thoughts on the character and fitness requirements of boards of law examiners.

The History of the Bar Examination

Between the late 18th century and the Civil War (1861–65), the bar examination was designed more to introduce the applicant to local judges and lawyers than to test the applicant about his (almost always a him) knowledge of law. Part of this was due to the local nature of bar admissions. Each court maintained control of those who were permitted to practice before it, which made sense when travel was arduous and most lawyers practiced in a relatively small geographic area. By the time of the Civil War, although differences existed, most states had adopted a "good for one, good for all" system. A lawyer admitted in one court was permitted to practice in all courts in that state (and sometimes out-of-state as well), at least in all trial courts.

The examination used to assess the knowledge of the bar applicant before the Civil War was usually an oral examination, often sloppily given and poorly thought through. Abraham Lincoln was an occasional examiner, and his style of judging applicants was informal at best. An applicant to the Illinois bar was informed Lincoln would examine him at Lincoln's hotel room. When the applicant entered, he found Lincoln taking a bath. "He asked me in a desultory way the definition of a contract, and two or three fundamental questions, all of which I answered readily, and I thought, correctly. Beyond these meager inquiries … he asked nothing more. As he continued his toilet, he entertained me with recollections—many of them characteristically vivid and racy—of his early practice and the various incidents and adventures that attended his start in the profession. The whole proceeding was so unusual and queer, if not grotesque, that I was at a loss to determine whether I was really being examined at all."

In an era in which most bar applicants were trained as apprentices, bar examiners often found themselves questioning applicants wholly unprepared to practice law. A bar examiner in Vermont, finding two candidates "as ignorant as so many Hottentots, … told them that for them to attempt to practice law would be wicked, dangerous, and subject them to suits for malpractice." The applicants begged the examiner to reconsider, and he signed their certificates on the condition that they buy several particular law books and "immediately emigrate to some Western town."

Shortly after the end of the Civil War, courts began replacing the oral bar examination with a written examination. While the first written bar examinations predated the Civil War, the written bar examination arose as the Harvard Law School introduced its system of final examinations for each course, and the further requirement that the student successfully complete his first-year exams before being permitted to continue to the second year. Much of the justification for the creation of the written bar examination was to enhance the prestige of the legal profession.

A substantial number of courts before the Civil War admitted to the practice of law those few graduates of law schools without first requiring them to take a bar examination. This system was called the diploma privilege system. Practitioners reacted against the modern law school (begun at Harvard in 1870) by urging the abolition of the diploma privilege. As of 1890, the graduates of twenty-six different schools located in sixteen different states were granted the diploma privilege. Even though a majority of states adopted a mandatory written bar examination in the quarter-century after 1890, that requirement was waived for many law school graduates. As late as 1951, fifteen states used the diploma privilege to admit 12% of all applicants to the bar. Today, Wisconsin is the only state that still uses the diploma privilege. Graduates of the two law schools in the state (the University of Wisconsin and Marquette University), but not graduates of ABA-approved law schools located outside of Wisconsin, are admitted to the bar without first taking the bar examination, provided they have taken a series of courses mandated by the Wisconsin Board of Law Examiners.

Despite significant changes to the bar exam, discussed below, the bar exam remains the province of the states. A person who is licensed in Arkansas may practice law in Arkansas. If a client of the Arkansas lawyer has a case in Kansas, the Arkansas lawyer may litigate that case in Kansas only with the permission of the Kansas trial court (this is called *pro hac vice* admission, admission for this matter only). That court is not required to give its permission, and if it does not, the client of the Arkansas lawyer will need to hire a Kansas lawyer to litigate the matter. A lawyer is permitted to advise a client on any federal matter, but to litigate a case in federal court the lawyer must be a member of the bar of that district court or be admitted *pro hac vice*. Each federal district court has its own admissions rules, for the effort to create a national federal district court bar exam fell apart about a decade ago. Most federal district courts will permit a lawyer to litigate a matter even if the lawyer is not a member of the bar in the state in which the district court is located, though this is not a matter of right. Federal courts of appeals allow lawyers in any state to obtain a license to practice upon completing an application and paying the application fee. The Supreme Court of the United States only requires the lawyer be in good standing, have three years of experience and pay the application fee. Finally, some states (but not Florida or Hawaii) will allow experienced lawyers to obtain a license to practice law upon a showing of sufficient experience (this ranges from three to seven years). This is called admission by reciprocity, which means that the receiving state must have an agreement with the state where the lawyer initially practiced law.

The Rise of the NCBE and the Objective (and National) Exam

The creation of the National Conference of Bar Examiners (NCBE) helped lead to the end of the diploma privilege everywhere but Wisconsin. The NCBE is a creature of one of the American Bar Association's (ABA) oldest sections, the Section on Legal Education and Admissions to the Bar. In 1898, at a meeting of the Section on Legal Education, participants discussed creating an organization of state bar examiners. The Section on Legal Education approved the idea in 1900, but the organization was not created immediately. Indeed, it wasn't until 1931 that the NCBE was created.

By the middle of the 20th century, the written bar examination was a one or two-day test exclusively in the form of essays, usually written and graded by practicing lawyers. The difficulties of the practitioner-crafted essay examination included both issues of quality control in the questions, and the variety of grading standards used by the graders. The sheer number of examinees required the use of multiple graders, most of whom were already busy with full-time jobs. Even if the state's board of law examiners included a grading sheet, the subjectivity of grading led to the quest for an objective examination.

At the first meeting of the NCBE in 1931, its executive director urged bar examiners to work toward a national bar examination. After forty or so years, this idea came to fruition. The NCBE decided to offer a standardized test on traditional common law subjects in the 1960s. This exam, the Multistate Bar Examination (MBE), was first given in February 1972. The MBE consists of 200 multiple-choice questions, each with four (4) answers, on six subjects: Constitutional Law, Contracts, Criminal Law, Evidence, Property, and Torts. It is given in two three-hour increments, which means the applicant is required to answer 100 questions in each of the two three-hour sessions. (Thus, finishing early in the morning session does not give you a head start on the last 100 questions.) When the MBE was first offered, nearly all schools required their 1L students to take courses in Contracts, Criminal Law, Property and Torts. Many also required Constitutional Law in the first year. Those that didn't ordinarily required 2L or 3L students to take Constitutional Law. All schools offered Evidence, and most required students to take the course as a condition of graduation.

The emphasis on traditional common law subjects by the MBE explains why much of the first-year curriculum at nearly all ABA-approved law schools remains as it was created in 1870 at the Harvard Law School. The NCBE's decision to test a student's doctrinal knowledge of the common law forces most law schools to continue to focus on those subjects in the first year of law school, even though the law has changed dramatically since 1870, and even though the kinds of legal work undertaken by lawyers today would baffle and astound a lawyer who practiced in the late 19th century.

The introduction of the MBE in 1972 was an immediate success. Within eighteen months, thirty-five jurisdictions had adopted the MBE as part of the bar examination; by 1976, forty-four jurisdictions had adopted it. Today, fifty-three jurisdictions use the MBE, including the District of Columbia and all states except Louisiana and Washington. The MBE is a *de facto* national bar examination. Even though the MBE is effectively a national bar examination, many state boards of law examiners refuse to allow an applicant to transfer her score from another state's examination, requiring the applicant to retake a test about which the applicant has already shown adequate mastery.

The MBE has also unified the dates of the bar examination across the nation, for the NCBE writes one examination for each examining period, which is then used by the fifty-three examining jurisdictions. Ensuring that applicants are taking the MBE at the same time reduces substantially the opportunity to cheat by sending questions (and answers) to other jurisdictions. Consequently, the NCBE offers the MBE on two days each year, on the last Wednesday of February and July.

The adoption of the MBE by nearly all state boards of law examiners led the NCBE to consider creating a multiple-choice test on legal ethics and professional responsibility. The NCBE began its work on what would become the Multistate Professional Responsibility Examination (MPRE) in 1976. The MPRE was rolled out in 1980, and by 2000, fifty-two jurisdictions had adopted it. The only states not to require a bar applicant to pass the MPRE are Maryland, Washington and Wisconsin.

The next uniform examination created by the NCBE was the Multistate Essay Examination (MEE). The MEE includes nine 30-minute essay questions. Those essay questions come from the following subjects: 1) the six areas of law tested on the MBE, 2) Business Associations, including agency and partnership, corporations and limited liability companies, 3) Conflict of Laws, 4) Family Law, 5) Federal Civil Procedure, 6) Trusts and Estates and 7) Uniform Commercial Code, including both commercial paper and secured transactions. The jurisdictions that have adopted the MEE can use all or some of those nine questions. Most use six, making the MEE a half-day examination. The MEE is scheduled for the Tuesday before the last Wednesday in February and July.

About half of the jurisdictions create their own essay examinations. The subjects tested in the MEE are similar to the subjects tested by those states, although that list can vary considerably. Check the website for your state's board of law examiners for a list of essay subjects.

Finally, after complaints that the bar examination failed to test practical skills used by lawyers, the NCBE created the Multistate Performance Test (MPT). According to the NCBE's website, http://www.ncbex.org/multistate-tests/mpt/, the MPT consists of two 90-minute "skills questions covering legal analysis, fact analysis, problem solving, resolution of ethical dilemmas, organization and management of a lawyering task, and communication." Like the MEE, the MPT is given on the Tuesday before the last Wednesday in February and July, and the states may use one or both of the MPT questions. Thirty-four jurisdictions have adopted the MPT either in part (one question) or in whole (both questions) for use in 2010.

Thus, much of the bar exam in most states is likely the creation of the NCBE. The NCBE offers for sale some of its past examinations, giving the applicant a good sense of how questions are framed. Some past examinations are available for download without charge, which may include model answers. Further, in perusing the NCBE website you will see that it provides a complete breakdown of the topics it tests on the MPRE and the MBE. For example, one-third of the Evidence questions on the MBE focus on the test taker's knowledge of hearsay and its exceptions, one-third focuses on relevance, privileges, expert testimony and writings, and one-third on presenting evidence (who is a competent witness? What is a permissible lay opinion? How are questions asked on direct and cross-examination?) and impeachment of witnesses. Your law school may have purchased one or more copies of past examinations. Whether by purchasing or downloading, you will be able to look at past examinations. Because the NCBE does not need to re-invent its questions in order to test applicants to the bar, a familiarity with past examinations will greatly facilitate confidence that one can pass the bar examination.

The NCBE offers informational booklets about each of its national tests, which includes detailed outline information regarding the topics tested. It also offers on its website examples of prior test questions for all of its test instruments. You should be aware of how past examinations were written well before you take the bar examination in February or July.

Bar Preparation Courses

Both the recent settlement of an antitrust lawsuit and the rise of the Internet have created the possibility of greater competition in bar preparation courses. For years the bar prep industry has been dominated by BAR/BRI, which offers a complete course for each state in which it operates. Before the antitrust settlement, PMBR (which stood for Preliminary Multistate Bar Review) offered a six-day course focusing wholly on the MBE, which began before BAR/BRI started, and then offered a three-day review after BAR/BRI concluded. Since the settlement Kaplan, which owns PMBR, has begun to roll out a complete bar review course in a number of states. BAR/BRI, which is now owned by West Publishing, a division of Thomson Reuters, and Kaplan remain the two largest competitors in the market. Because bar exam preparation is so boring, one significant factor in determining whether to take BAR/BRI or Kaplan is which will offer more live lectures. In cities other than the largest in the country, most lectures are taped, and shown on screen. If you live outside of an area which houses five or more law schools, you may be subject to bar exam prep by taped lectures. Although the lecturers are ordinarily quite good, much is lost in listening to a taped lecture. If BAR/BRI and Kaplan are truly going to compete in the same markets, one competitive approach is to offer more live lectures. Find out from your local student representative what percentage of lectures are live and what percentage are taped. Find out how many practice MBE questions are available for you to study, and how each is using the Internet to complement its lectures.

In addition to BAR/BRI and Kaplan/PMBR, several other bar prep programs exist, though these ordinarily eschew lecturers in favor of outlines and many sample test questions. Ameribar offers a full course with materials and an online format. Micromash is similar, as are Reed Law Group and Themis Bar Review. Each of these uses the Internet to support the study of its students. Finally, Adaptibar offers an online course on the MBE only. For some students, taking a bar prep course other than BAR/BRI and Kaplan/PMBR may not only make financial sense (the two largest bar prep providers are also the most expensive) but may fit the student's learning style as well. Before committing to any bar prep program, learn what the passing rate is for students at your school who took that particular bar prep course.

Students whose grades put them in the top half of the class ordinarily do very well on the bar exam of any state. Students in the third quartile vary substantially in their success on the bar, and students who graduate in the bottom quartile struggle the most on the bar exam. If you find yourself in the bottom quartile in law school at any time, you are at risk of failing the bar exam. You need to visit the Office of Academic Support or other counseling office at your school as soon as you can to learn more about your learning style and how to use it to your advantage during your remaining time in law school. You need to figure out which bar prep course best fits your learning style. In addition, if your school offers a bar preparation course or other test skills courses, you need to take it during your third year of law school. Much of the bar exam concerns the skill of taking a multi-day examination, and that skill can be learned.

The Bar Exam Structure

States differs on how they structure their bar exam, and you should go to the website for the board of law examiners for the state in which you plan to take the bar exam for specific information on how that state will structure its exam. Given the timing of the MBE, the MEE and the MPT, the structure ordinarily is something like this. Day 1 of the exam will be on the last Tuesday before the last Wednesday in February (early or late graduation) and July (regular graduation). It will consist of either or both the MEE (or a state-equivalent series of essay questions) and the MPT. On Day 2 (or Day 1 if your state has not adopted the MEE or MPT), the last Wednesday of February and July, you will take the MBE. A number of states have just a two-day exam, and the MBE is the final part of the exam. Some test on a third day. In those states, on Thursday, Day 3, you will be tested on your ability to answer a state-generated performance test or a state-generated essay exam. In Texas, for example, Day 1 begins with a half-day (three hours), a ninety-minute MPT exam followed by a ninety-minute exam requiring short, written answers to forty questions on Texas Procedure and Evidence. Each of those two exams is worth 10% of the applicant's score. Day 2 consists of the MBE, worth 40%, and Day 3 consists of twelve 30-minute state-generated essay questions, six completed in the morning and six completed in the afternoon, and divided into six subject categories. The Texas essay answers are also worth 40%. The California bar exam is three full days. Days 1 and 3 consist of three one hour essay questions in the morning followed by one three hour long performance test in the afternoon on California law. Day 2 is the MBE. Illinois offers a two day test. Day 1 (Tuesday) consists of a morning session of three 30 minute essays on Illinois law and one 90 minute MPT question. The afternoon consists of six 30 minute essays from the MEE. Day 2 (Wednesday) is the MBE, and each day is worth half of your score. Massachusetts begins its exam on Wednesday with the MBE and concludes Thursday with an essay exam. Massachusetts will accept an MBE score taken during a concurrent exam, so an applicant can take the New York (Tuesday essays and Wednesday MBE) and Massachusetts (Wednesday MBE and Thursday essays) bar exams at the same time. This is not advisable but is possible and has been done successfully.

Massachusetts accepts a concurrent MBE, but not a past MBE in its licensing process. Most states are more reluctant than Massachusetts to accept an applicant's MBE score if taken in another jurisdiction. Because each MBE is scaled to equalize any variances in the difficulty of the exam, a scaled MBE score in February 2008 is the same as the scaled MBE score in July 2010. The reason that states do not accept past MBE scores taken in another state is largely one of economic protectionism. By making it harder for a person to become licensed (that is, by making the person take an entire bar exam, not just a state's essay exam), those rules may discourage some would be lawyers from moving to that jurisdiction. Thus, a new lawyer who wants to obtain a law license in a second state will find it quite difficult to do so. The easiest location to obtain a second law license is the District of Columbia, which allows any person who has passed a bar exam in another jurisdiction and who received a scaled MBE score of 133 or higher and a scaled MPRE score of 75 or higher to be admitted by motion. Both of those scores are fairly modest scores. As a result, if you plan on practicing law in the District of Columbia you should strongly consider taking the bar exam elsewhere (say Virginia or Maryland) and then move for admission to the District of Columbia bar by motion.

February v. July Bar Exam

What differences, if any, exist between the February and July exams? Most states publish some data allowing one to compare bar exam results in February and July of each year. Those results usually show a disparity in passing rate between the two exams, with the February passing rate lower, sometimes markedly so. For instance, the February 2009 passing rate in Florida for first-time test takers was 70.7% and 80% in July 2009. Similarly, the passing rate for first-time examinees in February 2009 in California was 46.6%. The comparable number for July 2009 was 70.4%. Part of this is a consequence of who takes the exams. Graduates of ABA-approved law schools constituted 52% of the first-time test takers in the February 2009 California bar exam, but 85% of first-time test takers in the July 2009 California examinees. This difference may also somewhat reflect the fact that four times as many first-time examinees took the bar in July as in February in California (it was about three times as many in Florida), and the greater numbers of first-time examinees likely lessened the influence that fluke results may create. However, a common view of the difference between results in February and July, a view that has not been empirically verified, is that the applicants who take the bar exam in July are stronger applicants than the February exam takers. This common view is based in large part on the belief that those taking the bar exam in February are more likely to be repeat examinees. For example, repeat examinees taking the February 2009 California general bar exam were 64% of all test takers, while in July 2009 repeat test takers were just 29% of the total examinees.

Even if the assumption that February examinees are less capable than July examinees is inaccurate, the question remains whether this assumption is perceived by bar exam graders to be true. If those grading the bar exams (that is, the essay questions and any performance test) believe that February examinees are not quite as capable as July examinees, one possible consequence is that the graders of those essay exams (the MBE is scored by machine, of course) may grade more harshly in February than they do when grading July exams, on the belief that the test takers must know less than those taking the July exam. No empirical work has been done to determine whether any grading differences exist between the February and July exams.

For the student who graduates early, taking and passing the February bar gives the applicant up to a six month head start in the practice of law, for it usually takes longer to grade July exams than February exams, given the increased number of test takers. Particularly if the applicant is working for a small firm or beginning practice as a sole practitioner, that kind of head start can be valuable in building a legal business. Even if those taking the February bar exam are more stringently graded than July test takers, a graduate who performed adequately in law school (not superbly but not poorly either) should pass, as long as the applicant prepares thoroughly. The chief cost of taking the bar in February rather than waiting until July may be that failure will lead a good applicant to perform more poorly on the July exam than should be the case. This psychological cost, if any, is something an applicant should consider when deciding whether to take the bar early. If an applicant will not suffer from any psychological scarring should he fail a February bar exam, that applicant should take the exam early, for even if he fails he will not lose any more time in the practice of law if he then takes and passes the July exam.

What an applicant to the bar should avoid is skipping the July bar and waiting until February to take the bar exam. Not only will this create an unnecessary delay in entering practice, it may create greater anxiety given the lower passing rates. Of course, if an applicant passes the bar exam in July in one state and takes the bar in a second state in February, the lower passing rate will have little if any impact on the applicant, for she has already demonstrated an ability to surmount the difficulties of the bar exam. This experience should reduce considerably any anxiety the applicant may feel, in part because the applicant has already shown some mastery of the MBE (and MEE and MPT, if applicable) in passing the bar of the first state.

Scoring and Scaling

Each state can score its sections of the exam as it sees fit. However, the state's Board of Law Examiners does not want a section officially worth 25% to have a disproportionate impact on the scores of applicants. If the test takers overall did very well or quite poorly on a particular section, the raw scores in that section have to be "equated" and "scaled" so the weight of that section equals its predetermined value. If not, then that section will lead to a high or low passing rate, depending heavily on whether the section was difficult or easy. For example, assume the total raw score an applicant could receive was 1,000, and 675 was the passing score. Assume also that the exam consists of three parts, each worth 33.3%. A student might have the following raw scores: 225, 164 and 280. That raw score equals 669. Is that a failing score? It depends on how each section is scaled. If the first two scores (225 and 164) were both the median score (that is, 50% of test takers scored that number or higher and 50% scored at that number or lower), then those scores have to be "equalized," for otherwise the 164 score will have a disproportionate (and adverse) impact on an applicant's overall score. The goal is to keep like scores alike, so that scores in the 90th percentile are the same for each section, as are scores in the 25th percentile. Thus, if the 280 raw score on the final third of the bar exam is also a median score, that too must be scaled, though in this case it must be scaled downward rather than upward. Many examinees will do better or worse depending on the section (some, alas, do poorly on all sections, and a few perform excellently throughout), and those variations are not to count either too favorably or too adversely in the overall picture.

How a state scales its scores is usually not disclosed. However, the NCBE has published material on how MBE scores may be scaled, and states often scale using the MBE as their reference point. The amount of the scaling tapers as the examinee answers more questions correctly, and the scale differs depending on how "easy" or "difficult" the NCBE declared the particular exam in comparison with past MBE examinations. This was demonstrated in the NCBE's Sample MBE III, which was the examination given in July 1998. At the end of the Sample MBE III, the NCBE provided a Raw Score Conversion Table. For examinees who answered between 105–110 questions correctly, a result well below the median, the scaled score ranged from 126–130, a difference of 20–21 points. At the high end, examinees who answered between 167–173 questions correctly received a scaled score of 176–180, an increase of 7–9 points from their raw score. At the median, examinees correctly answering 124–129 questions received scaled scores of 141–145, an increase of 16–17 points.

The scaling of an exam easier than the July 1998 exam will mean fewer points are added to an examinee's raw score to obtain the scaled score. Conversely, more points would be added to an exam that was judged more difficult than the July 1998 exam. The difficulty the NCBE may find itself in is that, with the increasing emphasis of law schools and bar reviews on the MBE (due to declining bar pass rates in the 1990s), test takers may be better prepared for the MBE than they were in the past. Consequently, the median score might improve even if the exam is, in some absolute sense, more difficult than the July 1998 exam.

The board of law examiners takes the scaled scores and equalizes them in light of the percentage allocated to each section. A median scaled score for a section worth 50% of the applicant's score should be twice as much as the median scaled score for a section worth 25%. Once the scores are scaled and equalized based on the stated value of each section, they are ordinarily added together to determine the applicant's overall score. The total scaled score must exceed the stated minimum passing score listed by the board of law examiners.

In most states, once the bar examiners receive the scaled scores of students the scores of students in the essay examination is scaled to the MBE. Thus, if the scaled MBE scores in a state range from 100–165, with a median score of 140, and the raw scores on the essay exam range from 40–95, with a median of 60, those essay scores are adjusted to fit the scale of the MBE range, accounting for the value accorded each section. Those scores (plus scores on the Multistate Practice Test (MPT) and any other section) are added to determine if the total meets or exceeds the minimum passing score.

General Advice and Strategy

The bar exam is more about practice than it is about memorization. The number of rules of law appears endless, and you could spend years trying to memorize or master all of them. That extent of knowledge is wholly unnecessary to pass the bar exam, and indeed is more likely to lead to failure than success. By the time the bar exam begins you will know more law than you ever imagined, and that knowledge will be more than sufficient to pass the bar. Taking practice exams is just as important as learning or re-learning doctrine. You need to write answers to practice essay exams and performance tests (if applicable), and answer many multiple-choice questions. Practice may not make perfect, but it will make you capable of passing the bar. The number of past essay, performance and multiple-choice exams online is astounding, and answers to many of those questions are also freely available on the Web. Your bar exam preparation provider will also give you a host of practice exam questions with sample answers. Familiarize yourself with the time and other limitations (such as

closed book exams, or using only the materials provided you in the performance test) you will face in the bar exam. Regular practice in writing your essay
and performance test answers is crucial to reaching "good enough" answers.
Practice will make your answers to multiple choice questions highly educated
guesses rather than speculation.

Persons studying for the bar examination do so in a myriad of ways. Some will
do the same thing at the same time every day. Others will study in spurts. What
successful applicants know is how they best learn. Those who fail the bar exam
have often spent more time studying than those who passed, but they don't know
how they best learn. You must become aware of how you learn, especially if you
have struggled in law school. The bar examination is not a test of intelligence or
aptitude; it is a skills-based test that one can pass by learning those skills. Learn
how to read multiple choice questions discerningly. Understand how to appor-
tion your time. Learn how to answer the questions posed on the essay.

Preparing for the bar exam is much like preparing for a marathon. You must
take a sufficient amount of time to prepare, and you must be rested and fit
when the bar exam begins. Coming to the bar exam in an exhausted state is the
least likely approach to lead to success. You already know that test anxiety is unhelpful. If you have spent the time preparing for the bar exam, you should not
be anxious. If you have suffered from test anxiety in high school, college or
law school, see a counselor well before you graduate, and work with the counselor to try to reduce (if not eliminate) that anxiety you feel before and during exams.

You should be given a diagnostic test on the MBE subjects by your bar prep
course provider at the beginning of your bar prep course. If you are not, purchase past MBE exams from the NCBE and diagnose yourself in late December (for the February exam) or late May (for the July exam). You want to know,
what do I know about these six subjects without having studied them recently?
You should answer fifty questions on each of the six MBE subjects, which will
take a total of nine hours, for you should complete the fifty questions in ninety
minutes (if you don't complete those fifty questions in time, stop after ninety
minutes and count the unanswered questions as wrong). This will take roughly
three days, doing one exam in the morning and one in the afternoon. You
want to determine what your percentage of correct answers is, knowing that
getting 65% right will lead to passing the bar in any state. You also want to
know if you have any strong disparities in these subjects, because learning that
you correctly answered 55% of the Evidence questions but just 35% of the Real
Property questions tells you both that you need to study Real Property thoroughly and that you may have a knack for answering Evidence questions. If
you have the discipline, see if you can spot a pattern in the questions you get

right and the questions you answer incorrectly. Two patterns that may be relatively easy to ascertain are 1) is there is particular area of knowledge that I understand (or misunderstand)? and 2) are there types of questions that are harder for me to answer (either in length or type of style of question)?

You also want to take advantage of obtaining feedback on your practice essay answers (and performance test answers if applicable). Before you sign up learn what feedback services your bar prep company will provide, and at what cost.

Because practice is so important to passing the bar exam, during the two month period before the bar exam, you should complete at least three essays on each subject likely to be tested on the bar, and do so within the time constraints given in the bar exam. If your jurisdiction has adopted a performance test, you need to complete a number of tests comparable with the value given those tests (thus, if the performance test counts as 25% and the essays count for 50%, you should complete twice as many essay questions overall as performance test questions). You should also daily answer between 25–60 MBE questions. Again, because this is like a marathon, you should peak in the number of MBE questions you answer about two-three weeks before the bar exam. By a week before the bar exam, you should be in maintenance mode, answering no more than 25–33 questions each day. At the beginning of the bar prep process, it is usually better to group your MBE questions by subject, so that you answer questions on one MBE subject each day. After a while you should answer mixed MBE questions. The reason for this is simple: You are initially building both a book of knowledge of Constitutional Law, Contracts and other MBE subjects during the first half of your preparation for the bar. Once you have built up that knowledge, you want during the second half of your time preparing for the bar to replicate the conditions of the MBE.

As stated above, a number of states electronically publish their past essay exams. Some also provide representative answers. You may use this information in two ways. First, categorize the past essay questions. How often does the bar ask a question on secured transactions? How often is the business associations question about shareholders' rights? Particularly if the state asks fewer essay questions than subjects on which it may test (say the essay will comprise twelve questions on a possible sixteen subjects), getting a sense of what subjects are regularly tested and what subjects are occasionally tested gives you a good sense about how to allocate your study time. Some subjects also lead to similar types of questions. If family law is an essay exam subject, how often will a question on family law focus on the law of child custody? In other words, you can learn from past exams not only what subjects are likely to be tested, but what legal topics within the subject are likely to be tested. Further, actual past exams are a good source for practice, particularly if a sample answer is provided by the board of law examiners. If your jurisdiction does not post a representative answer to its questions you may look at similar essay questions and answers posted by the board of law examiners in another state. One caution if you do so: if the essay question from another state asks about state-specific law, avoid answering it.

Preparing for the bar exam is an eight hour a day, six day a week job beginning about nine weeks before the exam takes place. If you listen to a three hour lecture you have five hours to 1) review the materials discussed in the lecture, 2) preview the material to be discussed in the following lecture, and 3) to practice answering MBE, MPT and essay (MEE) questions. This is not difficult to accomplish. You should give yourself one day off each week to re-energize yourself. For most persons spending ten or more hours per day preparing for the bar is unproductive. You will learn the law of diminishing returns quickly comes into play should you spend that much time studying. Worse, you may trick yourself. You may spend a lot of time in the library, most of which is talking to friends, wandering about, taking breaks and doing relatively little studying. While preparing to take the bar exam you will have time to see friends and family. Do so. Becoming a hermit is not likely to improve your odds, as long as you keep to a timetable. You must find time for some physical activity. It matters less what activity you engage in than that you do something. Similarly, keep yourself mentally fresh by doing something other than reading bar exam materials and practicing exams. As long as you maintain a consistent approach to your "job," you can indulge yourself in your favorite hobbies. Eating well and limiting your alcohol intake are also simple but effective ideas.

If you spend just a little time at the NCBE website (www.ncbex.org) you will quickly learn what topics within subjects are heavily tested and what topics are lightly tested. Allocate your time based on what is likely to be tested. You do not need an "A" to pass the bar exam. You need a "C." If you come to the bar exam and don't understand the first essay question, do not panic. One question (even two) does not make or break any applicant's chances of passing the bar.

The MPRE

The MPRE is given by the NCBE thrice yearly, on the second Friday or Saturday in March, August and November. Nearly all states permit bar applicants to take and pass the MPRE before graduating from law school. Some, however, require the applicant to take the MPRE within two to three years of admission to the bar. Thus, if you passed the MPRE in August after your first year of law school, and didn't take the bar exam (or pass it) until a year after you graduated from law school, that three year and several month difference may result in you having to retake the MPRE. Check the rules for the jurisdiction(s) in which you plan to practice. Those rules are usually adopted by the state Supreme Court and on its website. The NCBE annually publishes a book titled *Comprehensive Guide to Bar Admission Requirements*, which lists the rules for admission in each jurisdiction. That book is available in every law school library. If you cannot find the book at your law school library, you can download the book from the NCBE. You must sign up for the MPRE through the NCBE, and pay the examination fee. Your score will be sent to the board of law examiners in the state you plan to take the bar examination. You can also have your score sent to other jurisdictions for a fee.

The MPRE consists of 60 multiple choice questions, of which ten are "unscored," with four answers offered for each question. After answering the 60 multiple choice questions, you are asked to answer ten questions concerning the test conditions. The examination must be completed within two hours and five minutes. This means a students has 2 minutes per question (30 questions per hour, with the extra five minutes either to answer the 10 test conditions questions, or as a hedge for those running out of time). Very few examinees report any time pressure on the MPRE. The raw number of correct answers (called the "standard score") is changed to a scaled score by the NCBE. The scale ranges between 50–150. The mean (average, not median) score of test takers was established as 100, based on the examinees taking the March 1999 exam. The passing scaled score for the MPRE varies by state, but ordinarily is set between 75–85. Consequently, you can pass the MPRE even with a score well below the mean scaled score.

As noted above, scaling raw scores helps account for the relative ease or difficulty of a particular examination. The harder the examination, the fewer the number of correct answers you need in order to pass the MPRE. A scaled score of 85, for example, may require you to answer correctly somewhere between 26–34 questions, depending on the difficulty of the exam. Ordinarily, 30–32 correct answers on the 50 scored questions will convert to a passing scaled score in any state.

When the NCBE crafted the MPRE, it made a conscious decision that this examination is not designed to prevent persons from the practice of law. Although some applicants have failed the MPRE on the first attempt, I have never heard of an applicant to the bar who has graduated from law school, passed a state bar examination, and remains unlicensed due to an inability to pass the MPRE.

The MPRE offers the bar applicant the opportunity to take an objective exam to use as a "dry run" before taking the MBE. The style and form of the questions in the MPRE is quite similar to the questions found in the MBE, but you have more time to answer each question in the MPRE than in the MBE, and you are tested on merely one subject rather than on six.

It is important to understand that the MPRE does not test your character or integrity as a professional. Those test takers who fail the MPRE often do so because they misunderstand the purpose of the test. An applicant's good or ethical character is not testable in a multiple choice examination. Instead, the MPRE is a test of your knowledge of rules. Those rules include the Model Rules of Professional Conduct of the ABA, constitutional rules applicable to lawyers and their clients and other decisions concerning the "law of lawyering" established by the Supreme Court of the United States or otherwise generally accepted by state courts, and the ABA's Code of Judicial Conduct. In addition, the Federal Rules of Civil Procedure and the Federal Rules of Evidence may apply to questions that concern Rule 11 sanctions, the attorney-client privilege and similar lawyering issues.

The NCBE offers an outline of the subjects tested in both the MPRE. The topics tested in the MPRE are found at http://www.ncbex.org/multistate-tests/mpre/subjects0/outline/.

In both the MBE and the MPRE, the exam taker reads a fact pattern. The question ends with the "call of the question," and provides four responses, which may or may not include the "best" or "right" answer. Instead, the answers may provide a "most accurate among the four options" answer, which is the answer you are to choose.

The types of MPRE questions, like the types of MBE questions, include the following: 1) definitional questions; 2) multi-definitional questions, and 3) application questions.

The easiest questions on a multiple-choice examination are definitional questions. These questions require you to show your knowledge of a specific doctrinal area of law. While these questions are occasionally designed to mislead you, they more often are designed to give you the chance to answer correctly.

For example, consider the following question:

> You represent Paddy's Beak, Inc., which has sued Dedrick Co. for product disparagement. Dedrick Co. and Paddy's Beak, Inc. are competitors in the plant seed business. Dedrick Co.'s ads falsely claimed that the seeds grown and sold by Paddy's Beak, Inc. were inferior. The complaint filed on behalf of Paddy's Beak, Inc. alleges damages and requests a permanent injunction prohibiting Dedrick Co. from making such false claims now or in the future. Dedrick Co.'s lawyer has called you to make the following settlement offer. Dedrick Co. will agree to the injunction, and will pay a total of $100,000 to Paddy's Beak, Inc. for the damages caused by the false ads. What answer is the most accurate?

A) You may reject the settlement offer because you believe the offer is insufficient to properly redress the injuries suffered by Paddy's Beak, Inc.

B) You must reject the offer as long as you believe in good faith that the proposed settlement is insufficient to properly redress the injuries suffered by Paddy's Beak, Inc.

C) You must let Paddy's Beak, Inc. decide to accept the offer, even though you believe the offer is unconscionably low.

D) You may accept the settlement offer, as long as you deposit the settlement check in your client trust account.

This question evaluates your knowledge of the duties of a lawyer when a settlement offer is made by the other side. Rule 1.2 of the ABA's Model Rules of Professional Conduct requires a lawyer to accept a client's decision whether to settle. Based on the rule, answers A, B and D cannot be correct, for the facts do not state that you have the authority from Paddy's Beak, Inc. to reject or accept settlement offers. Thus, answer C is correct.

Questions in the MPRE are often written in the "may" and "must" form, as found in the answers given above. The goal of the examiners is to assess your knowledge of what will cause the lawyer to be *subject to discipline* (thus the *must*), as well as knowledge of what discretion a lawyer has in terms of the ethical choices available to him or her (thus the *may*). Because the MPRE tests both what a lawyer must or must not do as well as what a lawyer is permitted but not required to do, answers are often phrased separated only by the use of the words *must* or *may*. Answers A and B above differ in part based on whether a lawyer "may" reject a settlement offer under certain conditions or "must" reject a settlement offer.

The "Two and Two" Definitional Question

Many of the definitional questions given in the MPRE as framed as two "yes, because" and two "no, because" answers. In these questions, the examiners are assessing your understanding of the policy or justification of the law. The advantage of this type of question is that the examinee can relatively quickly eliminate two answers. The disadvantage of this type of definitional question is that you must read both the facts and answers carefully in order to reach the correct answer. Consider the following question:

Lawyer represents the plaintiffs in a civil action. Her clients are three members of the congregation of the Divine Church, suing on behalf of themselves and others similarly situated. The defendants are Divine Church, Inc., a corporation, and Donald Davidson, the spiritual leader of the church and president of the church corporation. Davidson and Divine Church, Inc. are represented by separate defense lawyers. The complaint alleges that Davidson misappropriated substantial sums of money belonging to the corporation, and that the Board of Elders, acting as corporate directors, knew about it and failed to stop him. During discovery, Lawyer conducted a lengthy, private interview with the church bookkeeper, an employee of Divine Church, Inc. The bookkeeper brought the church books with her to the interview, and she and Lawyer went over them in detail. Lawyer did this without the knowledge or consent of either defense lawyer. Which of the following is most nearly correct?

A) Lawyer's conduct was proper, because the bookkeeper was not a party to the lawsuit.

B) Lawyer's conduct was proper, because the bookkeeper was neither an officer nor a high-ranking employee of the church corporation.

C) Lawyer is subject to discipline, because she should have obtained the consent of both defense lawyers before interviewing bookkeeper.

D) Lawyer is subject to discipline, because she should have obtained the consent of the church corporation's defense lawyers before interviewing bookkeeper.

The first determination is, was the Lawyer's action proper or subject to discipline? If the former, answers C and D are eliminated. If the latter, answers A and B are eliminated. Model Rule 4.2 concerns when it is permissible for a lawyer to communicate with a person represented by another lawyer in this matter. Is the bookkeeper a "represented" person? The bookkeeper is not a party in the case, but is employed by a corporation that is a party and thus a represented person. In cases concerning employees of represented persons, comment [7] to Model Rule 4.2 bars communication with a corporate employee either directing the lawyer's work (no) or who can obligate the organization (no) or whose actions can be imputed to the organization (seems likely). This strongly suggests that the lawyer may be subject to discipline, which eliminates answers A and B. Even if you were unsure about whether the bookkeeper's actions can be imputed to the organization, your knowledge of Rule 4.2 and Comment [7] eliminates answer A, for the fact that the bookkeeper is not a party is irrelevant. As for deciding between C and D, the difference is whether both defense lawyers need to give consent, or only the lawyer for the corporation. The bookkeeper cannot be prevented from speaking with the plaintiffs's lawyer by an individual defendant (that is, Davidson). Only the bookkeeper's employer, Divine Church, Inc., because it too is a defendant, may demand that Lawyer obtain its consent before speaking with bookkeeper. Thus, answer D is "most nearly correct."

The "Three and One" Definitional Question

A variation of the "two and two" is the "three and one." This occurs when the answers are framed as A) yes, because, B) yes, because, C) no, unless and D) no, because. Answer C, "no, unless," is similar to a "yes, because" answer. When this type of question is asked, the examiners usually (but not always) will draft it in such a way as to allow you to eliminate answer D, so you have three options remaining. As is the case in the "two and two" question, a correct answer will require you to understand the reason a rule exists and why it exists. Consider the following question:

> Lawyer Lynn represents plaintiff Paul for a contingent fee in litigation against Darwin Industries for breach of warranty. Attorney Avila represents Darwin Industries in *Paul v. Darwin Industries*. In an effort to settle the case, Darwin Industries' in-house counsel instructs Avila to offer a settlement of approximately $50,000. Avila calls Lawyer Lynn and makes the offer of settlement. Lynn tells Avila that she will take up the matter with her client Paul and get back to Avila as soon as she can.
>
> Avila hears nothing for three weeks, even after he calls Lynn several times. Avila then writes Lynn a formal letter making the settlement offer, requesting that she discuss the matter with Paul, and demanding a prompt response. Again, he hears nothing from Lawyer Lynn. When Avila reports the matter to in-house counsel for Darwin, in-house counsel says, "I think Lynn's not satisfied with her 'cut' and hasn't even told her client about the offer. Why don't you send an e-mail to Lawyer Lynn making a demand that she respond to the prior letter, attach a copy of the letter containing the settlement offer, and cc a copy of the whole thing to Plaintiff Paul. I think we have Paul's e-mail address right here." *May* Avila send Paul an e-mailed copy of an e-mail and letter sent to Lawyer Lynn, Paul's lawyer?
>
> A) No, because Avila is not allowed to communicate directly with Paul.
> B) No, because Avila cannot be sure that Lynn failed to communicate the settlement offer to Paul.

C) No, unless Avila reasonably believes that Lynn has failed to communicate the settlement offer to Paul.

D) Yes, because the e-mailed copy would simply advise the client, Paul, of the fact of Avila's prior communication with his lawyer, Lynn.

Each of the first two answers begins with "no, because." Answer D is framed as a "yes, because" answer, and answer C is crafted as a "no, unless" answer. As noted in the previous question, Model Rule 4.2 of the ABA's Model Rules of Professional Conduct concerns communications with a represented person. Paul is represented by Lawyer Lynn in *Paul v. Darwin Industries*, and Attorney Avila is asked by his client to convey the settlement offer directly to Paul (we already know it can be accepted only by Paul). Answers B and C suggest there exists some exception or limitation of the "no communication with a represented person" rule. Answers A and D are close to correlative opposites. Based on the facts in the question, Paul is a represented person (he's a party, which makes that determination simple), and the opposing lawyer wishes to communicate with him. Answer D seems wrong not only because it appears contrary to the no communication rule, but because it uses the word "advise" in relation to an interaction with the client of the opposing lawyer. Surely answer D is wrong. That leaves the question, is there some limitation or exception to the no communication rule that we need to be aware of, making answers B or C possibly correct? Certainly not in this case. Both of those limited answers are wrong. The statement of the no communication rule, found in answer A, is the correct answer.

One of the easiest ways for the examiners to draw test takers away from the most accurate answer is the use of what I will call *meaningless legalese*, an attempt to distract you from the most accurate answer. One of the first things law students learn as 1Ls is that the law is neither static nor certain, and exceptions to particular doctrines abound. By the time a law school graduate comes to the bar exam, the doctrine learned in the first year of law school has often faded from memory. But remnants of doctrine remain, including remnants of exceptions to rules. Answer C offers the enticement of a standard of "reasonable belief." It sounds good, but you should not be distracted by this enticement! This meaningless legalese is a classic distractor answer intended to confuse you.

The Multiple Options Definitional Question

A more difficult definitional question gives the examinee several options of law and professional duty listed as Roman numerals. The answers are then listed as combinations of the Roman numeral statements. This type of question is used more often in the MPRE than in the MBE. In order to answer this question correctly, you must assess the correctness of the statements given in the Roman numerals. Consider the following question:

> Clare is a new client of Lawyer, and has asked Lawyer to write a letter of recommendation supporting the application for admission to the bar of Anderson, Clare's cousin. Clare informed Lawyer she has not spoken directly with Anderson, but Anderson's father assured Clare that Anderson is hard-working, honest, and possesses good character. Which of the following would be proper for Lawyer?
>
> I. Write the letter based on Clare's assurances.
>
> II. Write the letter based on Clare's assurances if Lawyer has no unfavorable information about Anderson when writing the letter.
>
> III. Independently investigate and write the letter only if Lawyer is convinced Anderson is qualified to practice law in the state.
>
> A) III only.
> B) I and II only.
> C) I and III only.
> D) I, II and III.

The key to answering this question quickly is to look first at the options given in answers A–D, *even before looking at options I, II and III listed in Roman numerals.* Count how many times each Roman numeral is used. In this example, I is used three times, II is used twice and III is used three times. If either I or III is false, then the answer must be what is left standing. Because this gives the examinee the chance to answer the question by looking at just one of the three possible Roman numeral answers if the examinee guesses right, it is unusual to make an answer used three times an inaccurate answer. You could decide to begin by looking at either Roman numeral I or III, and you could get lucky. More likely, you will just eliminate one answer. The more efficient approach to take is to look at the Roman numeral option listed twice in answers A–D, because then you can eliminate two possible answers by looking at just one Roman numeral. Option II is used in two answers (B and D). If it is accurate, then you have eliminated A and C; if it is inaccurate, you have eliminated B and D. Option II is not accurate, eliminating answers B and D. Answer A states "III only." Answer C states, "I and III only." If you look at I and it is accurate, you have eliminated answer A; if I is inaccurate you have eliminated answer C. In either case, you do not have to look at III in order to answer the question.

In this case, option I is incorrect (because Clare is a new client and has had no contact with Anderson), and you will be able to answer this question (A is correct) after assessing just two of the three options given you.

Efficiently Using Your Limited Time on the MPRE

Instead of first looking at the answers to determine how you can most efficiently answer the question correctly, too often examinees begin by looking at the statements listed in the Roman numerals. That means that the examinee will first look at all three statements in the Roman numerals, then look at the answers, and finally match options I, II and III with the combinations given in the answers. This is an inefficient use of your time. What is worse, most examinees will look at the answers in the order the NCBE has arranged them. Thus, examinees will begin with answer A, "III only." Then the examinee may go back to option III, and determine that it is correct. In so doing, the test taker now knows that answer A *may* be correct, but he doesn't know what answers are incorrect until he goes back to the remaining answers, which means he has failed to eliminate any option. Consequently, the examinee will likely move to answer B. The test taker will note that because III is correct, answer B must be incorrect. But now the examinee has to move on to answer C, and in order to determine whether C is correct, he must now look at both options I and II. If either I or II is incorrect, that eliminates answer D (so that helps a little), but the examinee has now had to look at all three options, merely because he looked at the answers in the order the exam created, not the order that makes the most efficient use of your time. Again, count the number of times each Roman numeral is used before looking at the substance of what is written in the Roman numerals. Find a Roman numeral used twice in answers A–D, allowing you to eliminate two answers at one time. You will then need to look at only one remaining Roman numeral in order to answer the question correctly.

The Multi-Definitional Question

The multi-definitional question tests your knowledge of two or more legal doctrines or concepts. It is designed to assess whether, given the fact situation, you can correctly determine which of two possibly applicable areas of law is more likely involved. A multi-definitional question is more difficult than the definitional question because you must read the fact pattern even more carefully than is ordinarily the case when reading a definitional question. Consider the following question:

> You are employed as an associate in a law firm that limits itself to personal injury work. You represent individuals the firm has taken as clients in a suit against Diverse Industries, Inc. alleging chemical dumping. Diverse Industries, Inc. has proposed a settlement, but the name partner in the firm has instructed you not to communicate the offer to the clients because the partner believes the offer is too low to accept. You believe your clients want to settle. Which of the following is most accurate?
>
> A) You must withdraw as counsel.
> B) You may follow the directions given you by the name partner because those directions are arguably correct.
> C) You must communicate the settlement to your clients.
> D) You may sue for wrongful termination if the name partner fires you for communicating the settlement offer to the clients.

This question requires that you know several rules. Answer A requires you to know when you must withdraw as counsel. A lawyer must withdraw as counsel when the lawyer has a conflict of interest (Model Rule 1.7). In addition, Model Rule 1.16 concerns when a lawyer "*shall* not represent a client" (subdivision (a)) and when a lawyer "*may* withdraw from representing a client" (subdivision (b)). Rule 1.16(a) requires withdrawal when representation will result in the violation of the rules of professional conduct, when the lawyer is physically or mentally unable to represent the client, or when the lawyer is discharged from representation. None of those circumstances exist in this case, so A is not "most accurate." Answer B requires knowledge of Model 5.2, which permits the "subordinate lawyer" (an associate) to rely on a "supervisory lawyer's" (partner's) interpretation of an arguable question of professional duty. The failure to communicate an offer of settlement is not an arguable question of professional duty (see Model Rule 1.2), so answer B cannot be the most accurate answer. Answer C is correct. It simply restates Model Rule 1.2. Answer D concerns a matter of substantive state law, which varies among the states. Although the statement may be accurate in some states, it is a classic distractor answer. It is used to get you to think about how these events might affect you, an effort to distract you by getting you to think about self-interest. Because the law on wrongful termination claims by lawyers varies among the states, it cannot be the most accurate statement.

The Multiple Options Multi-Definitional Question

A more difficult multi-definitional question gives the examinee several statements of professional duty as Roman numerals. The answers are then listed as combinations of the Roman numeral statements of law or professional duty. In order to answer this question correctly and efficiently, you must look first at the number of times each statement given in the Roman numerals is offered as an answer. Consider the following question:

> Paula contacted Attorney Antoine and asked Antoine to represent her in a personal injury case. Paula was driving an automobile when her car collided with a truck driven by Daniels, a truck driver employed by Dotson, Inc. Antoine agrees to take Paula's case for a fee of 33% of any amount received from the defendants plus expenses. During discovery, Paula learns that Antoine represented Dotson, Inc. in a suit for damages caused by the spill of hazardous materials after a Dotson truck veered off an on-ramp and crashed to the roadway below. That lawsuit was settled for an undisclosed sum three months before Paula first contacted Antoine. Dotson moves to disqualify Antoine as attorney for Paula.

> I. The court should grant the motion to disqualify Antoine from the case if Antoine has not formally terminated his relationship as Dotson's counsel in the suit for damages for the spill of hazardous materials.

> II. The court should grant the motion to disqualify Antoine from the case if Antoine's agreement with Paula is not in writing.

> III. The court should grant the motion to disqualify Antoine if there exists a significant risk that Antoine's representation of Paula will be materially limited by Antoine's duties to Dotson, Inc.

A) I only.
B) II and III only.
C) III only.
D) I and II only.

In this example, options I, II and III are each used twice. When this is the case, no matter which Roman numeral answer you begin with, you can eliminate two answers. If you begin with Roman numeral I and determine it is a correct statement of law, then you can eliminate answers B and C. If it is an incorrect statement of law, then you can eliminate answers A and D. Assume option I is an incorrect statement of law, making the most accurate answer either B or C. All you need to eliminate a third option is to determine whether option II is correct. If so, B is the correct answer. If option II is incorrect, C must be the correct answer. In either case, you have reached the correct answer without having to look at III.

In the example above, only option III is a correct statement of one's professional duty. Option I is the better practice (to avoid having to prove that the opposing party is a former client rather than a current client), but it is not required as a matter of the Model Rules of Professional Conduct. Option II is a distractor, irrelevant to the call of the question. The absence of a writing when the lawyer and client agree to a contingent fee (as in this case) is a violation of the Model Rules. However, it is irrelevant, for the issue is whether Dotson can disqualify Antoine, not whether Antoine can collect his fee without the existence of a written fee contract.

As discussed above, most examinees look at the Roman numeral options in the order given, just as you look at answers A–D in the order given. Because most test takers do so, one of the ways for examiners to make sure you look at all three answers is to make the statement of law in option I neither obviously correct nor incorrect. "I don't know" is going to be a common response when you take the MPRE and the MBE. One way to avoid this waste of time is to vary your approach to the Roman numerals and the answers given. In this example, because each of the Roman numerals is used in two of the answers, it makes absolutely no difference which of the three options you begin with. If you began with Roman numeral III, you will again eliminate two answers once you determine that III provides a correct statement of law. After you make that decision answers A and D are eliminated. You now need to choose between answers B and C. This requires that you determine whether Roman numeral II is a correct statement of law. Again, you have not had to assess the accuracy of each of the three options (because in this case you did not need to look at I to reach the answer) in order to reach the correct answer.

A third, more devilish option occasionally used in the MPRE is the following:

> You have decided that the best way to increase your income is to divorce yourself from the yoke of the hourly rate. Instead of quoting prospective clients an hourly rate, you quote them a total fee with listed incentives based on result, efficiency and use of partners and senior associates rather than junior associates and paralegals. Which of the following is permissible?
>
> I. Taking and defending tort cases on a "reverse" contingent fee, that is, the difference between the assessed value of the claim and the ultimate award.

II. Taking as a fee an ownership interest in the transaction, as long as the fee is fair and reasonable, agreed to in writing and undertaken only after informing the client of a reasonable opportunity to seek the advice of independent counsel.

III. Taking contingent fees to recover past due alimony and child support amounts.

A) I only.
B) II only.
C) III only.
D) I, II and III.

Even in this example, you may need not have to read each of the three options. If option I is correct, then you have eliminated answers B and C. All you have to do is determine if option II or option III (your choice) is correct or incorrect. If II is correct, then the correct answer is D. If II is incorrect, then the correct answer is A. The converse holds if you choose to look at option II before looking at option I. If you are unsure of the correctness of option II, then you will have to look at option III. If option I is incorrect, then you have eliminated answers A and D, and again all you have to determine is look at one of the two remaining options to answer the question. In this case, each of the three statements of law is correct, making the correct answer D. Again, though, you only needed to look at two Roman numerals to reach that conclusion.

The most efficient way to answer these "multiple option" questions, then, is to begin by assessing how many times each Roman numeral is offered as an answer, and evaluate first the accuracy of the Roman numeral used twice. Ignore the option least used in the four answers. When examiners are limited to four answers, and they give you three options concerning the correct statement of law, the manner in which the options are paired (or go solo) will *always* allow you to eliminate two answers if you begin with the option used twice. If more than one Roman numeral is used twice, you get to choose which one to begin with. In order to avoid thinking about this choice, decide beforehand whether you will begin with the first or last available Roman numeral option (that is, if I and II are both used twice, do you automatically begin with the first available (I) or second available (II) option).

The Application or Analysis Question

The most difficult multiple-choice question to answer is the "application" question. The application question requires the examinee to engage in a two-step process to determine the correct (or least inaccurate) answer. First, you must know the correct rule of law, and you will likely be given at least three possible statements of legal doctrine. Second, you must correctly apply that legal doctrine to the facts given you in the question. Particularly in the MBE, as is discussed below, the examiners use carefully noted facts to make more difficult the examinee's work in answering questions. Although some questions have fairly lengthy fact patterns, the examiners are skilled at crafting application questions in relatively terse fact patterns. Do not let the brevity of the question fool you into thinking the question will be easier to answer.

Consider the following application question:

> Attorney represented plaintiff in a civil suit. During discovery, attorney obtained information that led her reasonably to believe that defendant had engaged in a criminal action. Attorney informed plaintiff of her findings and of her belief, and obtained permission of her client to inform local prosecutors of the information she had learned. Attorney did not notify defendant's lawyer before giving the information to the prosecutor. Defendant was indicted and acquitted after trial. Attorney for plaintiff did not use defendant's indictment to her advantage in the civil suit.
>
> Was Attorney's action in disclosing information to the prosecutor proper?
>
> A) Yes, because Attorney possessed a reasonable belief that defendant had committed a crime.
> B) Yes, because Attorney is required to report information of another's criminal conduct if Attorney did not obtain her information through attorney-client privilege.
> C) No, because Attorney failed to inform defendant's attorney and thus, defendant, before notifying prosecutor.
> D) No, because plaintiff's civil suit against defendant was pending when Attorney notified prosecutor.

The style of the question is the "two and two" approach, for each "yes" and "no" answer is followed by "because." To get to the correct answer (A), you must look carefully at the facts given you in the question to understand which rule should apply. One rule: A lawyer is not permitted to disclose client confidences except in very narrow circumstances, and information learned during the lawyer's representation of the client ordinarily may not be disclosed without the consent of the client. A second rule: Lawyers who know of another lawyer's misconduct must, in certain circumstances, inform "the appropriate professional authority." A third rule: Lawyers may not bring a claim or offer a defense that is frivolous. A fourth rule: Lawyers shall expedite litigation consistent with the client's interests. A fifth rule: Lawyers shall not falsify evidence nor allude in trial to a matter the lawyer does not believe is relevant. A sixth rule (usually understood in some vague form): Lawyers are officers of the court. With all of these possibly applicable rules, how do you reach answer A? The examiners offer facts that lead you to that answer, allowing you to dismiss the likelihood of the applicability of some of those rules listed above. First, the lawyer has a "reasonable belief" that the defendant committed a crime. Thus, no fact suggests that the lawyer is giving the prosecutor information known by the lawyer to be false. Second, the lawyer has learned of this evidence of the defendant's commission of a crime "during discovery," not through a conversation with the plaintiff. Consequently, issues of client confidences are not applicable (so too, the question notes that attorney obtained client consent to disclose the information to the prosecutor, further obviating any issue of a breach of client confidences). Third, the attorney did not use this information at the civil trial, which eliminates the applicability of the rules concerning fairness to opposing party and counsel and alluding to irrelevant matters at the trial. These facts eliminate answers B and D. Answer C is a kind of meaningless legalese distractor, suggesting some kind of due process duty is owed by one counsel to the opposing party and counsel. No such due process duty exists, so don't be distracted. That leaves answer A.

In addition to offering you several facts that allow you to apply the correct rule, the facts provide an irrelevant fact: "Defendant was indicted and acquitted after a trial." The result of the criminal trial is not the test of the propriety of the attorney's conduct. The earlier fact, that the attorney possessed a reasonable belief that defendant committed a crime, is sufficient. An additional reason why this fact is irrelevant is that none of the answers list a subsequent acquittal as important. So, why was this irrelevant statement of fact included in the fact pattern? Part of the goal of the first year of law school is to get students to think abstractly, to think less about the actual parties in the cases and more about the relevant facts and doctrine found in those cases. This de-sensitization project in law school has long been criticized, sometimes with good reason. Because most law professors teaching today have taken that criticism to heart, they want students to learn to recognize the humanity of the parties in the cases as well as to learn legal doctrine. The human factor in law remains central to its study, and many cases are better understood after considering the position of the parties than through understanding "dry" legal doctrine. The acquittal of the defendant raises the emotion of righteous indignation toward plaintiff's lawyer. Avoid that emotion.

The parties in the MPRE and the MBE are not human beings. They do not exist, and a test taker will do well to make the parties as abstract as possible. Showing sympathy for the defendant who during a civil case is charged with a criminal law violation after plaintiff's attorney gives information to the prosecutor will not help you succeed in answering these multiple choice questions. This person does not exist!

The examiners in the MPRE will occasionally attempt to elicit sympathy in the recitation of some facts. That is an emotional distractor. If you find a widow or orphan treated badly by his or her lawyer, it will likely be the case that the lawyer is not subject to discipline. Remember, that widow or orphan is merely a figment of someone else's imagination.

The MBE

The MBE is a 200 question multiple-choice examination, of which 190 questions are scored and ten are unscored. The MBE tests the applicant's knowledge of Constitutional Law, Contracts, Criminal Law and Procedure, Evidence, Real Property and Torts. The ten unscored questions are "pretest" questions "indistinguishable from the live test items," according to the NCBE. The 190 scoring questions are divided as follows: Constitutional Law (31), Contracts (33), Criminal Law (31), Evidence (31), Property (31), and Torts (33), which means that two of the "pretest" questions are included in four areas (Constitutional Law, Criminal Law, Evidence, and Property), while only one "pretest" question is included in the Contracts and Torts areas. Both the MPRE and the MBE give all plaintiffs names beginning with "P," defendants all names beginning with "D," and witnesses all names beginning with "W." Approximately 60 of the 200 questions have been used in previous examinations. The NCBE does this to assess the quality of the examinees, and to assess the difficulty of the remaining 140 questions. If an average or median raw score is 120 correct answers in the MBE given in July 2009, and the average or median raw score is 115 correct answers in the July 2010 examination, the NCBE has to determine whether the quality of the applicants differed between the two exams or whether the questions asked in the July 2009 examination were less difficult than the questions given in the July 2010 examination.

An applicant has 108 seconds (1.8 minutes) to answer each question in order to complete 100 questions in three hours. After the morning session, the examinees are given a one-hour break, and then must answer another 100 questions in three hours. Compared with the MPRE then, the MBE is more time intensive (108 seconds v. 120 seconds/question), more difficult (the MBE requires a knowledge of six subjects, not one as in the case of the MPRE), and requires a more sustained effort (200 questions in six hours v. 60 questions in two hours). Unlike the MPRE, the MBE is also used to keep some bar applicants from obtaining their law license.

The examinee's score is based on the number of questions correctly answered. Thus no penalty exists for incorrect answers. YOU MUST COMPLETE YOUR ANSWER SHEET. If you do not have the time to evaluate and answer the last ten questions, you need to have chosen a default answer before you entered the exam and pencil in that answer for the last ten questions. You have a 1 in 4 chance of getting the question right by guessing, so you may add 2–3 correct answers by completing the answer sheet. The other reason to fill in your answer sheet is a cautionary tale: You do not want to come to the end of the exam and realize that you are filling in the bubble for number 99 when answering question 100. Thus, if you are stumped by a question, use your default letter to fill in your answer sheet, and put a mark next to the question. You will only come back to that question if you have time.

The raw number of correct answers is equated with other MBE exams and translated into a scaled score. The scaled score is intended to make comparable different exams. An exam in which the median examinee achieves 130 correct answers will be scaled differently than an exam in which the median examinee answers correctly 120 questions. The NCBE and its constituent state boards of law examiners want consistency in scoring, if only to avoid charges that there exists a conspiracy to manipulate the passing score of bar applicants to limit the number of those admitted to the bar.

As discussed above, the bar exam passing rates in all states for all first-time examinees who graduated from an ABA-approved law schools is significantly higher than 50%. Even if your MBE score is somewhat below the median MBE score, you are still likely to pass the bar exam as long as your essay score (and any other parts of the exam your state requires) is comparable to your MBE score. In other words, your goal is to "pass," and you need not excel in order to do so. For purposes of the bar exam, the desire to excel may come at the expense of doing well enough. The old political saying is "the best is the enemy of the good." That is, the futile quest for only the best laws can frustrate the creation of laws or policies that, on balance, would do more good than harm. Trying to memorize all of the law of property or torts or evidence may result in an informational overload, leading the examinee to make some relatively easy questions appear more difficult than intended.

As a general rule the most difficult of the six subjects tested on the MBE is Real Property. A study of the July 2001 MBE found that the average number of correct answers was 19.2 in Real Property. The highest raw average score was in Constitutional Law, at 22.9. The other subjects, in order from next "easiest" to second-most difficult, were Criminal Law, Evidence, Torts and Contracts. You will find that the Real Property questions are often the longest-worded questions. Because the best is the enemy of the good, you may decide to use your default answer on some of those Real Property questions, which will better ensure that you finish the exam.

As is the case with the MPRE, the MBE offers three types of questions: 1) the definitional question, 2) the multi-definitional question, and 3) the application or analysis question. These types of questions are discussed below.

The Definitional Question

Consider the following "definitional" question testing the examinee's understanding of Evidence:

Plaintiff was injured in an accident involving Defendant. Plaintiff sues Defendant. Which of the following is an ERROR?

A) The trial court permits the Defendant's lawyer to ask the Defendant questions on cross-examination that go well beyond the scope of direct examination by Plaintiff, who has been called as an adverse witness.

B) The trial court bars Defendant's attorney from cross-examining Defendant by leading questions.

C) The trial court permits cross-examination concerning the credibility of a witness even though no question relating to credibility has been asked on direct examination.

D) The trial court, despite Defendant's request for the exclusion of witnesses, allows Plaintiff's eyewitness to remain in the courtroom after testifying, even though the eyewitness is expected to be recalled for further cross-examination.

The simplicity of the form of the question makes it clear that you will not have to apply facts to evidence law in order to answer the question correctly, because no facts are stated. Second, the call of the question indicates that you are to determine which decision would be "ERROR" by the trial court, not just poor trial management (a discretionary call that the examiners generally avoid). Because the focus of the question is merely testing your memory of the rules, you may have to look at each of the four answers in order to determine which is "ERROR."

Answers A, B and C all test your knowledge of Federal Rule of Evidence 611, which is why this is a definitional question. FRE 611(b), titled "Scope of

Cross-Examination," states, "Cross-examination should be limited to the subject matter of the direct examination and matters affecting the credibility of the witness. The court may, in the exercise of discretion, permit inquiry into additional matters as if on direct examination." Thus, although Rule 611 ordinarily limits cross-examination to 1) the scope of direct examination plus 2) questions concerning credibility, a trial judge may permit more extensive cross-examination under Rule 611. Consequently, answer A is incorrect, for it cannot be "ERROR." Answer B is incorrect, for on direct examination you cannot use leading questions for "your" witness unless that witness is declared "hostile." It is highly unlikely your client can be a hostile witness when questioned by the client's own lawyer. Answer C is incorrect for it misstates Rule 611(b). If all the others are wrong, then D must be correct. In a more positive manner, D is correct because the Defendant has made a proper request for the exclusion of witnesses under Rule 615, popularly known as "The Rule," and the trial court has denied that proper request, making the court's decision an "ERROR."

The Multi-Definitional Question

The multi-definitional question is, like the definitional question, a test of one's memory of doctrine. It differs from the latter only by testing the examinee's knowledge of more than one rule. Consider the following question:

> Plaintiff sued Defendant for illegal discrimination, claiming that Defendant fired her because of her gender. At trial, Plaintiff called Witness, expecting that Witness will testify that Defendant admitted firing Plaintiff because of her gender. Instead, Witness testified that Defendant stated that Plaintiff was fired due to Plaintiff's frequent absenteeism. During the direct examination of Witness Plaintiff offers a properly authenticated tape recording she secretly made during a conversation with Witness during which Witness spoke of Defendant's admission to discriminate on the impermissible basis of gender.
>
> The tape recording is
>
> A) admissible but only to impeach Witness's testimony.
> B) admissible to prove Defendant's impermissible motivation based on gender and to impeach Witness's testimony.
> C) inadmissible, because a secret recording invades Witness's right of privacy under the federal Constitution.
> D) inadmissible, because it is hearsay and no exception applies.

As shown in the examples concerning the MPRE, this is styled as a "two and two" question. In this case, though the initial inclination may be to determine first whether the tape recording is admissible or inadmissible. the question does not readily reveal an answer if approached in that fashion. Instead, the examinee should begin by mentally reviewing the rules of evidence. The examinee must first recall the difference between prior inconsistent statements offered as substantive evidence and prior inconsistent statements offered to impeach. Prior inconsistent statements offered as substantive evidence are admissible if they meet the requirements of FRE 801(d)(1)(A). One of those requirements is that the prior inconsistent statement be made "under oath." The statement made by Witness that was secretly recorded by Plaintiff was not made under oath, so answer B cannot be correct. Second, the examinee must know that evidence admitted to impeach is not hearsay, so answer D cannot be correct. Answer D is also a "residual" answer. It is the answer one uses when none of the other answers is accurate. A "residual" answer is similar to a "none of the above" answer, a specific answer the MBE does not use. Answer C is a classic distractor, causing you to think about constitutional law in the middle of an evidence question. Not only does it cause you to think about constitutional law while in the midst of trying to remember the law of evidence, this statement of constitutional law is an inaccurate statement, which makes it even more memorable, and thus distracting. A is the most correct answer, not only because it is the only answer left standing, but because the tape recording may be used to impeach Witness by use of a prior inconsistent statement. This multi-definitional question also raises another common aspect of the MBE: The "most correct" answer may not be a truly correct answer. Although the secret tape recording may be admissible to impeach the Witness, it is quite unlikely that a trial court would actually allow such impeachment, for the jury would be highly susceptible to misusing this evidence as substantive (that is, as demonstrating the defendant's liability) evidence. You cannot argue with the examiners during the exam (nor after it), and any disgust with the "unreality" of the question is simply costing you time. Accept the fact that these questions might never arise in "real life." Then answer them to the best of your ability. MBE questions are not about the realities of practice; they are highly stylized questions testing your knowledge and endurance.

The Application or Analysis Question

The application question requires you to engage in a two-step process. First, you must know the applicable doctrine. Second, you must correctly apply that doctrine to the facts given in the question. Consider the following question:

> Darwin is charged with aggravated assault. Darwin allegedly shot at Victoria in a road rage incident while both were driving on the freeway. The government offers evidence that five years ago Darwin fired a shot into Cutler's home while sniping and offers evidence that six years ago Darwin was accused of unlawful possession of a sawed-off shotgun.
> This evidence should be
>
> A) excluded, because it can be offered only in cross-examination.
> B) excluded, because it is improper character evidence.
> C) admitted, because it is evidence of Darwin's violent propensity.
> D) admitted, because it is relevant as showing Darwin's motive, identity or plan.

Again, the style of the question is a "two and two." To answer this question correctly, you must know 1) the character rule, found in FRE 404(a), and 2) the "exception" to that rule, the prior bad acts rule found in FRE 404(b). The character rule bars evidence of a person's character, which means that answer C cannot be correct, because "propensity" evidence for violence is never correct. The prior bad acts "exception" to the ban on character evidence allows evidence of specific prior bad acts on direct or cross-examination, so answer A cannot be correct. Answers B and D are opposing statements of law. That is, they are opposite sides of the same metaphorical legal coin. The question then is testing your knowledge of the law of character evidence, based on the facts given in the question. Which applies in this case? The better answer is B. The facts indicate that Darwin is charged with aggravated assault based on a "road rage" incident while Darwin and Victoria were driving. In the other two incidents of specific instances of prior bad acts, one occurred at a home and was a sniping, and the other was possession of an illegal weapon. These incidents are not factually close enough to meet the rule of 404(b), so the answer cannot be D. As was the case with the previous question, answer B is a type of residual answer, used only after eliminating the other possibilities.

The MPT

The Multistate Performance Test (MPT) is administered by participating jurisdictions on the Tuesday before the last Wednesday in February and July of each year. Thirty-two jurisdictions have adopted the MPT as of 2010, and California has its own state-created performance test questions. The MPT includes two 90-minute problems, and a state may offer one or both questions. The MPT examination is designed to test an examinee's ability to satisfactorily complete a skill expected of a practicing lawyer. That skill is a writing that may include statutory analysis, or a clear presentation of the state of the law on a contested legal issue. The MPT is a self-contained examination; the test taker is not required to memorize any law that may be applicable. The applicable law is provided in the *Library*, and the events are set in a fictitious state. The facts and context on which the assignment is based are given the examinee in a *File*. Most importantly, the File will include an instructional memorandum. That memorandum instructs you on your task. It is the equivalent of the call of the question of a multiple-choice or essay question. You must take care to perform the tasks asked of you in the instructional memorandum, whether that is to draft a memorandum (usually an "objective" memorandum but occasionally a "persuasive" memorandum), draft a complaint, write an opinion letter or draft a brief in support of or in opposition to some motion in light of the "firm's" rules on how such writings are performed.

The skills that may be addressed by the MPT include 1) fact gathering and analysis, 2) analyzing the law (taken from the Library) in light of the facts, and 3) problem-solving, including solving ethical dilemmas. The most important skills tested on the MPT are 1) your organizational skills, and 2) your written communication skills. Those drafting the MPT expect most bar exam test takers to competently analyze facts and law and propose solutions to legal problems. What an examinee can do to improve his or her chances of succeeding on the MPT is to organize the answer in light of the task the examinee has been asked to perform. Organize your answer in great part by completing that task. If the task is to write a persuasive memorandum rather than an objective memorandum, write persuasively in memorandum format.

How you divide the 90 minutes given you to complete your task for each MPT question is an individual decision. It should, however, be a decision based on how you should attack an examination, which requires you to engage in self-reflection about how you best complete an examination. In general, you should consider taking at least 30 minutes to read the instructional memorandum giving you your task, read the File and then read the Library, in that order. That reading may include your initial efforts to begin outlining your response. If it does not, spend ten minutes putting your outline together. This gives you 50 minutes to write your response, which may be enough time to give you a 3–5 minute cushion at the end.

The MEE and Essay Examinations

The NCBE also owns another standardized examination used in bar examinations. Twenty-six jurisdictions will use the Multistate Essay Examination (MEE) as part of the bar examination in 2010. The MEE is given uniformly on the Tuesday of the last week in February and July, the day before the MBE is administered. The MEE is a three hour test consisting of six essay questions (30 minutes per question), taken from a bank of nine questions provided to each jurisdiction's board of law examiners. The essay questions are drawn from the six MBE subjects, Business Associations, Conflict of Laws, Family Law, Federal Civil Procedure, Trusts and Estates, and the Uniform Commercial Code.

Even in states that have not adopted the MEE, the same model is often used. Essay questions are thirty minutes in length and the legal subjects tested in those states mimic much of what is tested on the MEE. Some states also test examinees on subjects such as Professional Responsibility, Taxation (either Federal or State), and state-based Civil Procedure, and some states offer essay question longer than thirty minutes. For example, New York gives examinees three hours and fifteen minutes to complete three essay questions and fifty multiple-choice questions, allocating forty minutes per essay question and 1.5 minutes per multiple choice question. (A New York examinee is permitted to allocate this time as she wishes.) California allots one hour for each of its six essay questions. Look at the board of law examiners' website for particular information on the essay subjects tested and the length of each essay if your state has not adopted the MEE.

The goal of a bar examination essay question is similar to an essay examination in law school. Both the bar examiner and your professor want you to determine which facts are relevant in giving rise to legal issues, to state clearly the applicable legal rule(s) based on the relevant facts, and to analyze the effect of these rules given the facts. In terms of facts, what is slightly different between the two types of essay questions is that professors prefer to use facts that give rise to "boundary" or "gap" questions of law or doctrine. That is, the facts may give rise to two legal rules, rules that may conflict, or to an absence of law in a particular area. If we return to the *Jasko* case discussed in detail in Chapter 4, the issue was whether the plaintiff's case could go to the jury even when she offered no evidence that the defendant Woolworth had either actual or constructive notice of the dangerous condition, the pizza on the floor. The Colorado Supreme Court held that the "well-known" rule of notice was inapt in this case for the defendant Woolworth had created the dangerous condition by its method of selling pizza by the slice to carry around the store. In this type of premises liability case notice was eliminated as an element of the tort.

A torts professor testing you on a premises liability case might give you a set of facts allowing you to characterize the facts so you can argue that either the well-known rule of notice or the *Jasko* exception applies to the matter. A successful answer would be a thorough analysis of both possibilities. The conclusion the student might reach is ordinarily less important to the professor than the demonstration by the student of her ability to analyze both sides of the question.

An essay question on the bar exam has a slightly different purpose. The examiners want specific legal conclusions rather than hedged or conditional conclusions ("if the facts are viewed this way, then.... If the facts are viewed another way, then...."). Bar examination essay questions are usually written with specific questions asked at the end of the fact pattern. Most essay questions ask the test taker to answer 2–5 specific questions. Many past MEE and state-created essay questions are available on the Internet. Both the NCBE and some boards of law examiners (*e.g.*, Minnesota and California) have posted model or "sample" answers to these essay questions, giving the test taker a good sense of the type of question and answer expected of her on the bar exam. Questions may be written in the following ways, "Did the judge correctly rule the evidence inadmissible?" "Did the attorney correctly preserve the plaintiff's claim of error on appeal?" "Is the property contested by the husband and wife community property?" "Does the federal district court have subject matter jurisdiction to hear the case?"

The most common number of specific questions asked on a 30 minute essay is three. This gives the test taker less than ten minutes to draft an answer per question. That means that the examinee should always begin his or her response by answering the question. The first sentence of the essay answer should directly restate and answer the question: "The trial court ruled correctly in sustaining defendant's objection to the plaintiff's credibility attack on Witness. Rule 609 of the Federal Rules of Evidence does not permit a party to attack the credibility of a witness for a conviction that has been the subject of a pardon if the witness has not been convicted of another crime punishable by imprisonment for more than one year. In this case the witness was convicted of fraud but was pardoned by the governor before Witness gave testimony in the current case. Witness has not been convicted of any subsequent crime. Witness is presently under indictment but Witness's trial has not taken place. This makes impermissible plaintiff's attack on the credibility of the Witness by prior conviction." The examinee should then move quickly to the second and third questions.

The examinee should consider using headers and sub-headers in writing an essay answer because this makes it easier for the grader to grade your answer. If the first question is, "Is the Bystander's statement to Defendant that Plaintiff ran the red light admissible?", then the response should begin with the header "Admissibility of Bystander's statement to Defendant." Within the answer to that question sub-headers may be helpful. If the question requires you to look at the doctrines of relevance, hearsay, and authentication, you might begin with "Relevance," or even "Logical Relevance" followed by "Legal Relevance," "Hearsay and Exceptions," and "Authentication." If another question is, "Was the police report properly admitted as evidence despite the officer's absence from the trial?", you can begin with headers that either focus on the legal (evidentiary) issues involved, or begin with headers categorized by facts stated in the report. Thus, if the police report included 1) statements from the Plaintiff and Defendant, 2) a statement from a Bystander who does not testify at trial, 3) a statement from Bystander #2 who does testify at trial, and 4) the officer's conclusion (that is, opinion) regarding who was at fault, the header might be "Admissibility of Report and Statements Within It," and sub-headers either by statement (*e.g.*, "Admissibility of Statement of Plaintiff," "Admissibility of Statement by Defendant") or by legal category (*e.g.*, "Hearsay," "Party Admissions," "Excited Utterance," "Expert Opinion").

One important reason for this approach to essay questions is the limited time graders have to evaluate essay answers. Each grader is looking at a checklist (or "marking formula") in scoring your essay answer, and the more clearly an answer lists in headers and sub-headers the issues raised by the facts, the easier it is to grade. The amount of time spent by a grader on each essay question will vary considerably, but it is a relatively modest amount of time. For example, if a grader is given just 200 answers to grade, and the grader spends just ten minutes per answer, the grader will spend over 33 hours grading essay answers, time that does not include necessary breaks during grading, nor the time needed for training. If that same grader spends just three minutes grading each answer, it will take 10 hours to grade those exams, still a significant amount of time, especially if the grader, as is true in some states, is a practicing lawyer. Consequently, the examinee needs to make it as easy as possible for the grader to give the examinee the full complement of points due the examinee's answer. A poorly organized examination may not receive as many points as it should because it is written in a fashion frustrating to the grader.

In terms of writing style, a clear and cogent style is always the best approach. However, writing style is less important than 1) answering the question posed, and 2) listing the issues raised by each of the questions. In some states it is official state policy to ignore spelling and grammatical errors when grading. And certainly an examinee's handwriting will not be used adversely to the applicant. However, you are again cautioned that you should make it as easy as possible for the grader to assess your answer, and that includes writing as clearly and legibly as possible.

Grading essay answers is difficult both because test takers organize their answers differently and because reading a large number of answers quickly becomes numbing. As a result most states will use a number of graders for each question. Some will also initially begin grading as a group to minimize differences in scoring. Despite these checks on grading, boards of law examiners regularly use scaling to equalize any scoring differences among graders.

A Sample Evidence Essay Question

Peter and Dana are involved in a car accident at the intersection of Norris and Kane. Both suffer serious injuries. Each claims the other ran a red light. Peter sues Dana, who files a counterclaim against Peter. Efforts to settle were unsuccessful and the case went to trial. At trial the following occurs.

On cross-examination during Peter's case-in-chief, Dana's attorney Albert asks William, a witness who claims Dana ran the red light:

Q. Isn't it true that you were convicted of driving under the influence two years ago?

Lara, Peter's lawyer, interjects, "Objection, your honor. This is clearly an impermissible character attack." The court overrules the objection, but Lara again stands and states, "I also object, your honor, on the ground that you cannot permit this form of impeachment until you have determined that the DUI was a felony conviction and that the probative value of this evidence is not substantially outweighed by its prejudicial effect. The DUI is not a felony, making it improper to allow this attack on William's credibility. The Court replied, "Counsel, that evidence comes in automatically. Overruled."

Later in the cross-examination of William, Albert asks,

Q. Isn't it true you didn't see the accident?

A. Yes I did. I had just left O'Mara's bakery shop after getting coffee and some donuts when I saw the accident.

Q. Isn't it true that O'Mara's is closed on Sundays, the day the accident occurred?

A. It was open.

In Dana's case-in-chief Albert offers the testimony of Walter O'Mara, the owner of O'Mara's, who will testify that the bakery is closed on Sundays. Lara objects to O'Mara's testimony, and the Court sustains the objection.

In Dana's case-in-chief attorney Albert offers the police report of the accident. It states in part, "An eyewitness named Wood stated his surprise that the white car [otherwise identified as Peter's car] just ran the intersection. I looked at the skid marks coming from Norris Street [otherwise shown to be the street on which Dana was driving] and the lack of skid marks coming from Kane Street [otherwise identified as the street on which Peter was driving] and as a result I gave a ticket for inattentive driving to Peter." The officer, Patrick Morrison, did not testify at trial. Albert offered the authenticated report through the testimony of the custodian of police records. Lara objected, claiming, "The officer's statement in the report about giving Peter a ticket for inattentive driving is hearsay. Further, the officer's statement concerning fault constitutes impermissible lay opinion." The court overruled the objection.

Assume the Federal Rules of Evidence apply.

Did the Court err in:

1. Overruling Lara's objection to the admission of William's prior conviction for driving under the influence? Explain.

2. Sustaining Lara's objection to the testimony of Walter O'Mara? Explain.

3. Overruling Lara's objection to the admission of the police report? Discuss.

The essay examination in the bar examination directs your attention to particular questions. YOU MUST ANSWER THOSE QUESTIONS. The essay may be in the form of a Q&A or in the form of several paragraphs creating a narrative, a story. Concerning Question 1, the first objection made by Lara is timely but inaccurate, making the Court's decision correct. But Lara's second objection is also timely and accurately states the standard of FRE 609 for all witnesses other than the accused if the prior conviction is not one of "dishonesty or false statement." Here it seems clear that DUI is not such a crime. That means it is admissible only if 1) it is a felony (in essence, that is) and 2) the court determines that the probative value of this impeachment evidence is not substantially outweighed by its prejudicial effect (the FRE 403 standard). The question does not state whether the prior conviction of DUI was a felony, though Lara's objection makes that claim. This requires a brief assessment of the difference. Even if the DUI is a felony the Court's refusal to exercise discretion is itself an abuse of discretion, making the Court's decision to admit the evidence error. On the second question William's presence in O'Mara's is a form of impeachment called contradiction. Because William's claim that he had just left the bakery is likely collateral to the case, you cannot use extrinsic evidence (the testimony of Walter O'Mara) to contradict William's statement that he had just left O'Mara's. On question 3, what you really want to talk about is the double hearsay problem of the eyewitness Wood, whose statement should not be admitted unless it is admissible as a hearsay exception (excited utterance?) *and* the police report is admissible as a public record exception. The question, however, only asks about the police report. Further, Lara's objection was not to the double hearsay problem but only to the hearsay of the officer's conclusion and his "lay" opinion. Consequently you must ignore the distraction of the double hearsay problem. The police report is hearsay but it is admissible as a public record (FRE 803(8)). Whether the statements found in the police report are admissible depends on whether those statements concern matters observed about which there exists a duty to report (FRE 803(8)(B)) or whether it is a factual finding (FRE 803(8)(C)). The lay opinion objection (FRE 701) is an odd one. The officer's statements concerning fault are likely factual findings. This skirts the limitations of opinion testimony altogether. Additionally, a conclusion of who was at fault is at least arguably permissible lay opinion testimony, though one could claim that the officer's conclusion is admissible only if he is qualified as an expert under FRE 702.

Character and Fitness

Even if you pass the bar exam you will not be licensed to practice law if the board of law examiners concludes that you lack the requisite character and fitness to practice law. During the last two decades most boards of law examiners have more stringently evaluated the character and fitness of those applying for a law license. The vast majority of bar applicants have little to worry about. Even those who have some blemish on their records will likely be admitted (even if conditionally) to the practice of law. Successful applicants to the bar have been arrested for, and convicted of, possession of illegal narcotics, driving while intoxicated and other crimes. The keys to the success of those applicants are taking responsibility and telling the truth. Accepting that you are responsible for the crime you committed (as opposed to blaming your actions on your addiction or blaming another person) allows the board of law examiners to see you as a mature person, one ready for the responsibility as a practicing lawyer of protecting a client's life, liberty or property. More importantly, covering up a crime (say, a crime that led a court to declare you delinquent in juvenile court) is always worse than the crime itself. Lying to the bar examiners is one sure way to fail the test of character and fitness to practice law.

An applicant to the bar who has been convicted of a violent crime or a crime of fraud may be unable to obtain a law license. As a state actor, the board of law examiners must create and follow fair procedures concerning its evaluation of an applicant's character and fitness to practice law as a matter of constitutional law. The failure to do so is a violation of the applicant's due process rights under the 14th Amendment to the Constitution. If you have been convicted of a felony you need to hire a lawyer who specializes in this type of case (your Associate Dean is one good source of the names of such attorneys) by the second semester of your 2L year. In some states you may need to hire such a lawyer in your first semester of law school, for those states conditionally certify law students as eligible to practice law at that time.

Chapter 8

Work (and Life) after Law School

In 1897, Oliver Wendell Holmes, Jr. gave a speech at the Boston University School of Law titled *The Path of the Law*. Holmes declared that in the rational study of the law "the man of the future is the man of statistics and the master of economics." Holmes's prophecy about the future of legal education was largely accurate. In the practice of law lawyers deal with a multitude of issues beyond parsing legal doctrine, from cost-benefit thinking to political analysis to strategic business planning. What Holmes may have implied by his statement was a proliferation of lawyers focusing on proliferating number of areas of law. Although the lawyer of the future is as likely to be a woman as a man, that lawyer will be a specialist. Part of your goal in your first job is to find an area of specialization you enjoy, and to gain the skills in the specialized practice that will allow you to build a career.

The rise of the administrative state has made lawyers an integral part of the operation of the levers of power in the United States. State and federal administrative agencies regulate much of our social and business relations. Further, administrative agencies rarely go out of business voluntary, and if they are to stay in business, they must have someone or something to regulate (or at least to propose to regulate). The *Federal Register* publishes a mammoth number of pages of proposed and adopted regulations every year. The tax code, it has been common to say in the last forty years, is an impenetrable mess. Retirement experts often speak of a trillion dollar transfer of wealth to occur in the next thirty years in the Unites States, an event that will be facilitated by the work of many lawyers. Our society remains a litigious society, and the peaceful resolution of disputes remains a mainstay of the practice of law. The jobs of lawyers are varied and vast, and the idea that a lawyer "knows the law" is a mere remnant from another era. Lawyers know parts of the tax code, or parts of securities law. Some criminal defense lawyers will know the practice of law in the juvenile courts, but not the work associated with parole hearings. Others will know felony practice but nothing about driving under the influence

(DUI) cases. The age of the legal specialist is at hand. In addition, the era of the wandering lawyer is also at hand. You are unlikely to remain in your first job for more than five-seven years (if you do, congratulations). That makes the job of obtaining transferable legal skills crucial to your development as a lawyer.

The idea of organizational loyalty between lawyer and law firm is at an end. Lawyers no longer expect to remain with a private law firm from cradle to grave, and even career government employees, who are neither required to generate business from paying clients nor to bill their hours, are less numerous today than even twenty years ago. The end of organizational loyalty halted the practice of paying lawyers based on their years of experience, with lawyers in their late 50s and early 60s receiving diminishing pay packages on their way to mandatory retirement. In most large law firms (it is impossible to generalize about medium or small law firms) the pay of partners is based on an "eat what you kill" (the title of a devastating book about the practice of law) idea. Partners in large law firms are paid predominantly based on the revenue they bring to the firm. The more revenue a lawyer brings to the firm the more that lawyer is paid. When an equity partner brings an insufficient amount of revenue to the firm the lawyer may be fired (the lawyer is not actually an equity "partner" but a shareholder in a corporation whose interest may be purchased). The failure of any equity partner to bring in sufficient revenue has even more pernicious effects on non-equity partners and associates, whose jobs are more vulnerable than the jobs of equity partners. Several legal publications estimate that over 5,000 lawyers lost their jobs with large private law firms during the Great Recession.

This change in the nature of the lawyer-private law firm relationship has also altered the client-private law firm relationship. The loyalty of a law firm in serving the interests of long-standing clients has diminished, to the extent that law firms have "fired" clients who do not generate enough revenue, no matter how long the firm has worked for the client. Not surprisingly, notions of client loyalty to a law firm rather than a lawyer at the firm have also diminished. Finally, the Great Recession has caused a number of organizational clients to re-think their loyalty to long-hired law firms in large part due to the ever-increasing costs of legal services. The changing economics of the practice of "BigLaw" has already caused several large law firms to file for bankruptcy. One important effect of this recession is that large law firms must practice law more efficiently, which will mean fewer new associates hired at lower salaries.

The decline of organizational loyalty makes it more imperative than ever that a young lawyer learn both to develop a list of clients whose legal needs the lawyer can serve and a set of legal skills that will make the lawyer valuable both to clients and a legal organization. The former will take years, and is easier said than done in the large organizational context. The latter is a necessary but not sufficient condition of successfully practicing law. Lawyers act as agents and fiduciaries for others. If a client no longer uses the lawyer's services, the lawyer must find someone else who will. Some lawyers, alas, are much better at marketing themselves than in performing legal work. This is not only true of those lawyers who advertise on television but also some who practice in large law firms. It was not just a stereotype that lawyers in many law firms were traditionally divided into "finders, minders and grinders." The finders were those lawyers who found clients and brought them to the firm, the minders were those lawyers who made sure the firm served the legal needs of those clients, and the grinders were those who performed the bulk of the legal work for those clients. Given the length of time it takes to develop a client base, you are better off initially focusing on creating a set of legal skills that are difficult for others to replicate.

The goal of this chapter is to assist you in thinking about the structure of the legal profession and how that may affect your ability to accomplish the goals you have for your first job. Although your first job should be the springboard to making a career in law, it may be a way station to a second or third job that actually allows you to attain those career goals. Forewarned is forearmed.

The Judicial Clerkship

The judicial clerkship has long been a viewed as a prestigious honor accorded a new law graduate. Judicial clerks spend one or two years serving as a legal assistant to a judge. In the federal system both trial and appellate judges hire law clerks. In most state court systems only appellate judges hire law clerks. A law clerk may write memoranda summarizing the briefs, draft initial opinions, write speeches and otherwise assist the judge. For those interested in litigation, a federal district court clerkship offers the opportunity to listen to good (and poor) advocacy and to understand how the mechanics of a judge's decision making process works. Appellate court clerkships provide an intellectual hothouse concerning both banal and new legal issues.

Federal clerkships are extremely competitive, and many state appellate court clerkships are quite competitive as well. To obtain one of these jobs your grades must be very good. Service on a law journal is usually required. A constant source of anxiety among federal and some state judges is the time frame used to choose judicial clerks. Despite several efforts, it appears that many judges will continue to hire during the applicant's fourth semester of law school. This essentially requires you to perform well during your first year of law school in order to compete for one of these jobs. In some cases judges wait until the fall of the law student's third year to hire, but you need to be ready to apply during the spring of your second year of law school. Some federal and a few state appellate judges hire from a pool of candidates who will have at least one year of experience as a law clerk before they begin their service. Thus, a student may obtain her first state appellate or federal district court clerkship in the spring semester of her second year of law school, a clerkship that will not begin until late August or early September after she graduates from law school. In the student's third year of law school she may apply for and receive an offer to serve as a judicial clerk to an appellate judge beginning after completion of the first clerkship.

Some judges will make an offer of employment at the end of your interview. It is considered very bad form to put the judge off by asking for time to consider the judge's offer. As a result, if you are lucky enough to obtain several interviews with judges, you should attempt to organize them according to your preferences on the type of clerkship (appellate or trial) and location.

Judicial clerks who join a private law firm after completion of the clerkship are usually given a year's credit as an associate for each year of service as a clerk. In addition, some clerks are given "signing bonuses" for agreeing to join a firm as an associate attorney. These benefits will likely continue even as the economic structure of large law firms changes, for law clerks are perceived as peculiarly talented new lawyers.

For those interested in teaching law in the law school setting, service as a law clerk is a valuable asset when looking for a law teaching job.

The Large Law Firm

The large law firm (100+ lawyers) has enjoyed a long, profitable run. Although lawyers for large law firms are not the highest paid lawyers in the United States (that would be high end personal injury/class action lawyers), lawyers at large law firms are paid very well, and partners in such firms are safely ensconced in the top 1% of those Americans earning an income. Even mid-level and senior associates are paid more than the vast majority of Americans who work. However, for most the pay is accompanied by significant amounts of stress and a great deal of work. These firms spend the bulk of their efforts doing work for some of the largest corporations in the world.

Most large law firms divide employed lawyers into three distinct groups: 1) equity partner; 2) nonequity partner; and 3) associate. Some firms now include a number of lawyers officially listed as "of counsel," which means the lawyer has neither a current or future ownership interest in the firm. Lawyers listed as of counsel may work for the law firm based on a personal services contract or be paid based on what the lawyer bills. The equity partner is a person who owns part of the law firm. Nearly all large law firms are structured as limited liability partnerships or as corporations, not as true general partnerships. In a general partnership each partner is responsible for the debts of the entire partnership, debts that may be repaid by taking the partner's personal assets. The corporation or limited liability partnership model allows those with an ownership interest to limit the extent of their liability for organizational debts to the amount of their ownership interest, not their entire net worth. The now misleading term "equity partner" is still used to describe these owners of the law firm, though these owners may be dismissed from most organizations. With the exception of law firms organized in the District of Columbia, only lawyers may own part of an American law firm. Nonlawyers own parts of law firms organized in Australia and Europe. The nonequity partner is a person who may share in some profits that associates may not be eligible to receive, and may have some claim to consideration as an equity partner. A nonequity partner is a misnomer in most instances, for the lawyer does not own any part of the entity (thus "nonequity") making the appellation "partner" inaccurate. These lawyers may, however, have an early opportunity to make equity partner, and the status of nonequity partner is often a way station between associate and equity partner. An associate is an employee paid a salary plus some possible year-end bonus. Associates may be divided into three categories: senior associates (those with seven or more years of experience), mid-level associates (those with four to six years of experience) and new (or low-level) associates.

New lawyers at large law firms can expect the path to partnership to extend to more than a decade. The supply of talented lawyers currently outstrips demand, and many large law firms are delaying the starting date of new hires. This will create a bottleneck for new law graduates in the next several years. The future of the large law firm is hazy, for the economic rationale of the large law firm model is broken and consequently, quickly changing. Large law firms have high fixed costs, and new lawyers constitute a high variable cost. The large law firm was able to hire thirty to sixty new law graduates annually at a starting salary of $145,000–$160,000 plus bonuses only because those lawyers could be billed at $200 or more per hour and new lawyers were expected to bill anywhere between 2,200–2,800 hours annually. That model is broken because clients are no longer willing to pay those rates for the work of new but naive (at least in law practice) lawyers. One initial response is that the starting salary of new associates in large law firms is likely to hover at slightly more than $100,000 plus possible bonuses for several years.

Clients of large law firms are interested in moving from an hourly rate model to some other approach. Two proposed models are a fixed or flat fee (at least fixed for some aspects of the representation) or a value-based fee, a fee predicated on the value added by the lawyer in representing the client. Any shift away from the billable hour will benefit lawyers in the long run by focusing on the lawyer's productivity, but will harm new associates in large law firms in the short run. A new associate may be very intelligent and very hard-working, but his or her legal skills are modest. When the representation involves a large or very small matter, using a new associate to perform some of the work makes sense for both the client and law firm. In too many instances, however, clients have complained that the law firm is billing the time of new associates for little purpose other than increasing the cost to the client. Not only was this work not helpful to the client, much of it was known by lawyers as "scut" work that did little to increase the legal skills of the new lawyers who performed the work. One consequence of the Great Recession may be that large law firms will hire fewer new associates and hire more mid-level associates with already-developed legal skills. This likelihood increases if, as has begun to occur, more basic work for corporate clients is either kept in-house by the client or performed by paralegals of the law firm. The reduction in starting pay of new large law firm associates will not alter the expectation that associates will continue to work punishing hours (70+ hour weeks are not uncommon). Large law firms will alter the economics of their practice in order to remain quite profitable, and that alteration will affect new law graduates unless and until those firms figure out how to make new associates a profit center without straining client relations.

The Medium and Small Law Firm

The demise of the medium-sized law firm (roughly speaking, from 25 to 100 lawyers) has been long suggested. This now appears unlikely. Well-run firms of this size are likely to prosper in the coming decade because they do not carry the same large fixed costs as large law firms and because they are slightly more agile than large law firms in adapting to changing business and economic climates. Lawyers (both partners and associates) at medium sized law firms generally do not earn as much as large law firm lawyers, though this generalization may best be proven by exceptions to the rule. The work of medium sized law firms can be very similar to large law firms: it can include transactional work, counseling businesses, acting in behalf of clients in various kinds of civil litigation and other work.

Specialization in the practice of law means that many medium sized law firms work only in certain areas of practice. Specialization joined by technological developments allow medium sized firms to compete for business with the largest law firms in the world. Some medium sized law firms, particularly those in cities with a metropolitan population of 500,000 or fewer people, may employ lawyers who can take on most litigation and office practice (writing wills, organizing entities, serving as outside counsel to medium sized corporations).

Learning the firm's culture is important if you are thinking about joining a medium sized law firm. Some firms are institutional in the sense of distributing profits on a fairly even basis, accounting for seniority and little else, and in treating clients as "firm" clients, not clients of the lawyers who serve those clients. Others are dominated by one or two "name" partners, partners who created and built the firm and who determine what lawyers will be paid, what bonuses (and how much) will be awarded and who will perform which tasks for clients. Some operate as fiefdoms, with partners operating their own departments of the firm independently of each other. Profits are largely divided as each unit of the firm prospers or falters. Some firms mix an institutional base with an entrepreneurial bonus for lawyers, including associates, who bring new clients or who obtain excellent results for the clients. The firm's culture will largely determine the manner in which the firm will handle growth. Medium sized firms that lack a strong institutional culture will reach a breaking point once they reach a certain size, with some group shearing itself off. These cultural factors may make a difference in your quest for partnership. The more a firm is dominated by a handful of partners, the more likely it is that partnership 1) depends wholly on how those partners rate your contributions, and 2) will not mean much in practical terms. That is, attaining the status of "partner" in a firm that lacks a strong institutional focus will give you little voice in the direction or future of that firm.

The small law firm (2–10 lawyers) will often practice in areas of law concerning individuals, from business counseling of small organizations to criminal defense to personal injury to elder law and wills and estates practice. Small firm lawyers are found in cities large and small. The breadth of law makes it impossible for a small law firm practitioner to focus on more than a couple of areas of practice. Some lawyers, as stated earlier, will focus on just one aspect of an area of practice, such as medical malpractice litigation or auto accident cases.

In both medium and small law firms, the relative "leanness" of the organization gives you the opportunity to gain legal skills at a rapid rate. This is one advantage of joining such a firm rather than a large law firm. The disadvantage, of course, has traditionally been the difference in salary between associates in large firms and associates in medium sized firms. If you join a small or medium sized firm it will be important for you to find a mentor to make sure you are performing as the firm desires. These firms will differ greatly in the extent to which you will receive either a formal or informal review of your work, making it important for you to seek reviews of your work.

Solo Practice

A plurality of lawyers practice as sole practitioners. They may (and as a new lawyer you should) share offices with one or more lawyers, but they are responsible for generating the revenues and paying the costs of their practice. A majority of sole practitioners work in areas of individual practice, such as criminal defense and personal injury. A significant number, however, engage in business litigation or business counseling work.

If you begin your legal career as a sole practitioner you will need to learn both how to operate a law practice (especially the part about not commingling client funds with your own, which gets many lawyers into trouble) and how to build a client base. You can build a very successful practice by adopting some or all of the thoughts below: 1) save on expenses by sharing office space with other lawyers. Your relationship with these lawyers may also result in receiving some business from those lawyers. Similarly, use the Internet and local law libraries for most of your legal research. The cost of using proprietary legal research engines (Westlaw and LexisNexis are the search engines law students are most familiar with) is dropping, but you may not need to adopt either, at least initially; 2) join the local bar association and, more particularly, the practice section of the local bar in which you are interested. Your client base and your legal interests may differ greatly as you begin to practice law. You need to focus first on what your clients need, while keeping in mind how to enter another area of practice; 3) consider taking court appointments, such as indigent defense work and guardian *ad litem* (usually for children) civil matters; 4) develop relationships with other attorneys including, if possible, a mentoring relationship with a senior lawyer. You might be surprised at how often experienced lawyers are interested in assisting new lawyers; 5) attend Continuing Legal Education (CLE) courses on subjects of interest to you and important to your clients as soon as possible. Most states that require CLE (those that do usually require fifteen hours per year) give new lawyers a grace period of a year before mandating CLE compliance. You do not need to take this grace period, and you probably should not; 6) use billing arrangements other than an hourly fee, and make sure you are paid for your work. If you collect your fee in advance, you must know your state's professional ethics rule on how advance fees are categorized. In some states, that money is yours because it is an advance payment of a fee to the lawyer. In a majority of states, even if it is called an advance fee, the rules of professional conduct consider it a type of "retainer," meaning some or all of that money must initially be placed in your client trust account at the bank; and 7) all clients rely on *you* to perform the work they need done. If you are not competent to perform that work, refer the prospective client to another lawyer, who will reciprocate in turn. Just a few clients will generate the largest challenges to your practice, in terms of time, loss of other opportunities and late payment of fees. Even if you think you desperately need any client to walk through the door, you are never so desperate as to take a client who begins by complaining about his last three lawyers failing to do the job. That client can and will poison your practice if you let him. You can and should turn down some clients, even at the start of your practice.

Because so many lawyers practice law as sole practitioners, a number of excellent books have been written about how to build a law practice. Just google that phrase and you will uncover several books that can assist you in creating a successful law practice.

Corporate Counsel

Corporate counsel now consist of slightly less than 10% of the legal profession. These lawyers are employees of the corporation which they advise, making for a close relationship between the lawyer and client. This often allows for a better understanding by the lawyer of the client's needs. It may also give rise to the possibility that the lawyer will align his or her interests too readily with the client's (that is, employer's) interests. The traditional role of a corporate counsel was in advising the corporation on routine legal matters. More complex legal matters were given to the corporation's outside counsel. This distinction is no longer tenable. Lawyers who work for corporations now undertake very complex legal tasks, which is one reason why the pay of corporate counsel has increased substantially in the past two decades.

The Great Recession is likely to lead to an increase in the size of corporate counsel offices. It is unlikely that most corporations will undertake their own litigation work, although corporate counsel may perform much more of the discovery work in litigation than outside firms. In terms of counseling work, corporate counsel are likely to perform most SEC and other administrative agency regulatory work, most tax work and much employment and labor relations work.

Traditionally lawyers did not join corporate counsel offices immediately upon graduation. Most corporate counsel came from private law practice, with anywhere between three and twenty years of experience. This has begun to change and is likely to change more rapidly in the next decade. Corporate counsel now realize the efficiencies they can generate by hiring new lawyers they can train at a significantly lower cost than that charged by large law firm associates.

Public Interest

Public interest law firms mushroomed beginning in the 1970s, but some began even earlier. The most famous public interest entity is the NAACP's Legal Defense and Educational Fund, the lawyers at which formulated and implemented the constitutional attack on the doctrine of "separate but equal." The work of Thurgood Marshall and other lawyers at LDF led to the constitutional end of separate but equal in *Brown v. Board of Education* (1954). Lawyers in public interest work make up fewer than 1% of all lawyers, and the pay of such lawyers is modest. Job satisfaction for many public interest lawyers is high, a likely result of their ability to mesh their personal and political ideals with their law work. The work of public interest law firms now spans the political spectrum.

The Legal Services Corporation (LSC) was created in 1974 by Congress. It is a private, non-profit corporation that is funded by appropriations by the federal government. LSC does not perform legal services itself, but awards grants to legal services grantees in the states. Those lawyers offer free legal services to the poor concerning civil (that is, non-criminal) legal problems.

It is quite difficult to obtain a job upon graduation with a public interest law firm, often due to budgetary limitations faced by many public interest law firms. Third-year law students may apply for the prestigious (and competitive) Skadden Fellows program, in which new law graduates receive a fellowship from the Skadden Fellowship Foundation to serve at a non-profit public interest law firm or non-profit organization performing legal work. If you are interested in joining a public interest firm you should contact the firm early in your law school career and ask if you can work as an intern during your summers while in law school (usually at no pay). You should also ask the office of career services if the school has alumni connections with the organization.

Government

The work of government lawyers varies tremendously. The work of a significant number of lawyers employed by the government can be placed in the following categories.

Assistant district attorneys (ADA)—if you are interested in quickly gaining trial experience, consider a job as an ADA. Although they pay modestly, these jobs are highly prized for litigators because ADAs quickly gain courtroom experience. At most larger district attorney offices you will begin as an intake attorney or as a second chair to the lead attorney (also called the "first chair") in misdemeanor matters. Differences among the several thousand offices makes it impossible to generalize, but most ADAs will be able to move within several years to prosecuting felonies, at least as a second chair. Some ADAs will serve as civil attorneys for the county or district, but most will work as criminal prosecutors. The District Attorney is elected to office, and an ADA's position may become less stable if a new District Attorney is elected.

Municipal attorneys—most cities of a significant size have a legal office headed by the City Attorney, usually appointed by the mayor or city manager. An assistant city (or municipal) attorney may be given the duties of prosecuting traffic violations, defending the city against civil negligence or civil rights claims, advising the city council on city, state or federal law (from the impact of environmental regulations and state property laws and administrative regulations to advising the city counsel how to interpret open meetings law and its municipal code), assisting in the drafting of municipal ordinances and defending the constitutionality of those ordinances. The work of municipal attorneys regularly varies between advising and litigating, and the legal work of municipal counsel reflects the variety of tasks municipal lawyers complete.

Legal work for state and federal administrative bodies—the rise of the administrative state includes an enormous rise in the number of lawyers who serve as counsel for state and federal administrative agencies. Administrative agencies promulgate regulations pursuant to statutory authority, and often enforce those regulations through quasi-judicial procedures. A lawyer in an administrative agency will likely specialize in performing particular work, whether counseling the body on proposed regulatory action, acting as a litigation attorney in quasi-judicial (or judicial) matters, or serving as adviser to those charged with implementing the law and duly adopted regulations. The most well known of these bodies is the office of the state Attorney General, which employs a large number of lawyers. However, the rise of other administrative entities has made it important for those agencies to hire their own attorneys.

The relationship between the work of agency attorneys and the office of the state Attorney General depends on each state's law. Some will give the Attorney General formal power over all administrative agencies, a power that is informally exercised by the local agency lawyers subject to occasional oversight by the Attorney General.

Department of Justice—the Department of Justice is the preeminent federal legal agency in the United States. The Attorney General of the United States serves the President and is a member of the Cabinet. The DOJ includes, among others, a civil division, a criminal division, a civil rights division, a tax division and an antitrust division, all of which have a number of branches. It also includes a number of offices that advise the Attorney General and other lawyers, including the Office of Professional Responsibility and the Office of the Pardon Attorney. The Office of Solicitor General, which represents the United States in cases before the Supreme Court, is also part of the Office of the Attorney General. The only way to obtain a job with the DOJ as an entry-level attorney is through its Honors Program.

United States Attorneys—there are 94 United States district courts. Each has a United States Attorney who is nominated by the President subject to confirmation by the Congress, and each has a staff of Assistant United States Attorneys. It is difficult to obtain a job as an AUSA immediately upon graduating from law school, but not impossible. Most AUSAs, like ADAs, will serve as criminal prosecutors.

Public Defenders—in a number of states and in the federal system indigent persons accused of a crime are represented by public defenders employed by the government. The Federal Public Defender system was created by Congress in 1964. Each federal district includes a Federal Public Defender appointed by the circuit court of appeals for that district for a term. The Federal Public Defender then hires attorneys as approved by the circuit court and the Director of the Administrative Office of the federal courts. The qualifications of those attorneys are similar to AUSAs. States and counties may also have public defender systems similar to the Federal Public Defender system.

Legislative work—many law graduates decide to work as legislative aides to members of Congress and members of state legislatures. These jobs do not ordinarily require one possess a J.D., but a law degree is helpful in understanding the work of the committees on which your employer sits. Hiring is idiosyncratic to each political office, and you should tailor your interest to those whose politics are not anathema to you.

Executive work—more administrative agencies means more power in the executive branch, both at the presidential and the gubernatorial levels. Governors and Presidents regularly need legal advice as well as political advice.

Some jobs are structured so that a law degree is necessary. In others a law degree is helpful but not a requirement.

Judicial staff attorneys—in most states the appellate courts have a group of staff attorneys who work for the court full-time. These lawyers may draft *per curiam* decisions, may assist in the docketing and channeling of cases to resolution, and may work on other projects as designated by the court. Many are hired after working as judicial clerks in that appellate court.

Teaching

The J.D. is a terminal degree, and many law professors have no other advanced degree. Very few law graduates immediately join law schools as professors. Most will work as judicial clerks and in some practice area before beginning teaching. A modest number will graduate and begin teaching undergraduates or community college students, though this is usually as an adjunct rather than as a tenure-track professor. Some law schools will hire their new graduates to work as fellows for one or two years. Those fellows may teach legal research and writing, serve as assistants in legal clinics or act as tutors to current law students.

Law-Related Work

About 25% of law graduates take jobs that do not formally require a J.D. Those jobs include public policy analyst, journalist or, more likely these days, blogger (or "blawger"), real estate adviser, accountant, lobbyist or agent, banker (investment or otherwise), trust officer and labor negotiator. Large legal publishers also hire new law graduates to write case and subject summaries for use by attorneys, draft model documents specifically tailored to local and state legal markets, operate bar exam prep courses and manage proprietary legal research. The pervasiveness of law in American society makes legal training useful in a variety of jobs. A graduate's interest in law-related but not law-practice work may be a result of a disdain for the banality of practice, serendipity, or finding a fit between your interests and your skills.

LL.M.?

For some students three years of law school is not enough. They decide to spend an additional year in law school in pursuit of a master of laws (LL.M.)

degree. Although it may seem odd to receive a master's degree after being awarded a doctorate (J.D.), the LL.M. harkens back to the era in which the first degree in law awarded by many law schools was called the LL.B., the bachelor of laws degree. In addition to spending another year engaged in full-time academic study, most LL.M. programs require their students to write the equivalent of a master's thesis as a requirement of receiving the degree.

The LL.M. is useful in two situations: first, if you plan to practice law in a highly specialized area of law, such as tax, an LL.M. is helpful. The LL.M. in taxation is the most commonly offered LL.M., in large part because it has been accepted within the field as providing expertise for those who obtain it, an expertise valuable to clients. An LL.M. in environmental law has also become relatively common. Environmental lawyers are a varied group, making an LL.M. beneficial in understanding both more of the subject as well as some particular subsets of this practice area. In fields such as international law, health law and dispute resolution an LL.M. may create better job opportunities or allow one to gain some traction as a practitioner in the field, but this is not the norm. An LL.M. in trial advocacy is also a hit-or-miss proposition, with more such graduates missing than hitting. Great trial advocates can be trained, so an LL.M. in trial advocacy can make sense. However, the National Institute for Trial Advocacy (NITA) has been successfully training advocates for years in intensive one-week (sometimes less) programs. This makes the prospect of a year long commitment to obtain an LL.M. appear much too long. It is unclear whether the receipt of an LL.M. in international law, health law, dispute resolution or trial advocacy provides a sufficient additional incentive for law firms to hire the LL.M. graduates. Even if it helps in some fashion, the cost, one year of time and foregone income plus the cost of tuition and living expenses, appears to outweigh the largely intangible benefits of the degree. The decision to obtain an LL.M. on a part-time basis while continuing to work may alter that calculus. If you really believe it important to obtain an LL.M. to succeed in a particular practice area, choosing a part-time program may be your best option.

The second reason to take an LL.M. is if you are interested in law teaching. Law school hiring is elitist, and a graduate of a regional law school can make herself a candidate for a teaching position if she receives an LL.M. from one of those elite law schools. An LL.M. in some specialized field may also make you more appealing to a law school looking for a faculty member interested in intellectual property, tax or environmental law. If you are looking for a "scholarly" LL.M. relatively few elite law schools serve the American J.D. looking to enter law teaching. Your best choice is likely between Harvard, which has the largest and best known program, and Yale. If you are admitted to the LL.M.

program at another elite school, find out the school's placement rate before entering the program.

Work and Life: Finding an Acceptable Imbalance

The practice of law is often very stressful. Lawyers suffer from substance abuse (alcohol, narcotics, chemical dependencies) in substantially greater percentages than the general public. Lawyers suffer from depression more so than the members of any other profession. Whether these illnesses are correlated with lawyers because a particular type of person is attracted to law is unclear. It appears that many lawyers are pessimistic creatures, a possible consequence of training in law in which you are to see how things could go wrong: "What's the worst that could happen?" is a question lawyers routinely ask, for we are trained to prepare for all contingencies. The practice of law is likely to remain very competitive for the next decade, a condition that likely will increase the stress faced by lawyers. How do you find ways to avoid substance abuse? To face depression? To learn how to create a proper "imbalance" in your life?

The bar associations of every state have worked for some time creating programs allowing lawyers to acknowledge and recover from substance abuse. Most of these programs are called lawyer assistance programs (LAP), which assist lawyers willing to acknowledge their addiction. These programs provide for crisis counseling and will refer the lawyer to a proper health care professional or facility. Most also offer a peer assistance program permitting the lawyer to reach out to another lawyer, a volunteer who may have suffered from alcohol or drug dependence. If necessary, LAPs aid lawyers in temporarily ceasing their practice without harm to clients. Calls to lawyer assistance programs are confidential. In addition to aiding lawyers who abuse alcohol and drugs, many states have extended their work to aid lawyers who suffer from depression. The ABA's Commission on Lawyer Assistance Programs offers publications and a resource library on the Web for perusal. It also offers contact information for LAPs in each state. No assistance can happen unless, of course, the lawyer acknowledges that he or she needs such assistance.

For some, the ability to ignore one's life outside of work is what makes the practice of law enticing. The lawyer who finds himself energized only when he is swamped with work, whether in closing a transaction or in preparing for trial, faces a different kind of addiction. His very existence and identity are premised on what he does to earn an income. This addiction can be fostered in the practice of law because it is often viewed as dedication, a virtue, not as a vice.

You may be able to find wealth, even comfort in such a life. Most lawyers, however, fail to find happiness or a sense of fulfilling purpose or meaning when work is all-consuming.

This is not to suggest that you must abandon your efforts to earn a healthy living in order to find a purpose in the practice of law. But the quest for wealth, which is always a quest for power, leads too many astray. The well-known Mississippi asbestos and tobacco lawyer Richard "Dickie" Scruggs now resides in federal prison after pleading guilty to efforts to bribe judges. The matters about which Scruggs offered bribes were themselves picayune, not worth the time for someone with Scruggs's massive wealth. In my view Scruggs attempted to bribe the judges not for the additional fees he would gain, but to demonstrate the extent of his power.

Lawyers can do good while doing well. Lawyers can also do ill (or even evil) while doing well. Lawyers provide life to the impersonal legal institutions that structures much of the lives of Americans. Lawyers infuse those institutions with the possibility that members of a community can live and work together. You have a choice to exercise your modest monopoly in the service of aiding clients by tempering the possible abuse of power or aiding clients in gathering and exercising power.

Why do you want to practice law? If your reasons for entering the practice of law have changed since you took the LSAT, how would those reasons appear to your pre-law school self?

The search for balance in one's life as a practicing lawyer is often (though not always) futile. An imbalance between work and your other commitments and interests is not by itself harmful, and acknowledging an imbalance provides the opportunity to reconsider why you do your job. Lawyers struggle to juggle the interests of clients, third parties, the legal system and themselves. Lawyers must also juggle the demands of work and the demands of one's other communities. These are nearly impossible tasks. However, the act of "juggling" those often conflicting commitments may be the best a lawyer can do, a condition the lawyer can accept. The act of juggling requires you to touch, even briefly, all of those aspects of your life. Juggling acknowledges one's different commitments and interests. It is thus wholly different from the decision to ignore any commitments or interests outside of the practice of law. Juggling is a credible form of imbalance allowing a lawyer to accept oneself as both a lawyer and a person with other statuses (spouse or partner, child, parent, friend, volunteer). Embrace (indeed enjoy) your juggling life, for it shall too soon pass.

Index